THE AMERICAN SHORT STORY SINCE 1950

BAAS Paperbacks

Series Editors: Simon Newman, Sir Denis Brogan Chair in American Studies at the University of Glasgow; and Carol R. Smith, Senior Lecturer in English and American Studies at the University of Winchester.

The American Short Story
since 1950

KASIA BODDY

EDINBURGH UNIVERSITY PRESS

© Kasia Boddy, 2010

Edinburgh University Press Ltd
22 George Square, Edinburgh

Reprinted 2011

Typeset in Fournier by
Koinonia, Manchester, and
printed and bound in Great Britain by
CPI Antony Rowe, Chippenham and Eastbourne

A CIP Record for this book is available from the British Library

ISBN 978 0 7486 2766 0 (paperback)

Contents

Acknowledgements

This book has its distant origins in my Ph.D. thesis, and while writing it I've tried to remember the good advice of my supervisors, Tony Tanner and Susan Manning, as well as that of Leonard Michaels, with whom I also worked briefly. I would also like to thank Robin and Tad Krauze, with whom I stayed in New York while doing some interviews, and Christina Büchmann for hospitality and book parcels from California. Pam Thurschwell and John Beck kindly invited me to give talks on some of this material, Alison Light commented very helpfully on the Introduction, and Janet Boddy did some inventive last-minute reference-chasing. I am very lucky to be able to draw on many years of conversations about short fiction with Ali Smith. My overwhelming debt is to David Trotter, without whom this book and, more importantly, I would be very much the poorer.

This book goes, with love, to my parents on whose well-stocked bookshelves I first encountered, and keep finding, American short stories.

Introduction:
The American Short Story to 1950

This book is about the American short story since 1950. It is a book about some of the greatest writers of the period, who consistently found in the short story a form well adapted to their most fundamental preoccupations, and about the literary cultures within which they wrote: the magazines they published in; the prizes they did or did not win; the university courses which taught them how to write, or enabled them to teach others how to write; and above all, or beneath all, the (more often than not disappointing) sales figures.

In order to understand fully both the quality of the short stories published in America since 1950 and their sheer quantity, it is first necessary to consider some historical context. This introductory chapter will explore some of the key issues raised by enduring debates about the genre's historical development and distinctive formal features. In particular, it will address the paradoxical status of the short story in American literary theory and practice during the past two centuries. How did the short story gain its reputation as a genre at once ancient and modern, formulaic and innovative, fragmentary and complete, local in emphasis and yet a means of understanding the nation as a whole?

While people have been telling each other tales since the days of cave-painting and publishing them since the days of Gutenberg, the term 'Short-story' did not appear in print until 1885, in an article by the American critic, Brander Matthews.[1] Matthews's use of capitals and a hyphen to join his two terms was a deliberate attempt to distinguish short stories from stories which merely happened to be short. In other words, he was arguing that short stories (I'll drop the hyphen) were not only different from novels in length but also in kind. A case was beginning to be made for the short story not just as a 'short prose narrative', but rather as the quintessentially modern literary form, ideally suited to the demands of both commerce and innovation.[2] For these, and other, reasons it was also often described as a quintessentially American form.

A National Art Form

In 1992, Richard Ford began his introduction to *The Granta Book of the American Short Story* by questioning the notion, proposed by the Irish writer Frank O'Connor some thirty years earlier, that the short story was a 'national art form'.[3] O'Connor's assertion of the 'superiority of the American short story over all others that I know' was not startling; indeed, since the early twentieth century, this opinion had become a bit of a cliché.[4] In 1912, Elias Liberman declared the short story the 'most typically American form of our fiction', a view echoed in 1925 by the Russian Formalist critic, Boris Eikhenbaum.[5] 'It may very well be admitted', wrote the British novelist Somerset Maugham in 1939, 'that in none of the countries of Europe has this form of fiction so assiduously been cultivated as it has been in the United States.'[6] By the end of the twentieth century, such exceptionalism was well established. In 1997, Kirk Curnutt prefaced an explanation of his critical approach to the subject by promising that it would allow readers 'to appreciate more fully the *sui generis* quality of American short stories'.[7] Richard Ford, then, is unusual in admitting that he couldn't 'even see in the great variety of American moods, hues, tones, effects, forms, and narrative strategies much difference between our short stories and, say, Irish ones, or ours and the Italian, or the French, or even ours and the English'.[8]

Back in 1884, Julian Hawthorne, son of Nathaniel, sought to explain his belief that Americans 'write the best short stories in the world'. The answer, he felt, lay in the lack of a 'fixed and settled condition of society'; American life to date had been 'nothing but a series of episodes, of experiments'. 'We cannot write American-grown novels, because a novel is not an episode, nor an aggregation of episodes.' Rather, he suggested, Americans must concentrate on the short story as a form 'needing no historical perspective, nor caring for any'.[9] If American identity was posited as an act of continuous restless invention, the American writer must continually start again. The short story was the perfect always-new form, and democratic too, for while not everyone had the technical skill to write a poem or the time to write a novel, surely everyone had a short story in them.

At the end of the century, Frank Norris advertised 'great opportunities for fiction-writers in San Francisco' on similar grounds. Unlike Eastern cities, such as Boston or New York, San Francisco was 'not settled enough yet for the novelist'. Why? Because the novelist, he argued, 'demands large, co-ordinated, broad and simple lines upon which to work, something far more unified than we can yet give him'. Seven years after the superintendent of the Census had announced that there was no longer a Western frontier, since the land mass had been settled from coast to coast, Norris presents San Francisco as the last bastion of 'hot-blood[ed]', 'vigorous', frontier virtues. For Norris, the form best suited to retain, or promote, unsettled manliness was short fiction. Only the short story, he claims, would allow the writer to express 'growing and living ... in spots, here a little, there a little, scattered bits of life and movement, quite independent of each other'. In advocating a return to the primitive – 'the swing and rush and trample of things that live' – Norris was behaving as a true modern. It is not the frontier that is obsolete, he suggests, but 'fine writing' and the genteel 'polish of literary finish'.[10]

Accounting for the 'Rise of the "Short Story"' around this time, Bret Harte also evoked frontier virtues. Americans liked the short story, he said, because it 'went directly to the point', always reaching its conclusion 'without an unnecessary word'; the 'proverbial haste of American life was some inducement to its brevity'.[11] For both writers and readers, the short story was literature for those who had more pressing concerns than literature.[12] 'The short story appeals to us just now', Esther Matson wrote in 1919, 'because it offers us recreation without too great a demand on our time.' The novel 'requires not only time for its perusal, but also a certain leisureliness of the soul', while the short story, as Edward J. O'Brien added in 1923, 'requires no leisure to grasp its point':

> To devote one's life to literature is to confess oneself a weakling and to be despised. But the short story from a pioneer's point of view has the merit of being brief ... Its chances of survival and development in a pioneer civilization was infinitely greater than that of the novel.[13]

Founder, and editor from 1915 to 1941, of the annual *Best American Short Stories* anthologies, O'Brien played a key role in what he saw as the form's 'advance'. Martha Foley described him as 'St Peter guarding the gates to a short story writer's heaven'; for William Saroyan, 'the very name in print, to my eye, means the Short Story'; Charles E. May recently declared him to be the 'greatest champion of the form America has ever had'.[14] Like Harte and Norris, O'Brien liked to think of the short story 'from a pioneer's point of view'.

In the 1890s, such a perspective was thought to provide a corrective to the fussy sentimentalism of the genteel tradition; in the early twentieth century, to the interlocked evils of commercialism and puritanism. In *The Wine of the Puritans* (1908), Van Wyck Brooks established 'puritan' as the epithet for all that was anti-intellectual, anti-art and anti-sex, for the sanctimonious and the commercially-minded. He developed this theme in *America's Coming-of-Age* (1915), and in 1918 published a kind of anti-puritan manifesto, 'On Creating a Useable Past', in which he called for a new 'generation' of writers to change things.[15] O'Brien was committed to this project, and further believed that the short story's 'progress' would be the best marker of America's gradual 'coming of age'. He would follow the genre's development, both on the level of the individual story and in a series of annual anthologies, each of which he described as striving towards a 'national unity of democratic utterance'.[16]

In the decades following the Civil War, a further debate had arisen concerning the respective claims on the imagination made by allegiance to the nation, on the one hand, and allegiance to region and locality, on the other hand. Which genre would strike the truest American 'note'? Should writers attempt one large, synthesising story (a 'Great American Novel' along the lines of *Uncle Tom's Cabin*)? Or would a proliferation of many stories better allow each specific 'people or locality' to 'voice' its own 'habits and thought'? Bret Harte supported the latter view, arguing that 'local color', which became the dominant mode of the short story in the 1880s and 1890s, enabled the Union, 'for the first time', to recognise 'its component parts'.[17] The proliferation of new magazines allowed particular groups of American readers to read, for the first time, about people like themselves – for example, the first Yiddish periodical, *The Post*, was founded in 1870, and by 1890, there were more than 150 Afro-American magazines.[18] Other magazines, however, specifically sought out scenes and settings that were different from those their readers knew – Western stories were largely popular in Eastern periodicals, and the Boston-based *National Magazine* did 'not care for stories about New England'.[19] In other words, local colour fiction often tended towards the ethnographic and educational. The short story informed one part of the nation about another, often by means of a case study of specific, and usually 'picturesque', regional, ethnic or racial 'types':[20]

> Their faces were interesting – of the dry, shrewd, quick-witted New England type, with thin hair twisted neatly back out of the way. (Sarah Orne Jewett, 'Miss Tempy's Watchers')

He one day found in his surgery a man of rude Western type, strong-limbed and sun-burned, but trembling, hesitating and neurotic in movement ... (Bret Harte, 'A Convert of the Mission')

... presently, with her mother, 'Tite Poulette would pass – tall, straight, lithe, her great black eyes made tender by their sweeping lashes, the faintest tint of color in her Southern cheek, her form all grace, her carriage a wonder of simple dignity. (George W. Cable, ''Tite Poulette')[21]

Of course, as Edith Maud Eaton (writing under the pseudonym Sui Sin Far) gently pointed out, what constituted a picturesque 'type' depended on one's point of view:

As [Mrs Spring Fragrance] walked along she meditated upon a book which she had some notion of writing ... She would write a book about Americans for her Chinese women friends. The American people were so interesting and mysterious.[22]

A glimpse of the typically particular seemed more modern than the generality provided by an all-encompassing overview. In July 1888, just a couple of months before George Eastman registered the name Kodak to identify his small, portable box-shaped camera, Henry James wrote to Robert Louis Stevenson announcing his intention to devote himself to 'short lengths':

I want to leave a multitude of pictures of my time, projecting my small circular frame upon as many different spots as possible and going in for number as well as quality, so that the number may constitute a total having a certain value as observation and testimony.[23]

The Eastman Kodak company was founded four years later, and Thomas Wentworth Higginson wasted no time in comparing 'the rapid multi-plication of the portable Kodak' to 'the swift growth of local writers, each apparently having the same equipment of directness and vigor'.[24] Bret Harte, too, made the comparison. The short story may have had its roots in oral culture, but it was also bang up to date, able to provide 'a striking photograph of a community or a section' in 'a few lines'.[25] For Higginson, the snapshot 'scarcely surpassed' the short story in its capacity to document the country, one frame at a time.[26] The short story, like the Kodak print, was modern in its vivid particularity. If, however, it was to teach the nation about itself, it might require a form of organisation and storage more coherent than the family photo album. To Edward O'Brien, an anthology of carefully selected pieces became the perfect vehicle for demonstrating American 'variety in unity and ... unity in variety'.[27]

A 'Poe-lemical' Theory of the Short Story[28]

If the short story was deemed to represent the nation to itself, it also provided many struggling writers with a living. It is not coincidental that the first theorist of the American short story, Edgar Allan Poe, launched his career at a time, the mid-1830s, when the United States was 'experiencing the early stages of an explosion in the production and transfer of print materials'.[29] The profession of authorship was not, however, straightforward. The absence until 1891 of international copyright law meant that American publishers often chose to pirate popular British novels rather than take a risk on local authors. 'Virtually the only avenue open to writers without capital or some alternative source of income was magazine work,' and even that tended to pay poorly.[30]

Turning necessity into a virtue, Poe became a great propagandist for magazines and 'magazine literature' to which, he argued, the 'energetic, busy spirit of the age' was tending: 'in preference to the old forms of the verbose and ponderous & the inaccessible', modern readers wanted 'the curt, the condensed, the pointed, the readily diffused'.[31] Writers of 'magazine literature', however, had to overcome a 'fatal and unfounded prejudice' – 'the idea that the mere bulk of a work must enter largely into our estimate of its merit'.[32] How might such a prejudice be overcome? How could the demands of the market and those of art be reconciled? Poe's writings are filled with references to the 'many' and the 'few'. He depended on the many – whom he described as an 'insolent, rapacious, filthy' mob – for his livelihood, yet he also believed that his art could only really be appreciated by a select few.[33] Poe saw this conflict as endemic to America itself, a consequence of the country's 'republican institutions'. Democracy, he argued, nurtured an insuperable 'evil': 'here a man of large purse has usually very little soul which he keeps in it. The corruption of taste is a portion or a pendant of the dollar-manufacture.'[34] Poe's theory of the short story was an attempt to resolve this conflict, a way of exploiting the 'republican' without giving up on 'soul'. Never forgetting what might appeal to magazine readers, he was none the less determined to 'surpass, by very much, the ordinary Magazine style'.[35] He would do this by adapting the modes and theories of European Romanticism to the demands of the disposable magazine.

On the one hand, Poe's criticism emphasised organic form and the necessity of brevity for an experience of 'intense' or 'elevating excitement'.[36] The novel was 'objectionable' because, as it could not be read 'at one sitting', it could not achieve 'totality'. 'Worldly interests, intervening during the pauses of perusal, modify, counteract and annul the impressions intended.' With the brief tale, or the short lyric poem, however, an author could 'carry out his full design without interruption'. What Poe means by 'one sitting' is something between half an hour to two hours. He didn't advocate anything that would take less time than that; extremely brief stories, he maintained, would 'degenerate into epigrammatism'. 'Without a certain continuity, without a certain duration or repetition of the cause, the soul is seldom moved to the effect. There must be the dropping of water on the rock. There must be the pressing steadily of the water on the rock.'[37]

Where Poe departed from the Romantic organic metaphor was in his view of the creative process. Unlike Coleridge, Poe does not maintain an 'essential difference' between the 'creative, productive, life-power of inspired genius' and the 'shaping skill of mechanical talent'.[38] With a magazine deadline in mind, one could not afford to wait for inspiration or to leave the end-product to chance. Once the writer had decided on a particular 'effect', he must 'build' the parts – 'atoms' and 'bricks' – according to a 'pre-established design'. '*No* word' should exist that 'does not tend ... to the development of the *dénouement*, or the strengthening of the effect.'[39] Brevity, then, was not enough. 'The first necessity of the short story', wrote Elizabeth Bowen, a hundred years later, 'is *necessariness*.'[40]

Since Poe, the notion that the short story 'abhors the idea of the Novel' and has instead a 'nearer kinship to poetry' has become a commonplace.[41] Less remarked on, but just as important to Poe, however, was the difference between the short story and the poem. Indeed, he believed that the 'writer of the prose tale' had a considerable advantage over the poet in that he could 'bring to his theme a vast variety of modes or inflections of thought and expression (the ratiocinative, for example, the sarcastic, or the humorous), which are not only antagonistical to the nature of the poem, but absolutely forbidden' by its rhythm.[42] Before Poe, short prose narratives had employed a rather limited number of modes, adapted from other literary and oral sources, including the essay, the sketch, the anecdote, the letter, the parable, the folk story and the *Blackwood's* 'article of the sensation stamp'.[43] Poe's tales varied much more widely in tone and style. His target 'effects' ranged from humour to psychological terror, and his inventions encompassed the psychological confession, science fiction and the detective story, 'woven for the express purpose of unravelling'.[44]

Poe's conception of the short story, and particularly its single effect, gradually gained ground through the second half of the nineteenth century, even as tastes turned away from what, as early as 1853, was described as the 'mechanical' art of plotting.[45] Although the 'direct, swift, inevitable' narrative remained popular, writers increasingly experimented with different kinds of effect.[46] 1853 also saw the publication of Herman Melville's 'Bartleby, the Scrivener' in which a Wall Street attorney struggles to understand what his employee has meant to him, is an early instance of the short story of 'implied' rather than explicitly stated 'significance'.[47] The narrator's purpose may have been to 'awaken curiosity' in the reader, but he remains wholly 'unable to gratify it'.[48] One of the reasons that 'Bartleby' has been so popular with twentieth-century readers is that Melville's way of bringing his tale to a conclusion has become a dominant modern mode: a story about the impossibility of telling the story.

A rather different take on the matter can be found in Mark Twain's 'A Story Without an Ending', first published in 1897. A group of men on a ship decide to pass the time with a game, 'the completing of non-complete stories'. It was a game that newspapers and magazines also liked to play, and that these were in Twain's mind is confirmed when one of the men introduces his example as a 'storiette', the term invented by *Munsey's Magazine* to refer to 1,000–2,000-word pieces.[49] The storyteller is unable to complete his tale, but not because (as the Romanticists would have it) 'some secrets ... do not permit themselves to be told'.[50] Rather, straightforwardly, 'when he read the story twenty-five years ago in a train he was interrupted': 'the train jumped off a bridge'. His audience try to complete the tale, knowing that 'none but a happy ending' would be acceptable. But narrative resolution is 'beset with persistent and irreconcilable difficulties'. At three in the morning, the men give up and the narrator concludes that 'it is the reader's privilege to determine for himself how the thing came out'.[51] Twain maintained that stringing 'incongruities and absurdities together' like this, 'in a wandering and sometimes purposeless way', was the 'basis of the American art'.[52] But *Munsey's*, and the many other magazines that suddenly burst on to the scene at the end of the nineteenth century, had rather different ideas. They wanted 'plots that went somewhere' and an unambiguously 'upbeat moral'.[53]

The Magazine Revolution

By the 1880s, the 'magazine revolution' was in full swing.[54] The spread of railways, cheaper postage and paper, advances in printing (including the half-tone process of reproducing photographs) and increased literacy were among the many factors that led to the proliferation of publications within which Gilded Age manufacturers could advertise their wares. Short stories began to replace serialised novels in these new magazines, partly because of a perception that the 'complete short story' was better suited to modern tastes.[55] Horace Scudder, editor of the *Atlantic Monthly* from 1890 to 1895, was one of the first to offer a not very flattering characterisation of short story consumption that was to become common-place throughout the twentieth century: 'a race of modern readers like ours ... educated upon the scraps into which newspapers are degrading is particularly caught with stories to be taken down with a gulp'.[56] Not everyone was happy to adapt to the demands of the gulpable story. In 1908, for example, Henry James wrote to his agent complaining that he had been asked by *Harper's* 'for a Tale in 5,000 words – one of their terrible little shortest of short stories'.[57] Nevertheless, despite his feeling that there was generally 'too little room to move around' in this 'detest-able number', James had no choice but to subject his prose to the process of 'innumerable repeated chemical reductions and condensations' neces-sary to produce a saleable 'short-story' (a phenomenon he quarantined in inverted commas).[58]

But for every James, frustrated by the demands of economy (financial and literary), there were numerous others, more than happy to produce 5,000 words (or the 1,000 of a 'storiette') on a regular basis. The scale of short-story production and consumption a hundred years ago is hard for us to imagine today, as increasingly few general magazines regularly feature fiction. 'The sad thing about writing short stories', complained Norman Mailer in 1981, 'is that you can't. I don't think there are more than four or five writers of short stories in this country who actually survive that way year after year.'[59] In 1900, things were very different. Readers bought magazines, and even newspapers, largely because

of their stories – and those magazines provided their targeted reader-
ships with reliable variations on their favourite formulae (romance,
crime, courtship, the Horatio Alger rags-to-riches tale, satire).[60] The
Smart Set, for example, usually published a dozen or so stories along
with a 'novelette'; its most popular author was O. Henry, whose tales of
New York supplied a satisfying 'semi-ironic, semi-sentimental twist'.[61]
Political magazines, too, acknowledged the draw of short stories. The
Crisis (the magazine of the National Association for the Advancement of
Colored People (NAACP)) and *Opportunity* (the Urban League journal)
were launched partly as 'periodicals for short fiction by black writers
who couldn't publish elsewhere'.[62] The market for short fiction seemed
insatiable, and if, as Frank Norris noted, 'the novelist may look down
upon the mere writer of short stories, or may even look down himself in
the same capacity', that object of contempt was none the less 'the man
who has the money'.[63] (Of course, the magazines' owners and advertisers had even more money, leading James T. Farrell to describe the
short story as 'a kind of literary pimp'.[64])

But tastes were beginning to change. If 1914 saw the launch of Edward
O'Brien's attack on the 'magazinable', it also heralded the arrival of new
editors at the *Smart Set*. H. L. Mencken and George Nathan wanted
to appeal to 'the civilised minority' who preferred satirical wit and the
occasional foreign author to sentiment and the surprise ending.[65] Within
a decade that audience gravitated to the *New Yorker*, and I'll consider its
version of sophistication in Chapter 2. But it's also worth considering
what the sophisticates were reacting against. Mencken's 1915 'Litany for
Magazine Editors' summed up, and dismissed, the various forms of the
commercial short story of the period with great thoroughness. Here is a
selection:

> from stories in which a rising young district attorney gets the dead
> wood upon a burly political boss named Terrence O'Flaherty, and
> then falls in love with Mignon, his daughter, and has to let him go;
> and from stories in which a married lady, just about to sail for Capri
> with her husband's old *Corpsbruder*, is dissuaded from her purpose
> by the news that her husband has lost $700,000 in Wall Street and
> is on his way home to weep on her shoulder … and from stories in
> which the dissolute son of a department store owner tries to seduce a
> working girl in his father's employ and then goes on the water wagon
> and marries her as a tribute to her virtue; and from stories in which
> the members of a yachting party are wrecked on a desert island in the

South Pacific, and the niece of the owner of the yacht falls in love with the bo'sun ... – good Lord, deliver us![66]

Never as witty as Mencken but twice as passionate, Edward O'Brien spoke about the evils of the magazine story in extreme (and mixed metaphorical) terms. It was not merely a 'clever form of trading, in which deceptive tricks are at a high premium'; commercial story writing was also a 'mechanical product' which shackled the writer, for the 'magazine of large circulation' would never let him 'practice literary birth control' on a product that pleased its advertisers. All the moral panics of the day (commerce, mechanism, 'levelling-down', and excessive population growth among the lower classes) seem to coalesce around the short story – and not for last time.[67] O'Brien maintained that the storyteller should be thought of as belonging 'to a profession that is a sort of priesthood, and not that he is holding down a job or running a bucket shop'.[68] The most priestly role of all was assumed by the devoutly Catholic O'Brien in creating his short fiction canon.

The *Best*

O'Brien began his rescue mission in 1914, selecting for special commendation, and a reprint in the *Illustrated Sunday Magazine*, twenty-one of the 2,000-plus stories that had been published that year.[69] The project was a success and for the following year he secured a book publisher. If magazines are understood to be, and appreciated as, disposable entities, anthologies – especially, handsome hard-covered books – promised persistence, permanence, posterity; all words commonly used by O'Brien.

The Best Short Stories of 1915 and the Yearbook of the American Short Story listed and ranked 2,200 magazine stories by American, British and Irish writers. Excellence in 'form' or 'substance' was rewarded with a single asterisk; excellence in both received two, and ninety-three stories achieved three and entry into the 'Roll of Honour' for possessing 'the distinction of uniting genuine substance and artistic form in a closely woven pattern with a spiritual sincerity so earnest, and a creative belief so strong' that each might claim 'a position of some permanence in our literature'.[70] The supreme honour was the dedication, to the 'best of the best'. Dedicatees in O'Brien's tenure included Sherwood Anderson, F. Scott Fitzgerald, Ernest Hemingway, Willa Cather, Ring Lardner, Richard Wright, Irwin Shaw, along with many others who have lost their 'permanence' along the way.

Like Poe, O'Brien realised that the 'magazine prison-house' was unassailable.[71] The critic could not simply ignore their presence, but rather must help the reader identify the aristocrats among the masses. *The Yearbook* included a number of league tables which directed the reader to the magazines which were said to have published either numerically or proportionally the larger percentage of distinctive stories. From 1920 to 1922, for example, the *Dial* had a 100 per cent rating for distinctive stories; an accolade that in 1939 went to the *Atlantic Monthly*.[72] It did not take very long for commentators to note the existence of a recognisable 'O'Brien story'. In his review of the 1916 (only the second) collection, James Thayer Gerould warned that 'young writers are getting into the way of writing with Mr O'Brien and his tastes and criteria in mind', while another reviewer, Mary Colum, complained that O'Brien was 'creating standards which a real criticism should resolutely reject'.[73] In 1919, William Dean Howells wrote to Edith Wharton to tell her that he was compiling 'a book of the really "best" American short stories'.[74] By 1922, O'Brien and his methods were ripe for satire, and Oliver Herford obliged with a piece in the *Ladies Home Journal* entitled 'Say It with Asterisks': 'Never, I think, were a mob of overworked employees so pitifully huddled together in an ill-vented factory as are the Asterisks in this Sweatshop of Twaddle.'[75] O'Brien responded by dedicating that year's collection to Herford.[76]

But not everyone laughed at O'Brien's classifications. In 1919, Blanche Colton Williams, a short story instructor at Columbia University and the author of *A Handbook of Story-Writing*, came out with a new book: *How to Study 'The Best Short Stories', An Analysis of Edward J. O'Brien's Annual Volumes of the Best Short Stories of the Year Prepared for the Use of Writers and Other Students of the Short-Story*.[77] What that meant was an analysis of four of O'Brien's collections from two perspectives: 'technique' and 'what is successful from an editorial point of view. For every short-story writer must be both an artist and a man of business.'[78] Williams went on to establish a rival annual anthology, this time one whose contents were selected by a committee rather than an individual, the also still-running *O. Henry Memorial Award Prize Stories*.

What might have helped you place a story in 1919 or 1939? For O'Brien, like his mentors, Van Wyck Brooks and Waldo Frank, the key was to distinguish 'organic' Americanness from 'inorganic' or 'standardised' Americanness. Dismissing 'short story engineers' in 1923, and 'the dance of the machines' in 1929, O'Brien claimed to be searching for 'the fresh, living current which flows through the best American work'. 'No substance is of importance in fiction, unless it is organic substance, that is to say, substance in which the pulse of life is beating.'[79] In practice this meant two things. First, the story had to resemble a 'closely woven' lyric poem. (O'Brien's appraisal of the best of 1915 even included two Robert Frost verse poems: 'In the Home Stretch', he said, was 'a masterpiece of the short story regardless of the fact that it is also an admirable poem,' while 'Snow' was even 'finer ... a short story full of skilfully suggested mystery, bitingly etched psychology and dramatic contrast'.[80]) Secondly, it had to be express the 'national soul' – not merely in setting, but in style and voice. He championed many writers, but always came back to Sherwood Anderson and Ernest Hemingway as the progenitors of the new 'generation'. 'Craftsmen' who had worked most 'experimentally' on the 'materials nearest to their hands', as well as the best of their 'tradition', they had 'rendered with the utmost economy of means the inarticulate thoughts and emotions of the little man in America'.[81]

O'Brien's model of literary history, as well as of form, was organicist: he liked to think of the American short story as a creature whose evolution he was simply 'encouraging'. By 1930, he felt confident that 'the period of ferment' was over and that, largely due to the advent of mid-western magazines such as the *Midland* and the *Prairie Schooner*, 'the period of integration' had begun. In 1931, after the launch of *Story*, 'the only magazine devoted solely to the short story', O'Brien announced that it was beginning to look 'as if the editorial dykes were breaking'. In 1935, he declared that the 'battle' for the American short story had been 'won' – although he also complained about the infiltration of political issues into the literary realm. The publication of a *Best American Short Stories 1914–1939* produced even grander claims: 'Twenty-five years have made a difference in the American short story comparable to the difference between the tone and feeling of Pope and the tone and feeling of Shelley.'[82] For rhymed couplet, read standard magazine story; for Wordsworth and Coleridge, read Anderson, Hemingway and *Story* magazine – all speaking the 'real language of men'.[83]

O'Brien's creation of a canon, like most such ventures, relied on personal taste and occasionally luck. He came across 'My Old Man', his top story of 1923, only because he met its author, Ernest Hemingway, on holiday. It took him a while to catch on to the little magazine phenomenon and even longer to acknowledge stories by black writers (although Sherwood Anderson's friend, Jean Toomer, featured in 1923).[84] In 1935, the *New Masses* accused O'Brien and the editors of *Story* magazine of working together to promote only plotless and 'introspective' tales.[85] This was not entirely true: *Story* published Zora Neale Hurston's 'The Gilded Six-Bits' in 1933 and numerous 'proletarian writers', launching the careers of, among others, James T. Farrell, Erskine Caldwell and Nelson Algren; while O'Brien's 1934 collection included Langston Hughes's influential 'Cora Unashamed', in which a black maid has a child by a white man, 'an I. W. W.', and 'didn't care'.[86] As the decade went on, O'Brien eventually extended his survey to the progressive and radical journals in which many of the most interesting stories were appearing. In 1939, Richard Wright's story of a lynching, 'Bright and Morning Star', from the *New Masses*, became the first story by a black writer to win his dedication.[87]

When O'Brien died in 1941, his friend Martha Foley left *Story* to become the anthology's editor (continuing until her own death in 1977). Foley remained loyal to O'Brien's memory – she mentioned him every year – and to his nationalist missionary work. 'Against the tragic backdrop of world events today,' she wrote in her first introduction, in 1942, 'a collection of short stories may appear very unimportant.'

> Nevertheless, since the short story has always been America's own typical form of literary expression, from Washington Irving and Edgar Allan Poe onward, and since America is defending today what is her own, the short story has a right to be considered as among the cultural institutions the country is now trying to save … In its short stories, America can hear something being said that can be heard even above the crashing of bombs and the march of Panzer divisions.[88]

In the second half of the twentieth century, this kind of patriotic rhetoric largely died out, with occasional exceptions. In the midst of the Cold War, for example, William Peden subtitled a survey of short fiction 'frontline in the national defence of literature'.[89] But if most Americans did not usually feel it necessary to make such an explicit case for the national distinctiveness of the short-story form, they nevertheless continued to think of it in terms of the debates outlined in this chapter. Thinking about the short story has continued to engage with the questions outlined here: about the regional or marginal in relation to the national, the ephemeral magazine in relation to the lasting book, the lyric in relation to the narrative effect; about craft as the route to organicism. O'Brien saw the short story as evolving and improving steadily through time. The argument of this book is rather less teleological. During the last fifty years, the American short story has been praised as a highly polished gem and derided as literary fast food. The short story is never just let be. For every complaint of stagnation, comes the announcement of a new dawn. In 2000, Joyce Carol Oates declared the form an 'endangered species' and doubted that the new century would be 'as hospitable to short story writers as the nineteenth and twentieth centuries' had been.[90] Surveying the same scene, however, Vince Passaro saw a 'quiet renaissance' in progress: 'American short story', he concluded, is 'an expression we can use with some degree of domestic pride, as when referring to jazz or liberty'.[91]

Notes

1. Brander Matthews, 'The Philosophy of the Short-Story', in May (ed.), *The New Short Story Theories*, pp. 73–80. It was not until the *O.E.D. Supplement* of 1933 that the term 'short story', designating a distinct literary product, gained formal admittance into the English lexicon. Reid, *The Short Story*. p. 1.
2. Poe, *Essays and Reviews*, p. 572.
3. Ford, *The Granta Book of the American Short Story*, p. vii.
4. O'Connor, *The Lonely Voice*, p. 41.
5. Lieberman, *The American Short Story*, p. 168; Boris Eikhenbaum, 'O. Henry and the Theory of the Short Story', in May (ed.), *The New Short Story Theories*, pp. 82–3.
6. Maugham, 'The Short Story', p. 84.
7. Curnutt, *Wise Economies*, p. 2.
8. Ford, *The Granta Book of the American Short Story*, p. vii.
9. Hawthorne, *Confessions and Criticism*, p. 56.
10. Norris, *Novels and Essays*, pp. 1112–14.
11. Harte, *The Luck of Roaring Camp and Other Writings*, pp. 250–8.
12. As early as 1843, Alexis De Tocqueville predicted that 'short works will be commoner than long books' in the new busy democracy. Scofield, *The Cambridge Introduction to the American Short Story*, p. 7.
13. Matson, 'The Short Story', p. 406; O'Brien, *The Advance of the American Short Story*, p. 26.
14. Foley, *The Story of STORY Magazine*, p. 97; Saroyan, *Sons Come and Go*, p. 73; May, *The Short Story*, p. 110.
15. Sprague (ed.), *Van Wyck Brooks: The Early Years*, p. 221.
16. O'Brien, *The Best American Short Stories of 1917*, p. xx.
17. Harte, *The Luck of Roaring Camp*, pp. 252, 254.
18. Sollors, 'Immigrants and Other Americans', pp. 581–2.
19. *1001 Places to Sell Mss.* (1912), quoted in Lieberman, *The American Short Story*, p. 98. On the popularity of black Southern local colour for white Northerners, see Lamplugh, 'The Image of the Negro'; on Harte's popularity in Britain, see Keating, *The Haunted Study*, p. 43.
20. 'Locality contributes to the short story typical settings, typical characters, typical

     situations and typical problems of conscience.' Lieberman, *The American Short Story*, p. 161.

21. Jewett, *Novels and Stories*, p. 680; Harte, *Barker's Luck and Other Stories*, pp. 142–3; Cable, *Old Creole Days* , p. 216.

22. Sui Sin Far, *Mrs Spring Fragrance*, p. 28.

23. Pattee, *The Development of the Short Story*, p. 205.

24. Smith, *The American Short Story*, p. 33.

25. Harte, *The Luck of Roaring Camp*, p. 252.

26. Smith, *The American Short Story*, p. 33. On O. Henry as the 'photographer of New York Life', see Lieberman, *The American Short Story*, p. 113.

27. Smith, *The American Short Story*, pp. 40–1.

28. Poe, *Essays and Reviews*, p. 1081.

29. Sandra M. Tomc, 'Poe and His Circle', in Hayes (ed.), *The Cambridge Companion to Edgar Allan Poe*, p. 22.

30. Sandra M. Tomc, 'Poe and His Circle', p. 23.

31. Poe, *Essays and Reviews*, pp. 1377, 1414–15; Charvat, *The Profession of Authorship*, p. 91.

32. Poe, *Essays and Reviews*, pp. 583–4.

33. Poe, *Poetry and Tales*, p. 880.

34. Poe, *Poetry and Tales*, pp. 385–6.

35. I quote from Poe's 1840 prospectus for *The Penn Magazine*. Three years later he published a prospectus for *The Stylus* promising even finer 'typography, paper and binding'. Neither magazine ever appeared. *Essays and Reviews*, pp. 1025, 1033.

36. Poe, *Essays and Reviews*, p. 15.

37. Poe, *Essays and Reviews*, p. 585.

38. Arac, *The Emergence of American Literary Narrative, 1820–1860*, p. 142. See also Rachel Polonsky, 'Poe's aesthetic theory', in Hayes (ed.), *The Cambridge Companion to Edgar Allan Poe*, pp. 42–56.

39. Poe, *Essays and Reviews*, pp. 1293, 148, 572.

40. Elizabeth Bowen, *The Faber Book of Modern Short Stories*, in May (ed.), *The New Short Story Theories*, p. 260.

41. Brander Matthews, *The Philosophy of the Short-Story*, in May (ed.) *The New Short Story Theories*, p. 75; Bowen, *The Mulberry Tree*, p. 128.

42. Poe's one complaint against Hawthorne concerned his 'lack of versatility' in 'subjects' and 'tone'. *Essays and Reviews*, pp. 573, 577.

43. Poe, *Poetry and Tales*, p. 281.

44. Silverman, *Edgar Allan Poe*, p. 172.

45. Robert F. Marler, 'From Tale to Short Story', in May (ed.), *The New Short Story Theories*, p. 171.

46. Matthews, *The Philosophy of the Short-Story*, p. 67.

47. Marler, 'From Tale to Short Story', p. 172.

48. Melville, *Short Novels*, p. 34.

49. In the 1930s, for example, the Chicago *Evening Post* included a 'Weekly Short Story', to which readers were invited to supply 'an appropriately melodramatic ending'. Mullen, *Popular Fronts*, p. 135. On Munsey and the storiette, see Ohmann, *Selling Culture*, p. 292. On writing storiettes, see London, *Martin Eden*, pp. 171–2.

50. Poe, *Poetry and Tales*, p. 388.

51. Twain, *The Complete Stories*, pp. 344–51.

52. Twain, *The Complete Essays*, p. 155.
53. Ohmann, *Selling Culture*, p. 324
54. Ohmann, *Selling Culture*, p. 234.
55. Keating, *The Haunted Study*, p. 39.
56. Ballou, *The Building of the House*, p. 444.
57. Horne, 'Henry James and the Economy of the Short Story', p. 5.
58. Horne, 'Henry James and the Economy of the Short Story', pp. 5, 9, 21. It was not until he was invited to contribute to the *Yellow Book* without concern for 'arbitrary' length that James felt the 'open[ing] up' of the 'millennium to the "short story"' or rather, more often, the 'beautiful and blest *nouvelle*'. *Literary Criticism*, vol. 2, p. 1227.
59. Mailer, *Pieces and Pontifications*, p. 178.
60. A division between the 10 cent 'pulps' and 25 cent 'slicks' or 'smart' magazines began in the 1890s. Douglas, *The Smart Magazines*, p. 9. See also Damon-Moore, *Magazines for the Millions*, and Ohmann, *Selling Culture*, ch. 10.
61. Dolmetch, *The Smart Set*, p. 16.
62. These magazines 'routinely devoted large space to black short fiction', mainly concerning middle-class life. Mullen, *Popular Fronts*, p. 128.
63. Norris, *Novels and Essays*, p. 1173.
64. Farrell, *The Short Stories*, pp. xxxi–xxxii.
65. Reviewing *Dubliners* in 1914, Ezra Pound praised Joyce's avoidance of both the 'types' of local colour and the 'tiresome convention' of the Maupassant-style story: 'Life for the most part does not happen in neat little diagrams and nothing is more tiresome than the continual pretence that it does.' *The Literary Essays*, p. 400. In 1915 Pound sent two stories to the *Smart Set*. 'A Little Cloud' and 'The Boarding House' were Joyce's first American publications. Dolmetch, *The Smart Set*, pp. 77, 48–9.
66. Dolmetch, *The Smart Set*, p. 51. The rejected romances and adventure stories were shunted off into a series of spin-off magazines such as *Saucy Stories*, *Parisienne*, and most successfully, from 1920, the crime pulp, *Black Mask*.
67. O'Brien, *The Dance of the Machines*, pp. 124, 152.
68. O'Brien, *The Best Short Stories of 1920*, p. xvi.
69. Simmonds, *Edward J. O'Brien*, p. 81.
70. O'Brien, *The Best Short Stories of 1915*, p. 19.
71. Poe, *Essays and Reviews*, p. 1036.
72. Simmonds, *Edward J. O'Brien*, pp. 164, 479.
73. Simmonds, *Edward J. O'Brien*, p. 103
74. Totten, 'Critical Reception and Cultural Capital', p. 115. Howells included Wharton's 'The Mission of Jane' in *The Great Modern American Stories* (1920).
75. Simmonds, *Edward J. O'Brien*, p. 155.
76. Simmonds, *Edward J. O'Brien*, p. 163.
77. On O'Brien and Williams, see Simmonds, *Edward J. O'Brien*, p. 108.
78. Williams, *How to Study The Best Short Stories*, p. viii.
79. In 1939, E. B. White pointed out that O'Brien recycled his introductory remarks. '"No substance," wrote Mr. O'Brien in 1916, "is of importance in fiction, unless it is organic substance." "No substance," writes Mr. O'Brien in 1939, "is of importance in fiction unless it is organic substance, substance in which the pulse of life is beating."' 'The Talk of the Town', p. 7.
80. Simmonds, *Edward J. O'Brien*, p. 102. O'Brien may have been influenced by Pound's

description of Frost's *North of Boston* as part of an 'effort to proceed from the prose short story to the short story in verse'. *The Literary Essays*, p. 385.

81. Simmonds, *Edward J. O'Brien*, pp. 314, 330–1, 481, 482.

82. Simmonds, *Edward J. O'Brien*, pp. 276, 278, 287, 314, 383, 479, 480.

83. In 1931, O'Brien declared *Story* the 'most important development in English literature since Wordsworth and Coleridge published "Lyrical Ballads"'. Quoted in Foley, *The Story of STORY*, p. 133. On Anderson and Saroyan as the American Wordsworth and Coleridge, see also Beck, 'The Real Language of Men', p. 737.

84. Toomer's 'Blood Burning Moon', which first appeared in *Prairie*, became part of *Cane* (1922).

85. O'Brien was an instant fan of *Story*. He selected four stories from its first issue in 1931; in 1932 he declared it 'now the most distinguished magazine in the world'; in 1933 he dedicated the anthology to its future. Foley, *The Story of STORY*, p. 127; Simmonds, *Edward J. O'Brien*, pp. 314, 329, 350; Anderson and Kinzie, *The Little Magazine in America*, p. 737.

86. O'Brien, *The Best Short Stories 1934*, p. 190. 'Cora Unashamed' opened Hughes's *The Ways of White Folks*, 'one of the key books of 1934's proletarian renaissance'. Denning, *The Cultural Front*, p. 217.

87. O'Brien also included 'Bright and Morning Star' in his *Fifty Best*. Another story from Wright's *Uncle Tom's Children* (1938), 'Fire and Cloud', won first prize in *Story's* 1937 W.P.A contest. See Bill Mullen, 'Marking Race/Marketing Race', in Brown (ed.), *Ethnicity and the American Short Story*, p. 29; Mullen, *Popular Front*, pp. 143, 132; Simmonds, *Edward J. O'Brien*, p. 479.

88. Foley, *The Best American Short Stories 1942*, p. ix.

89. Peden, *The American Short Story: Frontline in the National Defence of Literature*, p. 1.

90. Oates, 'An Endangered Species', p. 38.

91. Passaro, 'Unlikely Voices', p. 81.

CHAPTER I

How to Write Short Stories

The mutual dependence between the short story and the magazine was well established by mid-century and, during the 1940s and 1950s, it continued to flourish as the *New Yorker* became the magazine in which every writer wished to publish. Chapter 2 will consider some of the major writers, such as J. D. Salinger and John Cheever, associated with the magazine and ask whether it makes sense to talk of a '*New Yorker* short story'. But during this period, a rather different symbiotic dependence was also being forged: one between the short story and the university classroom. This chapter will consider what mid-century Americans learned about short-story writing in college.

A 'Teachable' Form

Education in how to write short stories began in response to the magazine-fuelled short-story boom of the late nineteenth century. The first textbook, Charles R. Burnett's *Short Story Writing*, was published in 1898, and looking back from 1923, Fred Lewis Pattee declared the first decade of the century to be the great 'era of the short-story handbook'.[1] And for those who wanted further instruction, there were correspondence schools. The first opened for business in Scranton, PA in 1889, and by 1924, Ring Lardner wryly observed that 'a glimpse at the advertising columns of our leading magazines shows that whatever else this country may be shy of, there is certainly no lack of correspondence schools that learns you the art of short-story writing.' In response Lardner offered his own spoof, 'How to Write Short Stories', ending up with the advice to the novice writer *not* to enclose a stamped, self-addressed envelope because 'this is too much of a temptation to the editor'.[2]

It didn't take long for colleges to realise how 'particularly teachable' the 'short-story art' was: perhaps because they didn't think of it as an 'art' but as an 'exact science' and one whose rules could be easily, and lucratively, applied. Some teachers even advertised their courses by quoting 'statistics of the number of stories published by the class the preceding year' and promised to instruct their students how better to exploit the market.[3] During the 1930s the young Carson McCullers benefited from the advice of her teachers at New York University and Columbia, where she took classes from Whit Burnett, editor of *Story* magazine. They advised her as to which magazines would be more likely to take, say, a 'picture story' rather than a 'special knowledge' story.[4] In 1936, McCullers launched her career by winning the *Story* annual competition with a special knowledge story, 'Wunderkind', about a pianist who realises at fifteen that the promise of thirteen has vanished.

Although many graduates of writing programmes – then as now – wanted to become professional writers, college 'creative' or 'imaginative' writing was not primarily conceived as a vocational subject. Rather, as D. G. Myers has shown, the introduction of imaginative writing into the university was the result of two educational trends which gained momentum during the early decades of the twentieth century: first, progressive educational theories about the value of self-expression (rather than rote-learning); and secondly, a turn towards a technically-orientated, or New, Criticism. Literary study had previously been dominated by historical philology: what the New Critics advocated instead was a method of reading grounded in the practical experience of writing. Students would approach literature 'from the inside': by focusing on the way that poems and stories were made, they would learn to read 'like writers' themselves.[5] By mid-century, the New Criticism had 'revolutionized the teaching of English literature in American colleges'.[6]

This pedagogic trend had a pragmatic, as well as a philosophical, basis. Access to higher education had been gradually developing before the Second World War, but the end of the war saw its massive, and rapid, extension and professionalisation, partly because a large number of demobilised soldiers took advantage of the 1944 Servicemen's Readjustment Act (the GI Bill) to pursue a free college education. One reason why the New Critics set the tone of literary study from the 1930s to the 1960s was that their methods worked so well in the newly crowded classrooms of America's colleges. Students didn't need any prior knowledge of 'extrinsic' factors – history, biography or literary history – in order to examine the 'intrinsic' features of a particular poem or short story.[7] Furthermore, 'by studying stories', those same students could become 'sensitive' to the 'principles' required to write their own.[8]

Writing also became a graduate degree, resulting in the award of the Master of Fine Arts (MFA). One of the first, and still the most famous, of MFA courses was that offered by the poet Paul Engle at the University of Iowa. Engle had been a good friend of Edward J. O'Brien, founding editor of the *Best Short Stories* anthologies. O'Brien described Engle as the equal of Whitman and Dickinson, and found in his poetry 'everything that the short story has been doing to interpret American conscious- ness'. The two men had similar views on the dangers of the 'machine age', the need to 'release poetic activity through the short story', and the importance of the Midwest in American literature's 'coming of age'.[9] Engle's Writers' Workshop would follow and develop the principles that O'Brien had set down in his anthology introductions.[10]

Named in 1939, with Engle taking over as director in 1942, the Iowa Writers' Workshop really came into its own after the war.[11] The 1945 class contained forty-five students, more than half of whom were returned servicemen keen to write about their war experiences; among only three women was a 20-year-old from Georgia called Flannery O'Connor, widely regarded today as one of the finest twentieth-century American story-writers.[12] But Iowa was not the only place where one could learn how to write: between 1946 and 1948, graduate writing programmes were set up at the universities of Johns Hopkins, Stanford, Denver and Cornell, each of which developed, at different times, a particular reputa- tion for its short fiction.

By 1950, Myers argues, the university had 'become the permanent center of artistic activity in America'. Others concur: Ted Solotoroff describes 'the rise of creative writing programmes' as 'the one genuinely revolutionary development in American letters during the second half of the century', while for Mark McGurl it is not only 'the most impor- tant event in postwar American literary history', but also the 'key' to understanding the distinctive features of postwar American literature.[13] The methods and impact of those writing programmes will be a theme throughout the rest of this book, but to understand how, and why, they developed as they did, it is first necessary to return to 1945, when Flannery O'Connor arrived at the University of Iowa.

'Long in Depth': The Short Stories of Flannery O'Connor

After a false start studying Magazine Writing (geared directly towards 'selling stories to magazines'), O'Connor enrolled in two courses in

which 'artistic standards prevailed over mere commercial publication':
Understanding Fiction (theory) and the Writers' Workshop (practice).[14]
The criticism class took its title from that of its textbook: an anthology of
stories arranged around topics such as 'how plot reveals', 'what character
reveals' and 'what theme reveals'. The book's editors, Cleanth Brooks
and Robert Penn Warren, declared their method 'inductive'; the close
study of 'concrete cases' would enable students to investigate, interpret
and make comparisons. Although it claimed to cover fiction in general,
the anthology's examples are all complete short stories – rather than
extracts from novels, which always require a context – and so it is in
effect a textbook on understanding *short* fiction. Moreover, Brooks and
Penn Warren realised that at least some of its readers would treat 'understanding' as the first step towards writing their own stories. Keen to
distinguish their approach from the how-to handbook – they reiterate
familiar complaints against the 'mechanical' methods and 'set formula'
of 'magazine fiction' and familiar praise for 'organic unity' – Brooks
and Penn Warren warned their readers that there was 'no ideal form,
or set of forms for the short story'. They did, however, believe that
certain fundamental 'principles' should be followed, and these were set
out in a helpful appendix. First published in 1943, *Understanding Fiction*
had an enormous influence on the development of the mid-century
American short story, far beyond Iowa. What the editors did not antici-
pate was how faithfully students would apply their principles, and how
easily the literary short story, as they conceived it, could itself become a
standardised magazine product.

Long after she graduated from Iowa, Flannery O'Connor acknowledged the 'invaluable help' provided by *Understanding Fiction*, and
in 1959 what John Barth was later to describe as the workshop graduate's ultimate dream – to find oneself included in the anthology one
had studied – came true.[15] The second edition of *Understanding Fiction*
included 'A Good Man is Hard to Find', the title story of her 1955 collection. (O'Connor later wrote that every time she learned that a story of
hers was to be included in an anthology, she had 'a vision of it, with its
little organs laid open, like a frog in a bottle'.[16]) Many of O'Connor's
early pieces are closely modelled on the stories she first encountered
in the *Understanding Fiction*: 'The Coat' reworks Maupassant's 'The
Necklace'; her first published story, 'The Geranium', takes Caroline
Gordon's 'Old Red' as a prototype. Other Brooks and Penn Warren
choices, echoes of which can be found in her stories, included Joyce's

'Araby', Faulkner's 'A Rose for Emily', Hawthorne's 'The Birthmark', and Poe's 'The Fall of the House of Usher' ('an influence I would rather not think about', she once said).[17] But O'Connor also learnt a great deal from the critical commentary that accompanied those stories and from the volume's discussion of 'technical problems and principles'. More generally, she later acknowledged, she was very much a part of 'that literary generation whose education was in the hands of the New Critics or those influenced by them'.[18]

For all their emphasis on technique, the New Critics were essentially moralists. They talked a lot about literature's value, which they maintained lay in its difference from science or sociology. Literature offered a 'special kind of knowledge', one which was not necessarily religious, but which was open to insights other than those available by means of everyday empirical observation (the New Critical understanding of the natural and social sciences).[19] This was an idea that had its origins in Romanticism or, more particularly, in Coleridge's desire to find in literature an 'ontological sanctuary' from 'secularising discourses', complete in itself.[20] The New Critics focused so much of their attention on the lyric poem and the short story, its prose equivalent, first, because the very brevity of those forms demanded the exclusion of discourses whose effect could only ever be cumulative, and, second, because it encouraged an alternative 'mode of cognition'.[21] On this view, what the lyric or short story worked to suggest, at the very least, was the incompleteness or inadequacy of empiricism. The first-person narrator of Melville's 'Bartleby' (discussed in the Introduction) submits both observations and an interpretation of those observations before finally acknowledging that he has nothing definitive to offer. The story has escaped its telling. Ideally, in the New Critical view, and this is often the case in the work of O'Connor, the short story provokes suspicion of the empirical claims it has itself made. The function of the artist, O'Connor said, is to 'penetrate the concrete world in order to find at its depths the image of its source, the image of ultimate reality'.[22] This move was essential, she thought, if the short story was to escape being merely 'slight'. A story must be 'long in depth'; that is, every detail must 'increase' it 'in every direction' in order that, finally, it can 'reveal as much of the mystery of existence as possible'.[23] The short story, thus conceived, ends up with a larger scope than a realist novel ten times its size.

I'll explore the implications of O'Connor's theory for her practice in a moment, but it's worth pausing to note how many other short story writers and theorists have evoked mystery as a way to avoid slightness. The 'first thing we see about a short story is its mystery', said Eudora Welty, another protégé of Penn Warren and Brooks who sought to create a 'confluence' in her fiction, 'a reality and a symbol in one'.[24] Two stories by Welty are included in *Understanding Fiction*, one of which, 'A Piece of News', is praised for offering a 'sense of illumination in which old and familiar things, by acquiring an altered focus, become mysterious and strange ... a recurrent theme in fiction as it is a basic fact in human existence'.[25] The New Critical 1940s and 1950s are long gone, but the jargon of mystery has proved remarkably enduring. In 1971, Joyce Carol Oates declared that the 'most interesting thing' about short fiction 'is its mystery'.[26] In a 1998 essay on the genre's 'future', Mary Rohrberger concluded that 'short stories question the existential world that the novel demonstrates' and that they are 'built on the metaphysical assumption that the ideal and the real merge at a moment of revelation'.[27] And in 2004, Charles E. May, perhaps the best-known recent short-fiction theorist, argued that the 'formal demands of the genre' – resulting from its 'compactness' – inevitably entail a focus on the 'mysteries of dreams, fears and anxieties' that exist 'outside the realm of familiar, everyday life'. For May, the form's 'basic sense of mystery' aligns it with religion 'in the most basic sense', that is, with 'those moments when we are made aware of the inauthenticity of everyday life, those moments when we sense the inadequacy of our categories of conceptual reality'.[28] The vagueness of this kind of formulation should not be allowed to conceal the history of its derivation from a highly specific literary philosophy and pedagogy. I'll say more about its endurance in today's workshop fiction in Chapter 5.

O'Connor embraced religion in more than its most basic sense. A committed Roman Catholic, she was steeped in theology and intolerant of the secular false 'prophesies' on offer in 1950s America. What she termed variously a 'grotesque' or 'deeper' realism provided an alternative to the 'social determinism' of 'abnormal psychology', 'Madison Avenue', 'men in gray-flannel suits', the 'mean average' of the 'poll-taker' and the 'middlebrow'.[29] 'Categories of conceptual reality', to recall May's phrase, proliferated during the 1940s and 1950s, and O'Connor was not alone in noting, and rejecting, many of these, in particular what C. Wright Mills named the 'sociological imagination'.[30] It became commonplace to complain about the 'tendency of modern industrial society' to 'transform the individual' into the 'mass' man or 'other-directed' woman, 'cheerful robots' defined by their peers, the media and a proliferation of socio-logical investigations into all aspects of their lives, from work to leisure to sex.[31] These trends were thought to encompass the whole country and O'Connor, like many of her teachers and mentors, was worried that the South in particular was losing its distinctive features; 'every day we are getting more and more like the rest of the country'.[32] Regionalism, for O'Connor and her teachers, was less a matter of local colour than of local 'sensitivity'. Southerners, she wrote, having experienced through defeat in the Civil War their own particular Fall, view the 'modern world' with an 'inburnt knowledge of human limitations and with a sense of mystery ... not sufficiently developed in the rest of our country'.[33] For her, the sense of mystery was political as well as religious.

O'Connor, and the Southern college-based magazines in which she mainly published – *Kenyon Review, Sewanee Review, Shenandoah* – tended to argue that the rest of the country, suffering a 'hangover' from 1930s 'social realism', treated fiction as nothing more than a branch of social science.[34] For O'Connor, any story that could be 'reduced' to an ideological 'statement' or abstract proposition or moral message was, by definition, no good, a 'dreary blight'.[35] In almost all of the many lectures she gave in later life, O'Connor chastised students who asked for interpretations of her stories: 'meaning', she said 'cannot be captured in an interpretation', only 'experienced'.[36] Like the critic, the author must never commit what Cleanth Brooks famously dubbed the 'heresy of paraphrase'.[37] Another way of putting this is to say that there should be no distinction between form and content. Form does not express meaning; 'form *is* meaning' said Allen Tate (after Coleridge).[38] O'Connor added her own echo. 'The more you write,' she told a class of students, 'the more you will realize that the form is organic, that it is something which grows out of the material, that the form of each story is unique.'[39] But if form grew like a plant, it was also, like a table or chair, reliant on careful and thrifty craftsmanship in the workshop or the Writers' Workshop. The old double-think, familiar from Poe's writing – advocating the fastidious chiselling of an *object* in order to produce a transcendent *experience* – formed the basis of New Critical discussions of the short story.

It has become commonplace to describe Flannery O'Connor as a pure product, perhaps *the* pure product, of Workshop New Criticism. Mark McGurl describes her stories as 'pre-packaged for close reading in the classroom', 'a systematic production of that institutional space, and of its virtual supplement, the New Critical textbook', while Frederick Crews asserts that even at their 'most impressive and original', they 'adhere to the classroom formula of her day':

> show, don't tell; keep the narrative voice distinct from those of your characters; cultivate understatement; develop a central image or symbol to convey your theme 'objectively' and point everything toward one neatly sprung ironic reversal.[40]

As we have already seen, O'Connor's own critical writings and lectures often repeat these injunctions: keeping everything 'under control', 'showing, not … saying', operating from 'behind the scenes, apparently disinterested', relying an 'elected image' to express and 'contain' 'thoughts and feelings'.[41] Her stories, however, are another matter.

Where O'Connor remains closest to the 'formula' is in her use of symbols. Her first few stories, submitted as part of her Iowa MFA thesis, identify their 'elected' images directly in the titles – 'The Turkey', 'The Train', 'The Geranium' – and use them in a straightforward way. In 'The Geranium', an old Southern man, living with his daughter on the sixth floor of a Manhattan apartment building, finds an affinity with a pot plant on a neighbour's window sill. Like him, the geranium is squashed, neglected and generally diminished by urban life and, not very surprisingly, it ends up 'at the bottom of the alley with its roots in the air'.[42] As O'Connor progressed as a writer, however, her symbols became less immediately identifiable *as* symbols. The trick, she said, was to make 'the concrete work double time', to allow 'details' to function naturalistically and then gradually to 'accumulate meaning from the story itself': 'when this happens, they become symbolic in their action'.[43] A symbol shouldn't be 'transparent', instructed *Understanding Fiction*; it must be 'prepared for' and it must contribute to the story's 'pattern'.[44]

Consider 'The Lame Shall Enter First' – a modern take on 'The Birthmark' or 'The Artist of the Beautiful', Hawthorne's parables about over-reaching rationalists.[45] We first meet Sheppard, a widower, while he's eating 'soggy' cereal 'mechanically' out of a 'pasteboard box', which he later throws into the garbage.[46] His son Norton's breakfast – a piece of stale chocolate cake smeared with peanut butter and then ketchup – is equally unsatisfying and Norton soon throws it all up, 'a limp sweet batter'. 'He hung over it gagging, more came, and he waited with his mouth over the plate as if he expected his heart to come up next.' Sheppard tells him it's 'all right' and that he 'couldn't help it'. The scene introduces the story's central subject: reason's inability to acknowledge or articulate the uncontrolled mess of human suffering. Norton, in fact, can 'help it': in throwing up the contents of his stomach, he may be struggling to express (to ex–press), in the only way he knows how, the contents of his heart. But Sheppard does not understand that his son's 'gorge' rises out of a despair which has not yet quite lost touch with hope. Nor is he any more attentive to his own gorge when it, too, rises, here and throughout the story. He thinks it's enough to clear the mess away. The problem with Norton, he decides, is greed and 'selfishness', especially when compared on a rational basis with Rufus Johnson, a boy he knows from volunteering at the town reformatory, and whom he had seen rifling for food in a garbage can. Sheppard exemplifies a recurrent O'Connor type: the self-satisfied liberal who reads about progress (here, the space race) in the *New York Times*, the intellectual equivalent of soggy cereal, who gains 'satisfaction' from helping those outside his family while showing no feeling for those within, and who refuses to acknowledge the power of evil in the world ('Nobody has given any reliable evidence that there's a hell,' he says).[47] When evil makes an appearance – here, and in many other stories – in the unlikely form of a literal-minded Protestant fundamentalist, it is welcomed as the only force that can shatter 'smugness', the 'Great Catholic Sin'.[48]

Sheppard thinks of Rufus as Norton's double: the boy who has nothing in contrast to the boy who has everything. One of the story's ironic twists is to turn this around; another is to suggest that Rufus, with his Protestant fundamentalist upbringing, is also Sheppard's doppelgänger, the 'prophet-freak' to his 'big tin Jesus'. Rufus's eyes become 'distorting mirrors' in which Sheppard sees himself made 'hideous and grotesque'. Different kinds of vision provide one metaphorical pattern in the story; eating, as we have seen, offers another. Sheppard eats from a box without paying 'attention to what he was eating'; Rufus eats out of a garbage can 'because I like to eat out of garbage cans'. In other words, O'Connor has created another kind of mirror, one which reveals cereal boxes to be like garbage cans, except less satisfying. Nor is food merely food. Sheppard finally acknowledges that he has neglected his child 'to feed his vision of himself', to fill 'his own emptiness with good works like a glutton'. The man's 'vision of himself shrivelled until everything was black before him', but the revelation has come too late. He climbs the stairs to the attic but finds himself, as in a story by Poe, 'like a man at the edge of a pit'. The hapless Norton, shepherded by Rufus rather than his father, made to believe he will find his dead mother in heaven, has hung himself. At this point another 'detail' begins to work double-time: the 'telescope', Sheppard's emblem of technology's promise of transcendence, has fallen off its tripod on to the floor.

In *Understanding Fiction*, Brooks and Penn Warren make a clear distinction between a story's 'denouement' – the 'point at which the fate of the character is clear ... or, perhaps, the moment when the character comprehends his own final position' – and its 'key moment', the moment of 'illumination' which 'brings into focus all previous events and inter-prets all previous events' and 'contains within itself, by implication at least, the total meaning of the story'. These two moments *'may or may not* coincide'.[49] In 'The Lame Shall Enter First', they almost coincide. The denouement is Sheppard's realisation that his son is dead. The key moment occurs when the narrator moves away from Sheppard's point of view and instead brings into focus and interprets for the reader the story's pattern of images: 'A few feet over [the telescope], the child hung in the jungle of shadows, just below the beam from which he had launched his flight into space.'

Considered in this way, O'Connor's story seems to fulfil the New Critical brief of a delicately controlled 'pattern of resolutions, and balances' developed through its 'temporal scheme'.[50] This was Cleanth Brooks's description of the unity required by a 'well-wrought urn'. But the third kind of pattern, after resolution and balance, that Brooks describes – 'harmonization' – doesn't really account for the incongruities that remain incongruous in the story: its moments of disgust and jarring comedy, its sensationally punitive ending, and our sense that the narrator does 'climb out' of the story 'into the meaning' (precisely what O'Connor says shouldn't happen).[51] Like Poe's, O'Connor's stories depend on the 'close circumscription of space' – in attics, closets, plant pots, cars, waiting-rooms, buses and the 'inner compartment' of the mind.[52] In the work of both writers, while each element (plot, pattern, tone) seems to be 'under control', the result is often a kind of furious explosion, like a 'piece of machinery that has been given one ounce of pressure too much', as the lid flies off the well-wrought urn.[53] Think of Mary Grace in 'Revela-tion' turning 'purple' as she hurls her book across the room, or Norton's gagging.[54] Moments like this, of sheer rage or disgust, burst out of the pattern. In each case, it is the protagonist who explodes – and the story itself which cannot altogether contain the damage.

For if O'Connor largely followed her teachers' advice on structure, she was more inclined to go her own way when it came to narrative voice and tone. Brooks and Penn Warren favoured 'suggestiveness' and 'ironical ambivalence' in 'subtle' shades of grey. They admired the 'reticence' of James, Chekhov and Mansfield and, among their contemporaries, praised Eudora Welty whose 'subdued' stories, they noted, develop 'delicately'.[55] O'Connor, however, is anything but reticent, delicate or subdued. Her stories present black turning to white and white turning to black against the background of a 'luridly bright pastoral world'.[56] 'To the hard of hearing you shout and for the almost blind you draw large and startling figures.' How else, she asked, could one make the 'distortions' of modern life clear to an 'audience which is used to seeing them as natural'?[57] It is hard to reconcile O'Connor's urge to 'shout' with her advocacy of 'apparently disinterested' narration in the Jamesian mode.[58] Indeed, while her essays celebrate detachment, her stories mock characters, such as Hulga, in 'Good Country People', or Julian, in 'Everything That Rises Must Converge', who think themselves 'clear and detached and ironic', and who observe others 'from a great distance' and 'with absolute clarity' and 'complete objectivity'.[59] The stories are on the side of those who shout.

Whatever she might say, O'Connor's fiction does not create a 'world apparently without comment'.[60] Her irony is 'militant'; her narrators 'strident' and 'fierce'.[61] Steering clear of a direct 'statement of meaning', as she was taught, she relies instead on what John Hawkes described as the 'devil's "demolishing" syntax'.[62] We see it in the mocking final sentence of 'The Lame Shall Enter First', in bathetic similes ('an honest look that fitted into his face like a set of false teeth') and in her favourite 'as if' construction.[63] Once, after her mentor Caroline Gordon complained that there were too many, O'Connor set to work removing these constructions from her page proofs, a task, she later recalled, that was 'like getting ticks off a dog'.[64] But here is one she kept, from 'The Lame Shall Enter First':

> An old gray winter coat of his wife's still hung there. He pushed it aside but it didn't move. He pulled it open roughly and winced as if he had seen the larva inside a cocoon. Norton stood in it, his face swollen and pale, with a drugged look of misery on it.

As we have seen, Sheppard tries to reason away his grief and, more importantly, that of his son – and for that he will be punished severely. But at the same time as the story moves through its pattern of images and ironic reversals towards the 'key moment' of understanding, it also presents moments of formlessness which punctuate the patterns favoured both by Sheppard and the story itself. First of all, the coat does not behave as a coat should. It seems almost animate in its refusal to move when 'pushed aside'. Then the sight of Norton inside forces from Sheppard a visceral reaction, comparable with the nausea he'd felt when staring at the boy's vomit: a sour-smelling 'puddle of half-digested food'. But, like Norton, Sheppard is unable to acknowledge his feeling; the 'as if' belongs to the narrator.

The use of 'as if' to undermine form is unusual in O'Connor's work. More frequently she uses the phrase to signal moments when one design gives way to another, when the secular concedes, rather straightforwardly, to the divine:[65]

> They stood looking at the artificial Negro *as if* they were faced with some great mystery, some monument to another's victory that brought them together in their common defeat. They could feel it dissolving their differences *like* an action of mercy. ('The Artificial Nigger')[66]

> The eyes that stared back at him were the same that returned his gaze every day from that mirror but it *seemed* to him that they were paler. They looked shocked clean *as if* they had been prepared for some awful vision about to come down on him. ('The Enduring Chill')[67]

This last example – emphasised by my italics – represents the turn-around of Asbury, another *New York Times* reader. Asbury had thought he was going to introduce his mother to 'reality', but he is the one who experiences the descent of the Holy Ghost and 'the last film of illusion ... torn *as if* by a whirlwind from his eyes'.

A similar process takes place in 'Everything That Rises Must Converge': a college graduate returns home, tries to teach his mother a lesson but is taught one himself. Published in 1961, six years after Rosa Parks refused to give up her seat to a white man on an Alabama bus, 'Everything That Rises' is set on an integrated bus. Julian's mother is torn between her desire to attend her 'reducing' class and her fear of the buses, so she asks her son to accompany her. This provides him with the perfect opportunity to demonstrate that, unlike his mother, he is 'free from prejudice'. His dream comes true when a black woman, wearing the identical 'hideous hat' to his mother, sits nearby.[68] His mother offends the woman by offering money to her child and Julian's expectations seem to have been fulfilled. But when the woman strikes his mother with her 'black fist' and she collapses, so does his smugness. 'Mamma', 'Darling, sweetheart!' he calls out, too late. The expected ironic reversal has occurred: in making his mother 'face a few realities', he finds himself facing the ultimate, the only, reality. Julian runs for help but the story ends with his feet moving 'numbly as if they carried him nowhere. The tide of darkness seemed to sweep him back to her, postponing from moment to moment his entry into the world of guilt and sorrow.'

The final two sentences clearly constitute the story's 'key moment', the moment which, according to *Understanding Fiction*, 'interprets all previous events'.[69] But what sense can we make of it? O'Connor might say that her subject is simply the 'action' or 'acceptance' of 'grace' and that the story's 'topical' setting simply provided a context in which that can occur.[70] If we accept this – as many critics have – then the black woman on the bus remains a faceless educational device, albeit one designed for Julian rather than, as he had intended, his mother.[71] While Alice Walker has argued that O'Connor should be commended for retaining a 'certain distance' from a character she knows nothing about, others have chastised her for opting out of politics.[72] But is this not a political story? From the very start, 'Everything That Rises' announces its preoccupation with change. 'The old world is gone,' Julian tells his mother, 'you've got to live in a new world.' He is right. By 1961, the momentum of the Civil Rights Movement was well underway, its 'progress' expressed in the figure of the 'huge' black woman 'disappearing down the street'. But what future was there for white Southerners? O'Connor provides two resolutions, one for each of her protagonists. The first answer to black momentum is white 'collapse', which finds its 'focus' in the image of Julian's 'immobile' mother with 'black apartment buildings' rising above her. She does not need to adapt or 'reduce' to a new world which promises salvation through the superficial secular communion of integration; she can escape by dying, her final words a call to her 'old darky' nurse to 'come get' her. In heaven, it is suggested, there is something better than social 'principles'. Julian's is a trickier case. His removal from the 'new world' is the result of metaphor rather than plot. In a story patterned by contrasting light and dark imagery, the narrator ends with a 'tide of darkness' – one that is travelling in the opposite direction to the integrated bus and that brings Julian 'back' to the family-centred values of the 'old' world, perhaps even as far as the antebellum estate for which he felt both 'contempt' and 'longing', as well as to the edge of mystery. All seems resolved, except for one detail and another 'as if'.

As she dies, Julian's mother's face becomes 'fiercely distorted'. One eye fixes on Julian's face, finds 'nothing' and closes. The other, however, 'moved slightly to the left *as if* it had become unmoored'. Thinking of this wayward eye – and it's hard not to – the story's resolution suddenly seems less certain. What exactly has been unmoored, here? A dead woman's eye? Or that bit of reality which will forever resist aesthetic or religious consolation? The trouble with the unmoored eye is that there's just no mystery to it.

'Everything That Rises' seems even more unsettling if we compare it with another story dealing with the Civil Rights struggle which O'Connor particularly disliked. Medgar Evans, field secretary of the Mississippi NAACP, was murdered on 12 June 1963. Eleven days later, Eudora Welty submitted to the *New Yorker* an internal monologue from the point of view of the killer. On the one hand, readers were encouraged to think of the piece as a 'story from the inside'; in other words, they were being given access to the kind of thoughts such a man might have had, expressed in the kind of language he would have been likely to use; this was, Welty said, a 'daring' attempt.[73] On the other hand, however, the story offered a reassuring interpretative framework familiar to any mid-century reader of New Critical short fiction. This reveals itself in several ways: in the title, 'Where is the Voice Coming From?' which has generally been thought to implicate the South, or even the nation, as a whole; in the name of the town, Thermopylae, which educated readers would recognise as the mountain pass where a small Greek force tried to resist a large Persian army in 480 BC, and thus appreciate an 'ironic reversal'; and in a metaphorical pattern of hellish heat, light and dark that the 'voice' presents, seemingly unaware of how literary he is being.[74] The shift between narrative styles is particularly striking in the description of the murder itself, when the killer's thoughts take the form of baroque simile:

> Something darker than him, like the wings of a bird, spread on his back and pulled him down. He climbed up once, like a man under bad claws, and like just blood could weigh a ton he walked with it on his back to better light. Didn't get no further than his door. And fell to stay.[75]

'Man is articulate and intelligible,' Welty once wrote, 'only when he begins to communicate within the strict terms of poetry', that is, in 'permanent' symbols.[76] But the murderer's articulacy is short-lived.

He thinks that he has expressed something 'for keeps, for good and all, for ever and amen', but his voice, or rather his deed, makes no lasting impression on the new media-saturated social order. The TV cannot be 'turned off'; the dead man's face is on screen before the murder and afterwards 'there it is again – the same picture'.

One can imagine that O'Connor disliked the story's claim to topicality and its insistence that we should try to understand the 'abnormal psychology' of murderers. The story exemplified what she saw as modern fiction's insistence on 'hazy compassion': that is, the excusing of 'all human weakness because human weakness is human'.[77] But what disturbed her 'most' was 'its being in the *New Yorker* and the stupid Yankee liberals smacking their lips over typical life in the dear old dirty Southland'.[78] O'Connor's sense of the story's reception was not far off the mark. Shortly after its publication, Welty received a phone call from a New York reporter asking whether she had suffered 'repercussions' and offering to call back 'in case anything develops': 'I told him I couldn't see any sense in his running up his phone bill. The people who burn crosses on lawns don't read me in the *New Yorker*.'[79]

Notes

1. Pattee, *The Development of the Short Story*, p. 364. See also Myers, *The Elephants Teach*, p. 68.
2. Lardner, *The Best of Ring Lardner*, pp. 207, 210.
3. Pattee, *The Development of the Short Story*, p. 364.
4. McCullers, *The Mortgaged Heart*, p. 100.
5. Norman Foerster, quoted in Myers, *The Elephants Teach*, p. 133.
6. Wellek, *A History of Modern Criticism*, vol. 6, p. 191.
7. Wellek and Warren, *Theory of Literature*, Pts 3 and 4. While working on the book, Warren taught a seminar in Literary Criticism at Iowa, which Flannery O'Connor attended. Her essay 'The Teaching of Literature' recapitulates many of these ideas. *Mystery and Manners*, pp. 121–34. Gooch, *Flannery*, p. 133.
8. Brooks and Penn Warren, *Understanding Fiction*, p. 571.
9. O' Brien, *The Best American Short Stories 1934*, pp. xv–xvii. See also Simmonds, *Edward J. O'Brien*, pp. 347–49, 390.
10. Engle also served as editor of the O. Henry Prize Stories from 1954 to 1959.
11. The first story-writing course was taught in 1900–1; the first short fiction MA thesis (Wallace Stegner's 'Bloodstain and Other Stories') was submitted in 1932. Wilbers, *The Iowa Writers' Workshop*, pp. 36, 57.
12. Gooch, *Flannery*, p. 131.
13. Myers, *The Elephants Teach*, p. 148; Solotaroff, 'Writing in the Cold', p. 266; McGurl, *The Program Era*, p. ix.
14. Gooch, *Flannery*, p. 121. O'Connor's contemporary, James B. Hall, recalled that

when another member of the Workshop published a story in the *Saturday Evening Post*, 'some people would not speak to him'. 'Recollections of the Iowa Writers' Workshop', in Dana (ed.), *A Community of Writers*, p. 17.

15. O'Connor, *The Habit of Being*, pp. 83–4; Barth, *Further Fridays*, p. 274.
16. O'Connor, *Mystery and Manners*, p. 108.
17. O'Connor, *The Habit of Being*, p. 98.
18. Asals, *Flannery O'Connor*, p. 130.
19. Brooks and Wimsatt, *Literary Criticism*, p. 601.
20. Lentricchia, *After the New Criticism*, p. 6.
21. Kermode, *Romantic Image*, p. 187.
22. O'Connor, *Mystery and Manners*, p. 157.
23. O'Connor, *Mystery and Manners*, pp. 94, 96.
24. Eudora Welty, 'The Reading and Writing of Short Stories', in May (ed.), *Short Story Theories*, p. 164; Welty, *One Writer's Beginnings*, p. 102. The *Southern Review*, edited by Penn Warren and Brooks, published more stories by Welty than by any other writer. See Penn Warren, 'Love and Separateness in Eudora Welty' in *Selected Essays*, pp. 156–69.
25. Brooks and Penn Warren, *Understanding Fiction*, p. 145.
26. Oates, 'The Short Story', pp. 213–14.
27. Mary Rohrberger, 'Where Do We Go from Here?', in Lounsberry *et al.* (eds), *The Tales We Tell*, p. 205.
28. Charles E. May, 'Why Short Stories are Essential and Why They are Seldom Read', in Winther *et al.* (eds), *The Art of Brevity*, pp. 16–17; May, 'The Nature of Knowledge in Short Fiction', in May (ed.), *The New Short Story Theories*, pp. 141–2.
29. O'Connor, *The Habit of Being*, p. 437; *Mystery and Manners*, pp. 39–41, 50, 58, 200. She is alluding to Sloan Wilson's best-selling novel, *The Man in the Gray Flannel Suit* (1955).
30. Mills, *The Sociological Imagination*, p. 14.
31. Macdonald, *Against the American Grain*, p. 8; Riesman, *The Lonely Crowd*, p. 151; Mills, *The Sociological Imagination* p. 171.
32. O'Connor, *Mystery and Manners*, p. 29.
33. O'Connor, *Mystery and Manners*, p. 59.
34. O'Connor, *Mystery and Manners*, p. 164.
35. O'Connor, *Mystery and Manners*, pp. 73, 38, 96, 102.
36. O'Connor, *Mystery and Manners*, p. 71; O'Connor, *The Habit of Being*, p. 437.
37. Brooks, *The Well Wrought Urn*, ch. 11.
38. Tate, *Essays of Four Decades*, p. 350.
39. O'Connor, *Mystery and Manners*, pp. 101–2.
40. McGurl, *The Program Era*, p. 144; Crews, *The Critics Bear It Away*, pp. 144–5.
41. O'Connor, *Mystery and Manners*, pp. 3, 98, 100, 74; Asals, *Flannery O'Connor*, p. 130.
42. O'Connor, *Collected Stories*, p. 14.
43. O'Connor, *Mystery and Manners*, pp. 70, 99–100.
44. Brooks and Penn Warren, *Understanding Fiction*, pp. 105, 86.
45. Gooch, *Flannery*, pp. 328, 340. Richard Chase's *The American Novel and Its Tradition* (1957) claimed romance – the exploration of the 'neutral territory' between the actual and imaginary (as Hawthorne put it) – as America's distinctive mode. O'Connor read Chase's book in 1960, thought it 'very good' and described herself

as working in the 'modern romance tradition'. *The Habit of Being*, p. 408; *Mystery and Manners*, p. 46.

46. O'Connor, *Collected Stories*, pp. 445–82.
47. Here, too, O'Connor's views chime closely with Tate's. If poetry is 'one of the sources of the knowledge of evil in man', he wrote, the 'graphs' and 'charts' of social science represent a 'powerful attempt to purify ourselves of that knowledge'. *Essays of Four Decades*, pp. 28, 29.
48. O'Connor, *The Habit of Being*, p. 131.
49. Brooks and Penn Warren, *Understanding Fiction*, pp. 583, 577.
50. Brooks, *The Well Wrought Urn*, p. 186.
51. O'Connor, *Mystery and Manners*, p. 73.
52. Poe, *Essays and Reviews*, p. 21; O'Connor, *Collected Stories*, p. 411.
53. O'Connor, *Mystery and Manners*, p. 100; O'Connor, *Collected Stories*, p. 418.
54. O'Connor, *Collected Stories*, p. 499.
55. Brooks and Penn Warren, *Understanding Fiction*, pp. 576, xvii, 144–5.
56. Hawkes, 'Flannery O'Connor's Devil', p. 399.
57. O'Connor, *Mystery and Manners*, pp. 33–4
58. O'Connor, *Mystery and Manners* , p. 74.
59. O'Connor, *Mystery and Manners*, pp. 285, 411, 412.
60. O'Connor, *Mystery and Manners*, p. 74.
61. Northrop Frye defined satire as 'militant irony' in *Anatomy of Criticism*, p. 223. See also, Brinkmeyer, *The Art and Vision of Flannery O'Connor*, p. 101; Gordon, *Flannery O'Connor*, ch. 2.
62. O'Connor, *Mystery and Manners*, p. 74; Hawkes, 'Flannery O'Connor's Devil', p. 399.
63. O'Connor, *Wise Blood*, p. 148.
64. O'Connor, *The Habit of Being*, p. 356
65. Kessler argues that the *as if* 'demands the death of the understanding before the reader can begin to evolve a new consciousness'. *Flannery O'Connor and the Language of Apocalypse*, p. 75. For a more nuanced reading, see McSweeney, *The Realist Short Story*, ch. 4.
66. O'Connor, *Collected Stories*, p. 269
67. O'Connor, *Collected Stories* , p. 382
68. O'Connor, *Collected Stories*, pp. 405–20. On doubles more generally, see Asals, *Flannery O'Connor*, ch. 3.
69. Brooks and Penn Warren, *Understanding Fiction*, p. 577.
70. O'Connor, *The Habit of Being*, p. 537.
71. Brinkmeyer compares the narrator with Julian – 'both are cynical authority figures' – and, less convincingly, argues that O'Connor deliberately chose a 'fundamentalist narrator to critique that fundamentalist part of herself'. *The Art and Vision of Flannery O'Connor*, pp. 72–3.
72. Walker, *In Search of Our Mothers' Gardens*, p. 52. See also Crews, *The Critics Bear It Away*, p. 159.
73. Prenshaw (ed.), *Conversations with Eudora Welty*, p. 94.
74. Jan Nordby Gretlund, 'Eudora Welty', in Gray and Robinson (eds), *A Companion to the Literature and Culture of the American South*, p. 504; Hargrove, 'Portrait of an Assassin', p. 82.
75. Welty, *Collected Stories*, pp. 603–7.

76. Welty, *The Eye of the Story*, p. 123.
77. O'Connor, *Mystery and Manners*, p. 43. Praising the 'virtuoso quality' of its 'sympathy and identification', Joyce Carol Oates included 'Where is the Voice Coming From?' in *The Oxford Book of American Short Stories*, p. 481. In March 2009, she read and discussed the story on the *New Yorker* fiction podcast.
78. O'Connor, *The Habit of Being*, p. 537. See also Bacon, *Flannery O'Connor and Cold War Culture*, pp. 108–10.
79. Prenshaw (ed.), *Conversations*, p. 35.

CHAPTER 2

The *New Yorker* Short Story
at Mid-Century

Flannery O'Connor had not always been hostile to the *New Yorker*. Before she went to Iowa, her big ambition was to become its resident cartoonist, the 'new James Thurber', and she submitted, unsuccessfully, a 'batch every week'.[1] She was also unsuccessful in placing her stories – in 1952, one was rejected on the grounds that its subject matter made it 'at best, a rather unlikely story' for the magazine.[2] The mismatch between author and magazine was confirmed three years later when the *New Yorker* published a dismissive review of *A Good Man is Hard to Find*.[3]

In 1955, the *New Yorker* was thirty years old. Born in the Jazz Age, its founder, Harold Ross, who remained editor until 1952, conceived it as a magazine 'of gaiety, wit and satire' aimed exclusively 'for a metropolitan audience'. Its ideal reader was defined from the start, both negatively – the founding prospectus declared that it was *not* for 'the old lady in Dubuque' (that is, Middle America) – and positively, in the figure of the monocled dandy, Eustace Tilley, the striking illustration on the first cover.[4] Rather than target subscribers, Ross appealed to those New York advertisers who didn't bother with national circulation magazines. But although it provided information about city theatres, galleries and restaurants, the *New Yorker* was much more than simply a sophisticated metropolitan listings magazine. It gained a reputation for factual reporting, for humour and cartoons, and for short fiction, and in doing so, cultivated an image of Manhattan that the rest of the country, including the old lady in Dubuque, found irresistible. Like 'the South', 'Manhattan' not only named a place but also a set of values or point of view, one that would find its consummate image in a 1976 cover by Saul Steinberg, 'View of the World from 9th Avenue'.[5]

The *New Yorker* grew steadily in circulation, advertising revenue and influence throughout the 1930s and 1940s and by mid-century, it had become a 'totem for the educated American middle and upper-middle classes'.[6] The magazine – large parts of which were written from the point of view of an institutional 'we' – offered its readers a sense of belonging to a 'unified and continuing entity': 'people raced home to read the latest issues, to be part of the community that read that latest issue'.[7] As the 'affluent society' prospered, so, too, did the *New Yorker*'s subscription figures. By 1965, 80 per cent of the *New Yorker*'s half a million subscribers lived outside the New York metropolitan area.[8]

Almost from the start, the magazine had a clear sense of the kind of short stories it wanted to publish – as early as 1929 one was rejected as not '*New Yorker*-ish – if that word means anything to you'.[9] It would be exaggerating to say that the 'special' quality that the phrase identified in 1929 was the same in 1959 or 1979 or 2009; perhaps Renata Adler puts it best when she says that if the inclusion of a story in the *New Yorker* meant 'acceptance by a certain sensibility', that 'sensibility in turn was formed and altered by the publication of each piece'.[10] Yet certain continuities can be observed through the decades, partly because the magazine has always been very aware, and proud, of its own heritage. As Adler put it, a 'particular context of achievements and expectations' was always in evidence. In the case of 'generation-defining' stories, such as Irwin Shaw's 'Girls in their Summer Dresses' (1939), Shirley Jackson's 'The Lottery' (1948) or John Cheever's 'The Enormous Radio' (1947) and 'The Swimmer' (1964), 'the context, the *New Yorker* itself, somehow, mysteriously, became part of the story, and not just part of its publishing history'.[11] Since the late 1940s, the magazine has maintained its reputation as *the* magazine for short fiction, 'the holy grail of the young fiction writer', as Stephen King put it in 2007.[12] The story of the approach to that grail features in the memoirs of countless writers. John Updike, whose story 'Friends from Philadelphia' was accepted by the *New Yorker* in 1954, the summer he graduated from college, later recalled that 'as a would-be writer' he had 'wanted little else'. In 1995 he could still remember opening the acceptance letter and feeling 'born as a professional writer'. He calculated that he could support his family if he sold six stories a year, and while there was no 'formula to adhere to', he felt he always knew when he'd 'conceived a story "they" would "take"'.[13] Sylvia Plath endured ten years of rejection letters for stories and poems – 'I would really like to get something in the *New Yorker* before I die' – before two poems were accepted in 1958.[14]

It's not just that the *New Yorker* paid, and pays, better than its competitors. A sense of being admitted to an exclusive 'great tradition' continues to inspire writers and readers alike. The magazine's historical milestones have become a crucial element in its ever more insistent marketing. Since 2007, current contributors have been invited to choose stories from the archive to read and discuss in podcasts, thus establishing a sense of lineage between (for example) Jonathan Lethem and John Thurber, Nathan Englander and Isaac Bashevis Singer, Donald Antrim and Donald Barthelme, or Richard Ford and John Cheever.

While there was never a *single* type of *New Yorker* short story, there were certainly identifiable varieties. Comic writing and 'talk stories' featured from the very beginning. The writer most associated with the former was James Thurber; the latter became the forte of John O'Hara. Marrying a snappy Hemingway tone with Fitzgerald's eye for the finer distinctions of social class, O'Hara's stories usually presented characters in a single scene, talking in restaurants, at cocktail parties or on trains. Long before Raymond Carver became famous for the practice, O'Hara titled his stories with conversational tags ('Common Sense Should Tell You', 'We'll Have Fun') and questions ('Are We Leaving Tomorrow?', Do You Like It Here?', How Can I Tell You?, 'Can I Stay Here?'); and long-before Bobbie Ann Mason and Bret Easton Ellis were chastised for using brand names as short-cuts to characterisation, O'Hara relied on Brooks Brothers suits and the Racquet Club – all things advertised in the magazine's pages. His characters don't pound their heels on the floor, they 'pound their Delman heels on the Penn Station floor'.[15]

With notable exceptions, the magazine's various fiction editors tend to choose stories that work through atmosphere rather than plot; stories that impart their meaning suggestively rather than through dramatic or surprise endings. 'The minor key, that was the essential matter,' recalled David Remnick, resulting in a 'profound inclination toward qualification or understatement', as Kay Boyle noted in a 1948 letter to the editor Harold Ross:

> If my hero wished to tell the girl he loved her, he would say so, right out, in my book – but for the *New Yorker* I am certain I would write, 'I love you, I think, somewhat' – or 'It feels a little like love'.[16]

The *New Yorker* generally had less tolerance than the editors of *Understanding Fiction* for the gothic, fantastic or allegorical, preferring stories to be grounded in recognisable aspects of contemporary life: what Frederick Crews, speaking dismissively of John Updike, termed the 'earnest mode of mimesis-cum-symbols', or what Updike himself described as a combination of 'a loving respect for facticity' and 'baroque, high-modernist effects, as were admired in college in the Fifties'.[17] That said, Shirley Jackson's parable of a small-town stoning, 'The Lottery', was a huge hit. Surrealism could also be acceptable (as we shall see in the next chapter), especially if its subject matter was urban and its tone ironic; that is, not too Freudian. As Updike and Cheever both found out, the *New Yorker* with William Shawn as its editor (1952–87), 'was a realm from which many types of unseemliness were excluded'.[18] The magazine's editorial 'squeamishness', combined with its scrupulous, some would say pedantic, approach to editing and fact-checking, gave it a reputation for prissiness. I'll say more about that too in the next chapter.

One of the founding principles of the *New Yorker* was a complete separation between the editorial and advertising departments. For readers of the magazine (of all magazines), the two inevitably inter-mingled: stories were encountered in the context of surrounding adverts; adverts were encountered in the context of surrounding stories. Super-ficially, editorial matter and adverts often seemed at odds with one another: a story satirising, with reference to brand names, the spiritual perils of materialism or drunkenness would appear next to advertise-ments for Brooks Brothers suits, Delman shoes, Tiffany bracelets or imported whisky. The disjunction seemed most apparent when the magazine featured serious articles – such as John Hersey's 'Hiroshima' in 1946 or James Baldwin's 'Letter from a Region of My Mind' in 1961 – which engaged with the wider political and social issues of the day. For Yagoda and Corey, however, the magazine's success was a direct result of its capacity to sidestep the seeming contradiction between 'goods and goodness', to reassure its 'bourgeois readers' that conspicuous consump-tion and anti-materialism, or elitism and egalitarianism, could co-exist with 'apparently seamless' ease, and thus 'fortify' them 'in their very bourgeoisness'.[19] Ultimately what connected and reconciled the adverts and the articles (whatever their topic) was their adherence to 'polished, rich, brilliant' style, to a 'touch of elegance'.[20] In prose, this often meant what Alfred Kazin termed the 'sudden drop shot – the ability to assert a smartly unexpected word or turn around a sentence so that the reader would think, "Um, how well written, how clever!"'[21]

Recently historians have used the *New Yorker*'s archive to chart changes in upper middle-class attitudes. In the 1950s and 1960s, as Corey has shown, stories, cartoons and advertisements were particularly concerned with the development, and etiquette, of the new suburbs, the burgeoning youth culture and the postwar realignment of gender, class and racial relationships. One of the seamless contradictions she notes is that at a time when the magazine's readership increasingly consisted of suburban women, the *New Yorker* retained its traditional 'chilling perspective' on domesticity.[22] Stories about sensitive, 'ineffectual and slightly resentful' men battling with, or trying to escape, their shrill, unfaithful, shopping wives had long been a staple of the magazine.[23] The laureate of the genre was John Thurber, best known today for 'The Secret Life of Walter Mitty' (1939), but the author of numerous stories and cartoons about the petty 'war between men and women'. In 'A Couple of Hamburgers' (1935), for example, a couple in a car, with 130 miles to go, bicker about where to get a snack and other matters:

> 'What's that funny sound?' she asked, suddenly. It invariably made him angry when she heard a funny sound. 'What funny sound?' he demanded. 'You're always hearing funny sounds.' She laughed briefly. 'That's what you said when the bearing burned out,' she reminded him. 'You'd never have noticed it if it hadn't been for me.' 'I noticed it all right,' he said. 'Yes,' she said, 'When it was too late.'[24]

In this talk story, it is the characters who take it in turn to deliver sudden drop shots.

After the war, Corey notes, the magazine was increasingly read by women, staffed by women and published women writers: eighteen in the anthology *55 Stories from The New Yorker, 1940–1950*; nineteen out of forty-seven in the 1950–1960 volume. Nevertheless, much of its content retained a tone of beleaguered (and now commuting) masculinity.

J. D. Salinger is sometimes described as the archetypal *New Yorker* writer because of the way his stories evoke the spiritual pain of the 'languid, sophisticated' types who frequent Lord & Taylor's, get drunk on good Scotch and then feel sick about the inauthenticity of their lives.[25] His 1953 *Nine Stories* was a huge bestseller, partly because of the success of *The Catcher in the Rye* two years earlier. In 'Uncle Wiggily in Connecticut', Eloise can't forget her lost 'sweet' soldier love especially now that she's unhappily married to Lew, a man she says is not 'even honest enough' to say that he likes a trashy book 'because it was about four guys that starved to death in an igloo or something. He was to say it was beautifully *written*'.[26] But Eloise is only in love with her own sensitivity. She won't let her housekeeper's husband avoid the icy roads by staying the night and when Lew calls asking for a lift, she tells him to walk. Devoid of attention, her daughter finds solace in an imaginary friend. Friendship with a child or adolescent (who if not always strictly imaginary seems, like the sweet young soldier, conjured up from a 'persistent longing to return to some state of purity and grace') tends to be the only consolation that Salinger's war-damaged protagonists find and then only fleetingly.[27] In another story, 'For Esmé – with Love and Squalor', a thirteen-year-old girl writes to Sergeant X to remind him of 'the extremely pleasant afternoon we spent in each other's company on April 30, 1944 between 3.45 and 4.15 p.m. in case it slipped your mind'.[28] It hadn't slipped his mind; that half-an-hour conversation is all that has kept his 'faculties intact'.

One of the *New Yorker*'s 'generation-defining' stories, 'A Perfect Day for Bananafish' (1948) is the story of two Florida conversations. The first takes place between Muriel and her mother. Waiting to be put through to New York, Muriel moves a button on her 'Saks blouse', tweezes stray hairs and polishes her nails. We know we are meant to be a little charmed even while disapproving of her complacency, even before the second paragraph announces that 'she was a girl who for a ringing phone dropped exactly nothing. She looked as if her phone had been ringing continually since puberty.' Finally connected, Muriel talks to her mother about her sunburn ('Didn't you use that jar of Bronze I put in your bag?'), 'that awful dinner dress we saw in Bonwit's window', adjustments to her blue coat, and among it all, her husband's psychiatric problems. The story then shifts to the beach where social satire (a brief mention of Martinis and olives) is quickly displaced by a very different kind of conversation between Muriel's bath-robed husband, Seymour Glass, and a five-year-old child called Sybil Carpenter. Sybil's pun with her companion's name – 'See More Glass' – highlights her difference from Muriel and all the story's adult women. Undistracted by the clichés of small talk, she and Seymour talk innocently and imaginatively. With Sybil, Seymour can express himself, albeit indirectly in the form of a fantastical story about bananafish, creatures whose 'tragic life' results from eating 'like pigs' and thus getting trapped in a banana hole. The story ends abruptly and shockingly when Seymour returns to the hotel, has an unpleasant encounter in the elevator, enters the room, which smells of 'new calfskin luggage and nail-lacquer remover', and searches among his undershirts for 'an Ortgies calibre 7.65 automatic'. 'Then he went over and sat down on the unoccupied twin bed, looked at the girl, aimed the pistol, and fired a bullet through his right temple.' Further stories about the Glass family followed, stories which looped back as if trying to explain this inscrutable moment. How did Seymour end up in his banana hole?[29]

Salinger's stories often explore the difficulty of achieving the 'fresh acuteness' of direct communication by evoking technologies of indirect communication.[30] Awkward dialogues occur at long distance, mediated by telephones or letters 'filled with triple exclamation points and inaccurate observations'; characters observe each through the view-finders of cameras or movie cameras.[31] 'What I'm about to offer,' says Buddy Glass, the narrator of a long story about his sister, 'Zooey' (1957), 'isn't really a short story at all but a sort of prose home movie'.[32] Salinger's sense that intimacy is always somehow technologically mediated also informed the increasing number of short stories that portrayed life against a backdrop of the radio or the new medium of television. (In 1950, only 9% of American homes had TV; by 1955, 55.7% had sets.[33]) In Grace Paley's 'An Interest in Life' (1959) – not published in the *New Yorker* – Ginny, abandoned by her husband and trying to bring up two sons alone, makes a list of her troubles which she plans to send in to *Strike It Rich*, a television programme in which prizes are won for the most interesting problems. 'The list when complete could have brought tears to the eyes of God if He had a minute,' she considers, and begins to feel better. But her lover is not convinced:

> 'They'd laugh you out of the studio ... Have you ever seen that program? I mean, in addition to all of this – the little disturbances of man' – he waved a scornful hand at my list – 'they *suffer*. They live in the forefront of tornadoes, their lives are washed off by floods – catastrophes of God.'[34]

Paley took 'the little disturbances of man' as the title for her first collection, although what the stories wryly suggest is that little disturbances do not affect man (he experiences TV-worthy catastrophes of God) so much as woman.

John Cheever's stories make a similar contrast, but examine it from a rather different (*New Yorker*) point of view.[35] His narrators often observe that their wives are suffering from what the sociologist David Riesman called 'suburban sadness': 'an aimlessness, a pervasive low-keyed unpleasure which cannot be described in terms of traditional sorrows'.[36] In 'A Vision of the World', the narrator's wife tells him that she has 'terrible feeling' that she's a 'character in a television situation comedy':

'I mean, I'm nice-looking, I'm well-dressed, I have humorous and attractive children, but I have this terrible feeling that I am in black-and-white and that I can be turned off by anybody. I just have this terrible feeling that I can be turned *off*.'[37]

In 'Where is the Voice Coming From?', the problem for Welty's murderer was that the TV is never switched off: his violent act can't remove his victim's face from the screen. The little disturbances of Cheever's housewife don't belong to the news programmes, but, as she sees it, to the episodic and trivial sitcom, a genre which, like the cathode ray tube, drains the colour of individuality from its protagonists. Her husband responds to this declaration by noting that her sadness is 'not a true sadness', 'not a crushing sorrow'. 'She grieves,' he says, 'because her grief is not an acute grief, and when I tell her that this sorrow over the inadequacies of her sorrow may be a new hue in the spectrum of human pain, she is not consoled.'

In 'The Season of Divorce', the narrator asks his wife, Ethel, why she is crying:

'Why do I cry? Why do I cry? I cry because I saw an old woman cuffing a little boy on Third Avenue ... I cry because my father died when I was twelve and because my mother married a man I detested or thought that I detested. I cry because I had to wear an ugly dress to a party twenty years ago, and I didn't have a good time. I cry because of some unkindness that I can't remember. I cry because I am tired – because I'm tired and I can't sleep.'[38]

A page later, however, Ethel has pulled herself together, cleaned the vegetables, bathed the children and she and her husband sit down to supper. Capturing rapid shifts in mood – in which 'a world that had seemed so dark could, in a few minutes, become so sweet' – is one of the things the short story does best.[39] More generally, Cheever's world is less susceptible to (*Strike It Rich*) catastrophe than to (situation comedy) 'sordid wrangle[s]' which end up with men sleeping on the 'living-room sofa' or women in the guest room, until they make-up and become once more, for a little while, 'the happiest married couple in the whole eastern United States'.[40] In one story, a man decides to leave home, walks a mile to the station, gets fed-up waiting, turns to walk home again and meets his wife coming toward him – 'and we walked home together and went to bed'.[41] In another, the wife is in the middle of issuing instructions, along with 'the name of the laundry and the maid's telephone number', to the husband she's decided to leave when he embraces her. 'I guess I'd better stay and take care of you a little while longer,' she says.[42] In 'O Youth and Beauty!', the 'quarrels and reunions' of Louise and Cash Bentley are compared with the hurdle race over the living-room furniture that Cash likes to perform while drunk; they 'didn't seem to lose their interest through repetition'.[43] The low-key repetitiveness of suburban sadness, and especially of marriage, becomes particularly apparent when several stories are grouped together (as in a TV series, perhaps) and in Chapter 6, I will consider Cheever's stories of Shady Hill, alongside John Updike's Maples series, and, by way of some contrast, Grace Paley's stories of the 'little disturbances' of Manhattan mothers and children.

A *New Yorker* contributor since 1935, Cheever's breakthrough came in 1947 with the publication of a fable of apartment life, 'The Enormous Radio':

> Jim and Irene Westcott were the kind of people who seem to strike that satisfactory average of income, endeavor, and respectability that is reached by the statistical reports in college alumni bulletins. They were the parents of two young children, they had been married nine years, they lived on the twelfth floor of an apartment house near Sutton Place, they went to the theatre on an average 10.3 times a year, and they hoped someday to live in Westchester.[44]

Statistical attempts to explain human behaviour are as much a satirical target for Cheever as they were for Flannery O'Connor. To say that the Westcotts are 'average', he implies, tells us nothing very interesting. Fiction, or fable, begins when it enters a realm that survey can't reach. The couple's one distinction is a love of music, and when their radio breaks they immediately get a new one. Large and ugly, it feels like an 'aggressive intruder' into their home. Instead of music, the machine broadcasts sounds from the other apartments in the building. It has a particular 'sensitivity to discord' and picks up every quarrel, confession and expression of anxiety or annoyance: '"I wish you wouldn't leave apple cores in the ashtray," a man said, "I hate the smell."' At first Irene find this amusing, but soon the 'restrained melancholy' of her neighbour's lives becomes 'horrible', 'dreadful', 'depressing'. She starts to imagine what she and Jim would sound like on the radio. 'Our lives aren't sordid, are they, darling? ... We're happy, aren't we, darling?' Yes, of course, Jim replies 'tiredly', and arranges for the radio to be fixed. When the apartment resounds with Beethoven's 'Ode to Joy', the problem seems to be over. But the radio has already done its work. The next evening the couple quarrel about money – 'all of my energies, all of my youth', says Jim, 'wasted in fur coats and radios and slipcovers and . . . .' When Irene tries to stop him, he angrily reminds her that she's never been 'a convent girl', and itemises her crimes: stealing jewellery; cheating her sister out of her inheritance; casually procuring an abortion. In the background, the radio reverts to its 'suave and noncommittal' broadcast of human disasters. It may have seemed like the snake in this Sutton Place Eden but the radio's presence merely brings to light the rottenness that was there all along. Cheever's setting may be very different from that found in an O'Connor story, but his intention here seems much the same as hers: to shatter the smugness of the 'satisfactory average'.

The figure of the 'aggressive', and educative, intruder – who can be found in the American short story as early as Washington Irving's 'The Little Man in Black' (1807) – appeared frequently in 1950s and 1960s fiction, much of which addressed the perceived conformity of American life. 'That peculiar American sweetness toward the stranger,' observed Frank O'Connor in 1963, in his now classic study of the short story, *The Lonely Voice*, 'exists side by side with American brutality toward everyone.'[45] Often the stranger was a refugee, or an allegorical representative of refugee, from the Second World War. In Bernard Malamud's tragi-comedy, 'The Jewbird', Harry Cohen, a frozen foods salesman, is disturbed when a talking Jewish crow flies into his Manhattan apartment. Fleeing 'Anti-Semeets', the bird has sought out a Jew, but in Cohen he inadvertently finds the worst kind of anti-Semite, a self-hating Jew.[46] A wannabe assimilated Jewish-American present is also challenged by its European past in Philip Roth's 'Eli, The Fanatic'.[47] Unhappy to be reminded of their not-so-distant roots, the 'modern' Jewish community of Woodenton appoint an attorney, Eli Peck, to get rid of the 'religious fanatics' in the local yeshivah. They are particularly perturbed by the presence of one of the teachers, a Holocaust survivor in a 'round-topped, wide-brimmed Talmudic hat … sidelocks curled loose on his cheeks': 'like in the Bronx the old guys who used to come around selling Hebrew trinkets … making a big thing out of suffering … going oy-oy-oy all your life'. Eli goes along with the plan to chase them out, although as his history of nervous breakdown indicates, he too is a misfit in the aptly named Woodenton. 'It's as if you don't think we deserve to be happy,' says his wife.

Eli becomes increasingly torn between the 'lights' of Woodenton and the 'shadows' of the yeshivah. Once more, this is a story of surface and depth, of ego and alter ego, as becomes clear when Eli gives the yeshivah director his suit to wear and in turn is presented with a gift of Hassidic garb. He puts it on, 'as if it were the skin of his skin', and wonders if he 'was two people'. When he goes to the hospital where his wife has just had a baby, his transformation into a fanatic is completed. By screaming 'I'm the father!', Eli affirms not only his new responsibility to his son, but, through his impersonation of the 'greenie', a man who had lost both wife and child in the Holocaust, his role as purveyor of a Jewish ancestry. The response of scientific, suburban America in what Robert Lowell famously called the 'tranquillized fifties' is to tear off the Hassidic coat and administer a sedative.[48] 'The drug calmed his soul, but did not touch it down where the blackness had reached.'

In these stories, as in those of O'Connor, the intruding antagonist is ultimately welcome because he is the antidote to tranquillisers. Because of the stranger, the mind's attention is awakened from the 'lethargy of custom'; only because of him 'man is at last compelled to face with sober senses his real conditions of life'.[49] In Cheever's work, however, the sober insight that the intruder allows is a mixed blessing. Perhaps, his stories sometimes suggest, it would be better not to know, better instead to have another drink. Read in this light, 'Goodbye, My Brother' seems like as a reworking of 'The Enormous Radio'. It's a more complex story, partly because it exchanges a detached satirical voice for an unreliable first-person narrator. (Along with O'Connor's 'A Good Man is Hard to Find', 'Goodbye, My Brother' was included in the 1959 edition of *Understanding Fiction*.)

The story is the account of an unnamed man and of the visit of his brother, Lawrence, to the decaying family home. Like Salinger's children, Roth's Hassidim or the enormous radio, Lawrence is sensitive to what lies beneath the surface of social niceties, what he calls 'the realities'. He walks around the house pointing out its pretensions and faults and those of its inhabitants. His sister is 'a foolish and promiscuous woman', his brother 'dishonest', 'Mother is an alcoholic' and 'the house is going to fall into the sea'. The siblings in turn think of him as 'Little Jesus'; a soubriquet which, like his supposed resemblance to a 'Puritan cleric', suggests a resemblance to Shepperd in 'The Lame Shall Enter First'. But Cheever does not want to re-educate Lawrence. Indeed, although the story is narrated by his 'fatuous' brother, Lawrence's perspective often comes across as the more compelling, even to him.[50] For example, he gives considerable space to Lawrence's view that 'we and our friends and our part of the nation, finding ourselves unable to cope with the problems of the present, had, like a wretched adult, turned back to what we supposed was a happier and a simpler time, and that our taste for reconstruction and candlelight was a measure of this irremediable failure.' This assessment makes a lot of sense – until, that is, we are told that Lawrence is 'lecturing' and that the alternative to feeling bad is swimming and Martinis on the beach. The narrator, and perhaps the story, can't make up its mind. There was, said Cheever, 'some ambiguity in my indignation', and it comes through in his use of 'as' and 'as if'.[51]

The siblings and their spouses attend the boat club dance, where many of the men dress up in college football uniforms and the women wear their wedding dresses:

> And I knew that Lawrence was looking bleakly at the party as he had looked at the weather-beaten shingles on our house, *as if* he saw here an abuse and distortion of time; *as if* in wanting to be brides and football players we exposed the fact that, the lights of youth having been put out in us, we had been unable to find other lights to go by and, destitute of faith and principle, had become foolish and sad.

This long sentence derives analogy (which is always conjecture) from repetition (which can be observed). It derives a statement about what Lawrence feels (it is as if he has lost faith in his generation) from a statement about his demeanor (he looks at the party in the same way as he had recently looked at the roof). But its own repetition, of 'as if', undoes the analogy, by expanding it into a hypothesis, more revealing, perhaps, of observer than of observed. It no longer matters what Lawrence thinks; the narrator is seeing himself *as if* through his brother's eyes.

Cheever may not have gone to college, but he knew how to intensify his fiction by adding layers of symbols and myth. If 'The Enormous Radio' alludes, at least by way of its apple cores, to Genesis, 'Goodbye, My Brother' encourages thoughts of both Eden (the family name is Pommeroy) and Cain (images of dark) versus Abel (light). In the story's dramatic denouement, the narrator attempts (and not for the first time) to kill his brother, but ends up tending his wounds. There is a genuine conflict here between Lawrence's 'facts are facts' and his brother's hopeless Romanticism. These contradictory impulses are never resolved but, in the final passage, somehow sidestepped. 'Eloquence,' as

Cynthia Ozick observed of Cheever's work more generally, 'cancels all things inscrutable.'[52] The passage begins with the narrator's exasperated exclamation:

> O, what can you do with a man like that? What can you do? How can you dissuade his eye in a crowd from seeking out a cheek with acne, the infirm hand; how can you teach him to respond to the inestimable greatness of the race, the harsh surface beauty of life; how can you put his finger on the obdurate truths before which fear and horror are powerless? The sea that morning was iridescent and dark. My wife and my sister were swimming – Diana and Helen – and I saw their uncovered heads, black and gold in the dark water. I saw them come out and I saw that they were naked, unshy, beautiful, and full of grace, and I watched the naked women walk out of the sea.

As Charles Baxter has noted, this passage feels 'a bit like an aria'.[53] Cheever moves away from a discursive tone towards grand statement ('the inestimable greatness of the race'), myth (Helen and Diana), incantation (through the repetition of 'and' and 'I saw') and abstraction (in the final sentence, 'they' are no longer his wife and sister but 'the naked women', black and gold, like something out of Botticelli). As in the passage discussed earlier, the narrator longer merely sees, but watches, and this conscious act brings about some kind of imaginative, and possibly redemptive, transfiguration, reminiscent of what Cheever elsewhere described as the 'calculated self-deceptions' with which his characters sometimes 'cheered' themselves.[54] For Baxter, 'it succeeds, but just barely'.

This finale recalls Scott Fitzgerald's *The Great Gatsby*, a story which its narrator decided not to end with the image of a man dead forever in his swimming pool ('material without being real'), but rather with a lyrical evocation of the Atlantic Ocean and the elusive 'orgiastic future that year by year recedes before us'.[55] More generally, Cheever shares with Fitzgerald a luxuriant melancholy about lost youth and a rueful admiration for futile attempts to stop time. Grey hair bothers him inordinately. In 'Goodbye, My Brother', the narrator's wife is thirty-eight and, he notes, 'her hair would be gray, I guess, if it were not dyed, but it is dyed an unobtrusive yellow – a faded color'. 'I'm not getting any younger,' says Jim in 'The Enormous Radio', 'I'm thirty-seven. My hair will be gray next year.' 'The Scarlet Moving Van' is about Gee-Gee (the 'Greek God at college') who's 'All-America twice' and still handsome 'though his yellow curls were thin'.[56] 'Stubborn youthfulness' is also what distinguishes Cash Bentley, a 40-year-old former track-star turned thin-haired suburban commuter in 'O Youth and Beauty'.[57] In his case, 'the realities' come in the form of the 'rank' and 'putrid' smells of spoiled meat and fading roses. He studies his friends' teeth and skin 'narrowly, as if he were himself a much younger man'. Cash's escape is the hurdle race that he performs over his neighbours' sofas and tables. 'There was not a piece of furniture in Shady Hill that Cash could not take in his stride.' That is, until he asks his wife to take a break from exorcising *Life* magazine of 'those scenes of mayhem, disaster, and violent death that she felt might corrupt her children' and shoot the starting pistol. She catches him 'midair' as he hurdles the sofa. The story ends with a neat ironic reversal – in running away from death, Cash unwittingly courts it.[58]

An attempt to arrest time is also undertaken in 'The Swimmer'.[59] While 'far from young', Neddy Merrill retains the 'especial slenderness of youth' and a perhaps misplaced belief in his own boyish charm; like Cash and the narrator of 'Goodbye, My Bother', he has a 'vague and modest idea of himself as a legendary figure'. The legendary quality of the story begins with its once-upon-a-time opening:

> It was one of those midsummer Sundays when everyone sits around saying 'I *drank* too much last night.' You might have heard it whispered by the parishioners leaving church, heard it from the lips of the priest himself, struggling with his cassock in the *vestiarium*, heard it from the golf links and the tennis courts, heard it from the wildlife preserve where the leader of the Audubon group was suffering a terrible hangover.

From the opening line, Cheever wants both to evoke a sense of ritual – 'everyone' is implicated, even 'you' who 'might have heard it' – and, by reminding us of priests and church, to suggest its debased nature. Nursing a hangover is not what Sundays used to be for.

We are then introduced to the Westerhazys' pool with its water 'a pale shade of green' and told that the day is 'fine' and 'hot'. Only then is the story's protagonist introduced: 'Neddy Merrill sat by the green water, one hand in it, one around a glass of gin.' At this point, his bifurcated desire – to 'get wet' in two ways – identifies him as a kind of community representative, its everyman. His separation from 'everyone' begins when he decides to swim home, making an 8-mile river (which he names

Lucinda after his wife) out of his neighbours' swimming pools. 'The day was beautiful and it seemed to him that a long swim might enlarge and celebrate its beauty.'

With this 'seemed to him', the story then shifts largely to Ned's point of view, although the legendary quality never fully disappears with the storyteller's voice coming to the fore at key moments. At first it seems that Ned is travelling through a paradise of 'light green water' and 'flowering apple trees', but it does not take long before he encounters a 'thorny hedge' and a gravelled path. These are momentary disturbances and half way through the journey he feels 'tired' and 'clean'. But, as the narrator of 'Goodbye, My Brother' noted, swimming provides only 'an illusion of purification', especially when, as in this case, the water has been subjected to suburban 'domestication'.[60] A storm brews and suddenly the time of day and even the season seem uncertain. Red and yellow maple leaves blow into the water. 'Since it was midsummer the tree must be blighted, and yet he felt a peculiar sadness at this sign of autumn.' Are the seasons really changing or does time speed up only for Ned? Midpoint in his journey, Ned needs to cross a busy road and, as he waits, we pull back from his perspective. The narrative voice of legend returns to address and implicate the reader: 'Had you gone for a Sunday afternoon ride that day you might have seen him, close to naked, standing on the shoulders of Route 424, waiting for a chance to cross.' Ned's bare feet are no longer in the green grass but 'in the deposits of the highway – beer cans, rages, and blowout patches'. And to the drivers of the cars that pass ('you', perhaps?), he is not an heroic pilgrim but a 'pitiful', ridiculous figure. There is, however, no turning back: 'in the space of an hour, more or less', he has 'covered a distance that made his return' to the 'green water' of the Westerhazys 'impossible'. In the second part of the story, the suburban odyssey becomes more definitely a descent into the underworld. The public pool is loud and 'stagnant' and by the time he gets to the next friendly house, where again he sees yellow leaves float on the pool (blight? or autumn?), he is 'cold', aching and confused. He doesn't understand why these neighbours sympathise with his 'misfortunes' (a vague mention of selling the house and the 'poor children'), or why others dismiss him as a 'gate crasher' and a fool. His 'gift for concealing painful facts' has become a kind of curse; he has been 'immersed too long'. 'Will you ever grow up?' asks his ex-mistress, but now, of course, he is growing up fast. The story ends in a tableau of despair: shivering, exhausted and 'stooped' like an old man, Ned pounds on his front door, 'and then, looking in at the windows, [sees] that the place [is] empty'.

It is perhaps a little melodramatic to say that this image also encapsulates Cheever's relationship with the *New Yorker* after 1964. But for the remainder of the 1960s, the magazine rejected many of his stories as too fantastical or sexually explicit. The *New Yorker*, after all, was not for the 'sort of people' who 'told dirty stories to mixed company' and anyway, Cheever complained, Donald Barthelme was now the magazine's 'chosen surrealist'.[61] Cheever turned briefly to teaching: at Boston University, Sing Sing prison and at the Iowa Writers' Workshop, where his pupils included T. C. Boyle, Raymond Carver and Allan Garganus. Garganus said that he ran his seminars like 'a very nice cocktail party'.[62]

Notes

1. Gooch, *Flannery*, p. 110.
2. Yagoda, *About Town*, p. 294.
3. Gooch, *Flannery*, p. 265.
4. Kunkel, *Genius in Disguise*, pp. 439–40.
5. See Jones, 'Mythologizing Manhattan'.
6. Yagoda, *About Town*, p. 24.
7. The 'we' remained until 1992. Yagoda, *About Town*, pp. 43, 105; Adler, *Gone*, p. 48.
8. Between 1941 and 1951, subscriptions doubled, from 171,000 to 325,000. Travis, 'What We Talk About', p. 254.
9. Yagoda, *About Town*, pp. 54–5.
10. Adler, *Gone*, p. 56.
11. Adler, *Gone* , pp. 51–3.
12. King, *The Best American Short Stories 2007*, p. xvi.
13. Updike, *More Matter*, p. 763. In 1946, Joseph Heller enrolled in a fiction-writing class at New York University hoping to become the next John O'Hara. *Now and Then*, pp. 96, 124, 194–7.
14. Plath, *Letters Home*, p. 207.
15. O'Hara, *Collected Stories*, p. 91.
16. Remnick, *Wonderful Town*, p. xi; Yagoda, *About Town*, p. 204.
17. Crews, *The Critics Bear It Away*, p. 176; Updike, *Hugging the Shore*, p. 848; Updike, *More Matter*, p. 782.
18. Updike, *More Matter*, pp. 779, 766; Shawn had 'never accepted a story about a homosexual'. Bailey, *Cheever*, p. 488.
19. Corey, *The World Through a Monocle*, pp. 181, 17; Yagoda, *About Town*, p. 121.
20. Plath, *Letters Home*, p. 207; Updike, *More Matter*, p. 766.
21. Kazin, *Writing was Everything*, p. 50.
22. Corey, *The World Through a Monocle* p. 179.
23. Yagoda, *About Town*, p. 88.
24. Thurber, *Writings and Drawings*, pp. 381–5.
25. Salinger, *Franny and Zooey*, p. 43

26. Salinger, *For Esmé*, pp. 38–44. The American edition was called *Nine Stories*.
27. Welty, *A Writer's Eye*, p. 110.
28. Salinger, *For Esmé*, pp. 97–125.
29. Salinger, *For Esmé*, pp. 7–23. For further stories of the Glass family, see *Franny and Zooey* (1961) and *Raise High the Roof Beam, Carpenters and Seymour: An Introduction* (1963).
30. Salinger, *For Esmé*, p. 106
31. Salinger, *For Esmé*, p. 119.
32. Salinger, *Franny and Zooey*, p. 43. In their combination of 'catalogs of items in the medicine chest' and 'long intimate family conversations', said Mailer, the Glass stories were 'not literature but television'. *Cannibals and Christians*, p. 155.
33. Rader, *In Its Own Image*, p. 18.
34. Paley, *Collected Stories*, pp. 50–65.
35. As early as 1939, Cheever's editor William Maxwell identified in his work 'that special quality … which is exactly right for the *New Yorker*'. The magazine ran 121 of his stories, 'more than any other author except John O'Hara'. Bailey, *Cheever*, p. 99; Donaldson, *John Cheever*, p. 61.
36. Riesman, 'The Suburban Sadness', p. 377.
37. Cheever, *The Stories*, pp. 512–17.
38. Cheever, *The Stories*, p. 145. Passages like this pepper Cheever's published *Journals*; see, for example, pp. 59–60.
39. Cheever, *The Stories*, p. 268.
40. Cheever, *The Stories*, p. 212.
41. Cheever, *The Stories*, p. 266.
42. Cheever, *The Stories*, p. 342.
43. Cheever, *The Stories*, p. 213.
44. Cheever, *The Stories*, pp. 33–41.
45. O'Connor, *The Lonely Voice*, p. 41.
46. Malamud, *Complete Stories*, pp. 322–30. Philip Davis points out that the story is 'in mute counterpoint' with 'Angel Levine', in which the stranger is a large black Jewish angel. *Bernard Malamud*, p. 274.
47. Roth, *Goodbye Columbus*, pp. 187–221.
48. Lowell, *Life Studies*, p. 99.
49. Coleridge, *Biographia Literaria*, vol. 2, p. 6; Marx and Engels, *The Communist Manifesto*, p. 223.
50. Cheever, 'What Happened', in Brooks and Penn Warren, *Understanding Fiction*, 2nd edn, p. 571.
51. Cheever, 'What Happened', in Brooks and Penn Warren, *Understanding Fiction*, 2nd edn, p. 571.
52. Ozick, 'Cheever's Yankee Heritage', p. 159.
53. Baxter, *Burning Down the House*, p. 59.
54. Cheever, *The Stories*, p. 245.
55. Fitzgerald, *The Great Gatsby*, pp. 153–4, 171.
56. Cheever, *The Stories*, pp. 15, 41, 360–1.
57. Cheever, *The Stories*, pp. 210–18.
58. Updike's first *New Yorker* story, 'Friends from Philadelphia', was a response to 'O Youth and Beauty!': 'I thought there must be more to American life than this'. *More Matter*, p. 764.

59. Cheever, *The Stories*, pp. 603–12.
60. Cheever, *The Stories*, p. 10.
61. Cheever, *The Stories*, p. 610; Bailey, *Cheever*, p. 586.
62. Bailey, *Cheever*, p. 475.

CHAPTER 3

Experimental Fiction in the 1960s and 1970s

In *Advertisements for Myself* (1959), a kind of autobiographical anthology of the evolution of a writing style, Norman Mailer included some examples from his brief 'interim career as a writer of short stories'. Following the poor reception of his second novel, *Barbary Shore*, Mailer wrote, he had decided to pursue a 'New York career' – 'I would get myself printed in the *New Yorker*, in *Harper's Bazaar, Mademoiselle*'.[1] Perhaps because no more than a day was to be spent on each story, they generally 'didn't do too well'. Mailer was sure he was through with 'short stories and markets and editors and agents ... done with trying to write less than I knew'. The epiphany complete, he woke up the next day with thoughts of Joyce, Zola and Melville, and 'the plan for a prologue and an eight-part novel in my mind'.[2]

I start this chapter with Mailer because his 1960s distaste for the 1950s magazine story – 'they are respectable. They make no attempt to raise the house an inch or two' – was not untypical.[3] His objection, however, was not just to the short story's association with commercial magazine publishing. Arguing that the artist should not view the age 'statically' but confront it, Mailer complained that:

> The short story has a tendency to look for climates of permanence –
> an event occurs, a man is hurt by it in some small way forever. The
> novel moves as naturally as flux. An event occurs, a man is injured,
> and a month later is working on something else. The short story
> likes to be classic. It is most acceptable when one fatal point is made.
> Whereas the novel is dialectical.[4]

This distinction was formulated in relation to Philip Roth's second novel, *Letting Go* (1962) which Mailer regarded as a 'collection of intricately interconnected short stories' rather than as a proper novel. In *Letting Go*, Roth himself had expressed doubts about the New Critical emphasis on 'all that *form* crap' and its impetus towards 'completeness

and the ends tucked in'.[5] One of the novel's central characters, Paul
Herz, is an English instructor and 'creative writer' who worries that his
students think that 'writing is like tapestry-weaving; a kind of construction work'.[6] Roth was partly reacting against his own collection of short
stories, *Goodbye, Columbus* (1959), which included, as we saw in Chapter
2, the tightly-patterned, ironically reversing 'Eli, the Fanatic'. On the
strength of that collection, Roth had been invited to teach at the Iowa
writing programme. He stayed a year, wrote a disparaging article about
the experience and thereafter 'let go' of tapestry-like form to devote
himself to the impermanent 'dialectical' novel.[7]

Thomas Pynchon abandoned short fiction for similar reasons. In
1984, he collected the short stories he had written in the late 1950s and
early 1960s, mainly while a student at Cornell University, with the aim
of identifying and exemplifying in his own work a transitional period in
American literature, during which writers had tried to negotiate between
'traditional' and 'Beat' influences. Pynchon's first published story 'The
Small Rain', he was later embarrassed to observe, contained 'a whole
extra overlay of rain images and references to "The Waste Land" and *A
Farewell to Arms*. I was operating on the motto "Make it literary".'[8]

'Entropy', published in 1960 and subsequently much anthologised,
represents an ambivalent departure from literary tradition thus understood. On the one hand, Pynchon recalls, it was 'as close to a Beat story
as anything I was writing then'; on the other hand, it worked hard to
achieve formal intricacy (a 'fugue' of 'counterpoints' and 'correspon-
dences') and a central 'symbol' (entropy) acquired from 'second-hand
science' to which the behaviour of its characters had to 'conform'.
Looking back after twenty-five years, Pynchon thought the story 'a good
example of what can happen when you spend too much time and energy
on words alone'.[9]

The Beat Spirit comes in the form of Meatball Mulligan's 'lease-
breaking party', a frenzy of tequila, jazz and benzedrine which has been
going for forty hours and shows no sign of ending. His guests are in a
limbo of lethargy. It's a 'false spring' in 1957 and Washington is full of
'American expatriates who would talk, every time they met you, about
how someday they were going over to Europe for real but right now
it seemed they were working for the government.' The second-hand
science comes from Callisto, the man who lives in the apartment upstairs
from the party. He is obsessed with the idea of entropy or the tendency of
an isolated system towards disorder, and finds in it an 'adequate metaphor

to apply to certain phenomena in his own world'. In an attempt to resist entropy, Callisto has transformed his apartment into a 'hothouse jungle'. 'Hermetically sealed, it was a tiny enclave of regularity in the city's chaos, alien to the vagaries of weather, of national politics, of any civil disorder.' What Callisto does not realise is that what he has created is as much an analogue of social 'heat-death' as the chaotic party downstairs.[10.]

In 1984, Pynchon was struck less by the story's 'thermodynamical gloom' than by the way it reflected 'how the '50's were for some folks'.[11] The story juxtaposes two different responses. Callisto's is that of an older generation that has lived through the Depression and the Second World War, and now bemoans 'the end of ideology'.[12] He hides from the changing world in his womb-like room, a 'closed circuit' consisting of himself and his girlfriend, Aubade. But his failure is inevitable. Aubade (as her name suggests she should) initiates a new dawn by breaking out of the 'airless void', artfully smashing the glass, 'with two exquisite hands which came away bleeding and glistening with splinters'. The young people at the wild party demand much less than Callisto – only that 'in its lethargic way their life ... provided kicks' – but when the noise reaches a 'sustained, ungodly crescendo', Meatball, too, faces a choice:

> The way he figured, there were only two ways he could cope: (a) lock himself up in the closet and maybe eventually they would all go away, or (b) try to calm everyone down, one by one. (a) was certainly the more attractive alternative. But then he started to think about that closet. It was dark and stuffy and he would be alone ... the other way was more a pain in the neck, but probably better in the long run.[13]

Mulligan chooses the 'other way' and so would Pynchon. The 'academic enclosure' and stasis of the short story proved too stuffy for him and after publishing *The Crying of Lot 49* (1966), which he described as a long story 'marketed as a "novel"', he gave up short fiction altogether. 'I wasn't,' he later recalled, 'the only one writing then who felt some need to stretch, to step out.'[14]

By the early 1960s, it became fashionable to dismiss the *New Yorker*'s formulaic qualities in terms previously reserved for *Collier's* and the *Saturday Evening Post*. James Purdy complained that the *New Yorker* exerted 'the worst influence [on the short story] in America today', while James Laughlin maintained that 'if you read all their stories every week for a year you'd begin to think that most of them were written by the same person using different names'.[15] The complaint was partly about the magazine's preference for stories with a narrow class and social setting, its own specific version of 'local colour'.[16] But it was also a matter of stylistic uniformity. The *New Yorker*, its critics felt, went too far in trying 'to iron all the writing out' so that, as Edmund Wilson put it, nothing 'vivid or startling or personal' remained.[17] Strict adherents to the rules of 'modern English usage', the magazine's editors added commas and informative sub-clauses to avoid the very ambiguities and uncertainties that their fiction contributors had worked so hard to cultivate. In 1955, Elizabeth Bishop complained about one such intervention. 'The idea underneath it all,' she concluded, 'seems to be that the *New Yorker* reader must never have to pause for a single second, but be informed and reinformed comfortingly all the time.'[18] 'Why not have the reader re-read a sentence now and then?' asked another bemused contributor, Vladimir Nabokov; 'it won't hurt him.'[19] By the mid-1960s, the argument had taken on a rather macho tone: the magazine's perceived 'stylistic timidity' (despite its inclusion of the surely idiosyncratic Nabokov) was increasingly associated with its adverts for luxury goods and thus 'coded as feminine' or gay.[20] Seymour Krim complained about the 'punctuation castratos who have gone to bed with commas for half a century', while Tom Wolfe mocked its qualifying subordinate clauses and 'bourgeois sentimentality': too many stories of 'inchoate longing Young Homemakers [and] unrequited flirtation ... add up to the perfect magazine for suburban women'.[21]

One reason why the *New Yorker* became the focus for such concerted attack was that, by the 1960s, there were far fewer magazines publishing short fiction than there had been ten or twenty years previously. Another was the turn, by the self-described New Journalists and others, towards narrative non-fiction. Magazines that once published short stories now preferred personal essays by writers such as Annie Dillard, Joan Didion and Tom Wolfe, many of which adopted the devices and strategies of short fiction to tell a 'true story'.[22] But it was not only magazine editors who were impatient with the short story's timidity, its 'water color realism', its 'understated perceptiveness'.[23] A great deal of the grumbling also originated in the fiction workshops, where a second edition of *Understanding Fiction* (1959) was still very much in use. Since 1945, America's colleges and universities had gradually reinforced their position at the nation's cultural centre. As creative writing programmes proliferated and gained in influence, elements of 'bohemia' shifted to the campuses.[24] In the classroom setting, the sprawling dialectical novel wasn't really an option. Unwilling or unable to abandon the 'most conservative art of mid-century', teachers and students on writing programmes chose instead to transform it from within.[25] By the end of the 1960s, the short story's reputation had shifted from that of most conventional of contemporary literary genres to a position at 'the fore of the avant-garde'.[26] The aim of this chapter is to explain how and why that transformation came about. Enclosure – in a time, a space or a literary form – was bad. But liberation proved to be harder to achieve in the short story than it often was in life.

'On with the Story'[27]

While Mailer complained about the short story's desire for permanence, others suggested how it could be made 'more flexible and open to experiment than the novel'.[28] A novel might progress fluidly or dialectically, but it did require some kind of unifying idea. A collection of stories, on the other hand, as Poe had pointed out, could try out a 'vast variety of modes or inflections of thought and expression'.[29] During 'the American High Sixties' (1965–73), variety was the order of the day.[30] Short rather than longer forms seemed better suited to 'an age in which the new tends to be obsolete by tomorrow, in which change seems more relevant than order, and eventual destruction the only reality'.[31] Discussion about short fiction's appropriateness in capturing the disruptions and uncertainties of the era – from the Civil Rights Movement and Black Power to Vietnam and the Women's Movement – recalled that of the 1890s when the short story was championed as an 'unsettled' frontier form suited to the expression of diverse marginal voices. 'The world is new,' proclaimed one early 1970s anthology, 'and its experiences must be known by a new epistemology. Story writers experiment with new systems, coming to know the irrational or relativistic through something other than the older rational forms.'[32]

As ever, the short story's status depended on economic as well as epistemological concerns. With writers relying increasingly on academic tenure and promotion structures, rather than high-paying commercial magazines, 'the size of the direct payment of any given magazine' became 'secondary in importance to the fact of being published'. The university 'publish-or-perish' culture, argues George Garrett, led many writers to the 'regular writing of short stories and to the task of finding (sometimes creating) places to publish them'. The demise of mass-market magazines was off-set by a 'fantastic growth in the number and kinds of quarterlies, literary magazines and little magazines'.[33]

There were lots of stories about the difficulty of writing (or typing) stories, with titles such as 'What's Your Story', 'Ernest Hemingway's Typist' and 'Storytellers, Liars, and Bores'.[34] Others, more interestingly on the whole, parodied or reduced particular generic conventions or narrative components; including such basics as beginning, ending, character and plot. What, asked writers, was the bare minimum (of, say, exposition, duration or dialogue) needed for a narrative to work? One of Stephen Dixon's experiments was to see if he could write a story without any reported speech. 'Said' is the story of a married couple's quarrel, the joke of which is how predictable – 'She said, he said, she said' – such quarrels are.[35] In other words, it works because we are so familiar with what the couple *would say* in a more conventional story. The title of Richard Brautigan's one-paragraph tale, 'The Scarlatti Tilt', on the other hand, seems to promise a detective story. This is what we get:

> 'It's very hard to live in a studio apartment in San Jose with a man who's learning to play the violin.' That's what she told the police when she handed them the empty revolver.[36]

The two sentences include a dead body in a particular setting, the means and motive for a murder, a confession and the apprehension of the perpetrator. What more, Brautigan asks, does a detective story need?

Much of this interrogation of genre was conducted (and published) within universities and drew on (as well as parodied) new trends in literary criticism, in particular its shift in emphasis from symbol to structure. In some ways, story-writing itself became a form of literary criticism.[37] While Roland Barthes drew an analogy between the sentence and the narrative – 'a narrative is a large sentence, just as any declarative sentence is, in a certain way, the outline of a little narrative' – Donald Barthelme wrote 'Sentence', a six-and-a-half page fiction made up of a single, unfinished sentence, and dealing with the process of writing a sentence.[38]

What short-story writers most wanted to do was escape enclosure in existing literary models. All sorts of alternatives were proposed. Some writers revived pre-modern forms such as the fable or fairy tale or drew upon short fiction's links to the discursive essay and Kafkaesque philosophical parable. Others looked further afield. Why not write a story in the form of a questionnaire or footnotes or a TV game show? Why not make collages combining words and images? Why not write fiction for 'tape' and 'live voice' as well as for print?[39] In other words, just about anything went – except, that is, the mood-driven, slice-of-life realist short story. The urge to distinguish their work from New Critical or *New Yorker* paradigms led many authors to search for new names for their short prose pieces. This was a great era of manifestoes, as writers vied with each other to label, and anthologise, the mood of the moment: new fiction, neo-narrative, anti-story, surfiction and superfiction were some of the contenders. *Anti-Story* highlighted experimental fiction's 'contrariness': its stance 'against' event, subject, analysis, meaning, mimesis, scale, 'reality' and the 'middle range of experience'. *Superfiction or The American Story Transformed* was more positive, if less definite, in its sub-headings: Fantasy-Fabulation-Irrealism; Neo-Gothic; Myth-Parable; Metafiction. Others revived the nineteenth-century term 'tale' or, following Samuel Beckett, talked about 'texts'.[40] The most popular designation, however, was 'fictions', after Jorge Luis Borges's *Ficciones*, which had appeared in English translation in 1962 and which was often declared the single book that broke through the parochial complacency of mid-century American writing.[41] In the 'High Sixties', no one wanted to talk about the Americanness of the short story or even its distinctness from poetry or non-fiction. Internationalism and intermediality were now the rage. It was often difficult to distinguish the parables, fables and 'exemplary fictions' produced by people who called themselves poets from those written by people who called themselves fictionalists. For example, Robert Coover's special issue of *TriQuarterly*, 'Minute Stories', includes prose poems by Francis Ponge as well as stories by J. G. Ballard. In Klinkowitz and Somer's anthology, *Innovative Fiction*, W. S. Merwin's 'poetic' parable of a man communing with a boulder, 'Tergvinder's Stone', sits inconspicuously between two pieces of 'fiction': Coover's labyrinthine 'The Babysitter' and Donald Barthelme's surreal fable of 'Porcupines at the University'. The promise was a release from genre itself.

'Lost in the Funhouse'

> Like everybody else in post-World War II America, I started out writing short stories in an entry-level creative-writing workshop.[42]

John Barth was one of the first writers to spend his whole career in the creative writing world: he graduated from Johns Hopkins in 1947, then taught at Penn State (1953–65) and Buffalo (1965–73), before returning to Johns Hopkins until his retirement in 1995. The university context should perhaps be remembered when considering his influential 1968 essay, 'The Literature of Exhaustion', in which Barth spoke of the 'used-upness of certain forms, of exhaustion of certain possibilities'.[43] Modern fiction, and the short story perhaps most of all, was 'never far from parody, sensing itself anticipated, overdone, exhausted'; nevertheless, Barth insisted, there was 'there was no need to despair'.[44] Exhaustion itself could be a subject, a provocation to new forms.

At the heart of Barth's essay is a discussion of Borges's short story, 'Pierre Menard, Author of the *Quixote*'.[45] Pierre Menard, a turn-of-the-century Symbolist poet, has written some pages which 'coincide – word for word and line for line' with Cervantes's novel, *Don Quixote*. A later critic reads Menard's version alongside Cervantes's original and finds that words written in the twentieth century mean something quite different than those same words written in the seventeenth century. The point of the story is not simply that interpretations change. Rather it suggests, even as the critic asserts that Menard's 'fragmentary *Quixote* is more subtle than Cervantes's, that in the twentieth century, literary ambition must inevitably be reduced, become modest. The modern writer can do no more than imitate and miniaturise the great works of the past; her creations are mere 'palimpsests'.[46] Announcing that one's story was wholly 'anticipated', that originality was now impossible, but that one would nevertheless carry on – 'aware of where we've been and where we are' – became a standard move in what was then becoming known as post-modernism.[47] The writer could not transcend or abandon the past, only 'revisit it with irony, not innocently'.[48] Thus, Richard Brautigan's 'A Short Story about Contemporary Life in California' begins: 'There are thousands of stories with original beginnings. This is not one of them.' Instead the narrator decides that 'the only way to start a story about contemporary life in California is to do it the way Jack London started *The Sea-Wolf*'. But all is not lost: 'It worked in 1904 and it can work in 1969.'[49]

It is no coincidence that so many stories about the difficulty of writing stories were short. Metafiction works best when restricted in length. As Robert Scholes points out, 'when extended', the self-reflexive story 'must either lapse into a more fundamental mode of fiction or risk losing all fictional interest in order to maintain its intellectual perspectives'.[50] What Scholes calls fiction's 'fundamental mode' is one that encourages the reader to suspend disbelief and 'lose' herself in a narrative. When we read a short story, however, 'there is no time … to forget it is only "literature" and not "life"', which is why, says Tzvetan Todorov, 'the public prefer novels to tales, long books to short texts'.[51] Another way of putting this is to note that framing or narrative enclosure, the conscious act of selecting a fragment, is inevitably more apparent in a short piece than a long one, and not only when its author chooses a title such as 'An Episode from the Life of Professor Brooke', 'Two Short Sad Stories from a Long and Happy Life' or 'Five Signs of Disturbance'.[52] As we spend time with a lengthy novel, and become familiar with the protagonists and their world, we are more likely to forget the frame and concentrate on the 'fictional interest'. The short story, by its very lack of length, forestalls that immersion process and so we are more likely to retain a critical perspective. Aware of the enclosure in which we are trapped, we are, metafiction argues, released from its power.

An exemplary piece of metafiction, John Barth's 'Lost in the Funhouse' seems to be narrated by a writing-school student trying to remind himself how to go about his task. He often interrupts his narrative with passages that might have come from his lecture notes or from *Understanding Fiction*. The advice may be good, but it's hard to follow:

> Description of a physical appearance and mannerisms is one of several standard methods of characterization used by writers of fiction … The brown hair on Ambrose's mother's forearms gleamed in the sun like. Though right-handed, she took her left arm from the seat-back to press the dashboard cigar lighter for Uncle Karl … The smell of Uncle Karl's cigar smoke reminded one of.[53]

It is not only figurative language which proves difficult. The narrator contemplates the use of italics for emphasis, wonders how to present dialogue, and asks himself whether diving 'would make a suitable literary symbol'. He also worries that he might be straying too far from a teenager's point of view. Part of the story's problem is its used-up subject matter: an account of a day trip to the Ocean City boardwalk made by 13-year-old Ambrose, his elder brother, Peter, his parents, his Uncle Karl and a 14-year-old neighbour called Magda. It is Independence Day, sometime during the Second World War. 'What is the story's theme?' asks the narrator. 'Is the war relevant?' 'It's all too long and rambling,' he worries, 'as if the author.' But he can't finish that sentence either.

The narrator's awkwardness and inability to get going with his story mirrors Ambrose's awkwardness and inability to get going with Magda, with whom he had had a sexual encounter in the tool shed when he was ten. 'I shall never forget this moment,' Ambrose had solemnly told her. Three years on, he is paralysed by self-consciousness. Ambrose enters the amusement park's funhouse, which features in the story both literally, as a building containing 'various devices designed to startle or amuse' (in *Webster*'s definition), and metaphorically, as an analogue of fiction itself. Quickly lost in its maze-like corridors, Ambrose comforts himself by making up stories about his future, drawn from the standard Hollywood repertoire. He fantasises about a time in which, now 'quite famous in his line of work' and 'gray at the temples', he reminds Magda of 'his youthful passion' or reassures their son that 'it' is 'perfectly normal. We have all been through it.' The convention that the story most depends on, and which its narrator least trusts, is that of the teenage *turning point* (his italics): 'either everybody's felt what Ambrose feels, in which case it goes without saying, or else no normal person feels such things, in which case Ambrose is a freak.' Even the rhetorical question 'Is anything more tiresome, in fiction, than the problems of sensitive adolescents?' is such a cliché that the narrator puts it in quotation marks. In standing back from its own effort and making this point, however, the story draws attention to the distinctive pathology that literary fiction shares with sensitive adolescents: that of trying to be normal while also trying to be distinctive.

For all that it mocks the conventions of realism, 'Lost in the Funhouse' retains an element of the normal. The narrative, despite its wrong turnings, follows a definite arc, ending with the family driving home in the evening, and with Ambrose having experienced some kind of intellectual initiation or turning point: a recognition of the fact that while he would rather be 'among the lovers for whom funhouses are designed', that is, 'a regular person', he will probably end up as their constructor and 'secret operator'. The narrator quotes *Ulysses*, but it is the more conventional *Portrait of the Artist as a Young Man* to which he has added 'an "exhausted" footnote'.[54]

Ambrose recognises that the main difference between life and fiction is that in fiction anything can happen, whereas in life, 'no one chose what he was' and that, to him, was 'unbearable'. The world of the funhouse might be 'incredibly complex' and initially confusing, but compared with the world-at-war outside, the funhouse, like the hothouse apartment in Pynchon's 'Entropy', offers a space that is 'utterly controlled'. Another Barth story, 'Anonymiad', makes a similar point. A minstrel from the time of Homer finds himself exiled to a 'Zeus forsaken island' where he invents 'what [he] came to call *fiction*':

That is, I found that by pretending that things had happened which in fact had not, and that people existed who didn't, I could achieve a lovely truth which actuality obscures … It was *as if* there were this minstrel and this milkmaid, et cetera; one could I believe draw a whole philosophy from that *as if.*[55]

Of course, as least some of Barth's original readers would known, a whole philosophy of 'as if' had already been developed. Hans Vaihinger's *The Philosophy of 'As If'* had appeared in German in 1911, but 'remained in obscurity' until 1967 when Frank Kermode discussed it in *The Sense of an Ending*, a book whose admonition not to 'forget that fictions are fictive' chimed with, and influenced, a great deal of late 1960s metafiction.[56] The value of fiction's 'as ifs' (as opposed to those of science) does not lie in their truth-claims (which might be subjected to empirical verification) but, for Barth at least, in their fun-claims. Fun is not merely 'amusement'; fiction-making is 'called into play by the "assaults" upon it of a "hostile external world"'.[57] In other words, as Barth and his contemporaries often emphasised, the construction of funhouses was not mere 'intellectual fun and games'.[58] Indeed, the formalism of the 1960s metafictionalists was as morally driven as that of the 1940s New Critics. Like their predecessors, they believed that in finding its ideal form, literature could offer a 'special kind of knowledge' unavailable elsewhere.

A great deal of experimentation in short-fictional form presented itself as a direct response to the various 'assaults' of the American 1960s and 1970s. In Grace Paley's work (which I'll discuss in Chapter 6), the closure provided by the single story comes under pressure when it tries to accommodate the voices of a new generation and those of women. In James Alan McPherson's 'Elbow Room', it is America's changing racial situation that challenges existing models. 'Elbow Room' enacts the struggle between a narrator and his editor about the correct form in which to tell the story of Virginia Valentine, an idealistic black woman from Tennessee in search of 'different ways of looking at the world', and Paul Frost, a white man from Kansas, 'trying desperately to unstructure and flesh out his undefined "I".' The narrator's task is to find a way of conveying the complexities of their relationship, a form that breaks through literary as well as social 'caste curtains', one which doesn't restrict 'black folk' to 'entertaining with time-tested acts'. 'I needed new eyes, regeneration, fresh forms, and went hunting for them out in the territory.' Along the way, however, he is challenged by an editor unable to see what imagination or form might have to do with 'caste restrictions' and why 'conventional narrative conventions' and 'traditional narrative modes' won't work. The narrator just needs a little 'elbow room', just needs to become 'nimble enough to dodge other people's straightjackets'. But like many narrators of short stories, he declares himself unsuccessful in his task. 'I lack the insight to narrate its complexities,' he concedes, 'But it may still be told.' The editor interrupts: '*Comment is unclear. Explain. Explain.*'[59]

Perhaps the most philosophical of the 1960s moralists of form was William Gass. The author of numerous essays on aesthetics, and three novels, including the 650-page *The Tunnel* (1995), he is still best known for his 1968 collection of short stories, *In The Heart of The Heart of the Country*. The title story, which Tony Tanner described as 'one of the most distinguished American short stories written this century', generates new form out of the exhaustion of pastoral and interrogates the consolation offered by the aesthetic 'as if'.[60] A story about 'retirement from love', it can also be read as a war story with 'no mention of the war in it'.[61] The poet-narrator has, in his own Yeats-inspired words, 'sailed the seas and come ... to B ... a small town fastened to a field in Indiana', happy to see 'the country sail away'. The fragmented and confused experiences of war are often made sense of through reference to an unchanging pastoral existence, which provides some kind of stable moral touchstone from which to view the whole enterprise. But the Midwest in which the narrator finds himself is a 'dissonance of parts and people' and the 'rural mind' is 'narrow, passionate, and reckless':

> The air nimbly and sweetly recommends itself unto our gentle senses. Here, growling tractors tear the earth. Dust roils up behind them. Drivers sit jouncing under bright umbrellas. They wear refrigerated hats and steer by looking at the tracks they've cut behind them, their transistors blaring. Close to the land are they? good companions to the soil? Tell me: do they live in harmony with the alternating seasons? ... The modern husbandman uses chemicals from cylinders and sacks, spike-ball-and-claw machines, metal sheds, and cost accounting. Nature in the old sense does not matter. It does not exist. Our farmer's only mystical attachment is to parity.[62]

The promised pastoral space, it turns out, is not opposed in spirit and essence to the war, but rather crucial in its engendering. It is, in fact, 'surly Christian' Midwesterners who most strongly urge the 'smithereening, say, of Russia, China, Cuba, or Korea'. That 'say' is rather coy, as is the absence of Vietnam from the list. But Gass, like so many short story writers, was adamant that fiction should not have a 'message' for, in his view, that entailed replacing the 'work with its interpretation' which became a 'way of robbing it of its reality'.[63]

If pastoral reveals itself to be no more than a 'lie of old poetry', the only refuge to be found is within one's own mind and linguistic creations. The story suggests that nothing exists outside the paragraphs the narrator invents; it is a self-sufficient system, a 'geography of the imagination', a consoling 'as if'.[64] For Gass, the writer's task is not to comment on the world, 'where you have very little control', but to take it 'apart' and 'replace it with language over which you can have control. Destroy and then repair.'[65]

This is what the story's narrator does. He replaces B, Indiana with thirty-six discrete blocks of prose, each clearly labelled and each describing, or rather inventing, some aspect of the town: business, education, church, politics and so on. For many critics, this process represents a 'new' and 'life-enhancing solipsism'; optimistic because 'it has more to do with the actuating and liberating imagination than with the entrapment of selfhood'.[66] Imagination, Gass argues, is the 'unifying power, and the acts of imagination are our most free and natural; they represent us at our best'.[67] Even listing can become an act of imagination because lists, says Gass, 'are for those who love language, the vowel-swollen cheek, the lilting, dancing tongue, because lists are fields of words'.[68]

Among the champions of lists that Gass identifies is James Joyce; he notes that the word 'and' occurs 7,170 times in *Ulysses*. Joyce, of course, was also interested in elaborating the details of a town, but cataloguing 'Dublin's street furniture' was only the first step in his 'unifying' imaginative process. The next, at least for Stephen Dedalus, was to 'see it and I know at once what it is: epiphany.'[69] The transcendent knowledge afforded by epiphany, as many short story writers know, allows an escape from enclosure. But Gass's narrator, for all that he strives for epiphany or some other 'unifying' principle (such as *Ulysses*'s myth), struggles to get beyond 'lumps and pieces in piles'. Each paragraph is a visual image of the isolation and enclosure it describes. The town itself is isolated: 'you can reach us by crossing a creek'. The houses originally built by farmers 'to contain them in their retirement' are now abandoned, with 'vacant lots' on either side of any that remain inhabited. Teenagers sit in the protective shells of their 'darkened cars', and 'no one touches except in rage'. The heart of the country is vacant, barren and loveless, and, most strikingly, inert.

The narrator presents various attempts at movement, both in the town and in himself. For example, he notices a long line of parked cars:

> In a moment one will pull out, spinning cinders behind it to stalk impatiently up and down the dark streets or roar half a mile into the country before returning to its place in line and pulling up.

In the section that follows this – 'My House, My Cat, My Company' – his description of the town is interrupted by what seems like the beginning of a narrative. 'I must organise myself', he asserts. 'I must, as they say, pull myself together, dump this cat from my lap, stir – yes, resolve, move, do.' And so he gets up and wanders 'from room to room, up and down, gazing through most of my forty-one windows'. In other words, like Callisto in 'Entropy' or Ambrose in 'Lost in the Funhouse', he is trapped within a closed circuit. From that safely enclosed space, he observes movement: 'Leaves wiggle. Grass sways. A bird chirps, pecks the ground. An auto wheel in penning circles keeps its rigid spokes.' But this is movement within stasis. Viewed through the frame of the window, wiggling, swaying and pecking become 'images', 'stones', 'memorials'.

In order truly to move and thus 'restore' himself, the narrator must 'pass the glass' (exit the frame) and enter the outside world. But his attempts are thwarted from the start; he tries to talk to the old woman who is his neighbour, but her talk's 'a fence – a shade drawn, window fastened, door that's locked'. The story ends with the narrator listening to a Christmas carol: 'Yes, I believe it's one of the jolly ones, it's "Joy to the World". There's no one to hear the music but myself, and though I'm listening, I'm no longer certain. Perhaps the record's playing something else.' This is not an optimistic solipsism, but one wracked with profound scepticism, and not only about which carol is playing.

As its opening line suggests, 'In the Heart of the Heart of the Country' translates the dialectic of descriptive stasis and narrative movement into terms established by Yeats's 'Sailing to Byzantium', between stone-like memorial ('monuments of unaging intellect') and the human body (which is 'begotten, born and dies').[70] It also reworks the long-standing debate between the two most common analogies for the short story: its approximation to a picture (framed in space) or an oral tale (framed by a voice in time). On the one hand, then, 'In the Heart' is a static visual object, a fixed and finished 'thing' among the many things it enumerates, and on the other hand, it is an event that is happening to someone, a communication, by 'vowel-swollen cheek' and 'lilting, dancing tongue', from 'I' to 'you'. In its attempt to create a 'semantics of sound' to counter the inevitable 'whole' of the printed text, 'In the Heart' can be read in the broader context of 1960s adaptations of the traditional modes and values of oral storytelling.[71] Historical and anthropological works, such as Albert B. Lord's *The Singer of Tales* (1960), which emphasised the importance of performance and participation in oral culture, provided models for a new trend in literature and criticism.[72] Marshall McLuhan's championing of TV as a form of 'secondary orality' was one manifestation of this; others included performance art, action painting, living theatre, happenings and the oral poetry movement.[73] Metafiction had transformed the short story from within, but only by a kind of self-mirroring and a constant provocation to imagery of spatial enclosure. The performative narrative voice promised an escape from the claustrophobia offered both by the traditional short story and by the solipsistic spaces of Pynchon's hothouse apartment, Barth's funhouse and Gass's geography of the imagination.

Low-grade Mystery and Mess: Donald Barthelme

Today Donald Barthelme is known as an exemplary *New Yorker* comic writer, in the tradition of S. J. Perelman, E. B. White and James Thurber. The magazine published 130 of his stories and unsigned 'casual' pieces, many of which highlighted the non sequiturs of urban life.[74] By the end of the 1960s, Barthelme had become the 'most imitated short fictionist in America', and writers today such as Donald Antrim and George Saunders continue to acknowledge his influence.[75] Although he briefly studied creative writing (and produced some obligatory 'ersatz Hemingway' pastiches with added imagery from Eliot's 'Prufrock'), Barthelme's fiction owes as much to his more cosmopolitan early career as a museum curator and editor of small art magazines.[76] Many of his stories appeared alongside, and were informed by, the work of his friends from the intertwined New York worlds of painting, poetry and art criticism: Robert Rauschenberg, John Ashbery, Kenneth Koch and Harold Rosenberg. 'Will You Tell Me?', for example, first appeared in the inaugural (March 1964) issue of the Paris-based *Art and Literature: An International Review*, preceded by an extract from Gaston Bachelard's *The Poetics of Space* and followed by an essay by Jean Genet. Elsewhere in the issue, Cyril

Connolly declared that little magazines were the 'pollinators of works of art' without which literature 'could not exist', while Marcelin Pleynet argued that the value of James Bishop's painting was its 'particular and insistent questioning of all aspects of pictorial language' and 'refusal to admit that any of these aspects' could be 'taken for granted'.[77]

'Will You Tell Me?' also works hard to stop the reader from taking fictional language for granted.[78] The story disrupts 'causality, continuity, cohesion, consistency in point of view – all the attributes', says David Lodge, 'that bind together the ingredients of realistic fiction into a smooth, easily assimilable discourse.'[79] It opens with the statement 'Henry gave Charles and Irene a nice baby for Christmas', and although we are then told that Charles and Irene were 'puzzled' to learn that Henry got the baby 'from the bank', no further explanation is given. The next, one-line, paragraph reports that 'Eric was born'. To whom? When? We don't know. The third paragraph moves on to the subject of an affair between Irene and Henry. As Lodge says, while we learn about the couple's bed ('small but comfortable enough'), we are told 'little about their emotions, sexual pleasure, means of deceiving Charles, and all the other details we would expect of an adultery story'. The paragraph ends by declaring that the affair lasted twelve years. A one-word fourth paragraph introduces another character; the fifth tells us that 'To begin with she was just a baby, then a four-year-old, then twelve years passed and she was Paul's age, sixteen.' Paul, the paragraph concludes, 'had already bitten the tips of Helen's pretty breasts with his teeth.' In five short paragraphs, Lodge notes, 'we have covered enough events to fill an entire novel'. The story's parodic effect, moreover, depends on our familiarity with realist novels that explore this kind of material at length. 'Deviations', says Lodge, 'can only be perceived against a norm.'[80]

All sorts of metaphors can express the relation of norm and deviation, the fact that that 'writing remains full of the recollection of previous usage'.[81] Cynthia Ozick's 'Usurpation (Other People's Stories)' considers the way in which stories are always 'acquired, borrowed, given, taken, inherited, stolen, plagiarized, usurped'.[82] Joyce Carol Oates prefers to think of the relationship as one of *Marriages and Infidelities*, the title of a 1972 collection which reworked such classic 'inspirations' as 'The Lady with the Pet Dog' and 'Metamorphosis'.[83] The marriage between texts enables the writer to 'transcend the limitations of the ego', yet it also opens the way to infidelity.[84] For Barthelme, however, the contemporary writer was less like an unfaithful spouse than like a child living in the shadow of his father. Even when the father dies he remains powerful, 'an inner voice commanding, haranguing, yes-ing and no-ing'. 'At what point do you become yourself?' Barthelme asks, 'Never, wholly, you are always partly him.' All that the son can do then is reproduce paternal action 'in attenuated form'.[85] Sometimes Barthelme makes this explicit in the Menard/Cervantes mode. 'At the Tolstoy Museum we sat and wept', begins one story, biblically, before moving on to provide, in ten pages, an illustrated biography of Tolstoy and a retelling of his 'The Three Hermits'. Considering 'the 640,086 pages (Jubilee Edition) of the author's published work', some museum visitors want Tolstoy to 'go away', while others 'were glad we had him'. The narrator, however, hasn't made up his mind.[86]

For Barthelme, fatherhood does not simply represent any writing from the past; more specifically, it is a metaphor for the principles of narrative order and coherence associated with the unachievable, out-of-date, big novel.[87] Like the man at the Tolstoy museum, Barthelme has mixed feelings about the extended, explanatory narrative of the novel and its corollary, a conception of the self as stable and continuing over time. On the one hand, his stories seem to accept that in the post-modern world, 'small is one of the concepts that you should shoot for'; on the other hand, they often express nostalgia for some large organising principle. Barthelme is aware that he is not only writing after Tolstoy and Balzac, but also 'after Joyce' and Beckett.[88] While he wrote novels and was 'always working on a novel', Barthelme confessed that they 'always seem to fall apart in my hands'.[89]

Barthelme's stories are often about a thwarted quest for structure and meaning. Like Flannery O'Connor, he was keen to distinguish the insights available through art from those associated with 'journalism or sociology'.[90] What she called mystery, he named 'not-knowing': the not-knowing, he argued, is 'what permits art to be made'.[91] But if O'Connor saw mystery as eventually giving way to religious enlightenment, Barthelme – also brought up a Catholic – tends to deny that final step. 'Paraguay' begins with a description of a plain that is 'white with snow'. By the end, the snow is red which, as someone points out, '"like any other snow … invites contemplation"'. 'It seemed to proclaim itself a mystery', decides the narrator, 'but one there was no point in solving – an ongoing low-grade mystery.'[92] Many tales enact the inevitability and absurdity of Samuel Beckett's 'I can't go on. I'll go on.'[93] In one of the several question-and-answer stories, 'Kierkegaard

Unfair to Schlegel', Q challenges A's ironic stance and A responds 'I turn my irony against others. But I accomplish nothing. I march, it's ludicrous.'[94] In 'The Catechist', two priests meet and have a conversation. At the end we are told that 'there is no day on which this conversation is not held and no detail of this conversation which is not replicated on any particular day on which this conversation is held.'[95] To recall Mailer's distinction between novelistic flux and short-fictional permanence, what we have here is the permanent, repetitive flux of not knowing but wanting to know, and the pleasure of 'speaking about that which I do not know'.[96]

The knowing pursued by the narrator of 'See the Moon?', in anticipation of the birth of his son, seems arbitrary and esoteric. He attempts 'lunar hostility studies' – why the moon hates mankind – and 'cardinalogy' – the scientific study of cardinals, which involves testing the acidity of their stomachs, and finding out how many gallons of water it takes to fill their baths. 'It's my hope', he says, 'that these ...souvenirs ... will someday merge, blur – cohere is the word, maybe – into something meaningful. A grand word, meaningful. What do I look for? A work of art, I'll not accept anything less.'[97] But whereas souvenirs of experience in the classic modernist works of Joyce, Faulkner or Ellison eventually come together under the aegis of an explanatory discourse – myth – all that results from the efforts of Barthelme's narrator to connect the discontinuous pieces of his life are the fragments with which he began.

> Here is the world and here are the knowledgeable knowers knowing. What can I tell you? What has been pieced together from the reports of travelers.
> Fragments are the only forms I trust.[98]

Fragments can relate to wholes in three main ways. First, they can be collected by 'some process of unification' (as Georg Lukács described the practice of the novel); secondly, they can operate as nostalgic reminders of a remembered or imagined whole (as is the case with Menard's *Quixote*); and, thirdly, they can be 'pieced together' without any hope of unification by a method that rather 'accommodates the mess'.[99] For Barthelme (and for many of his contemporaries – from Rauschenberg to Ashbery to Bob Dylan) – that method was collage.[100]

'You don't know how I envy [painters],' says the narrator of 'See the Moon?':

They can pick up a Baby Ruth wrapper in the street, glue it to the canvas (in the *right place*, of course, there's that), and lo! People crowd about and cry, 'A real Baby Ruth wrapper, by God, what could be realer than that!' Fantastic metaphysical advantage. You hate them, if you're ambitious.[101]

Although sometimes striving for purely visual effects – integrating graphics or typographical experiments – into his stories, Barthelme's (near) equivalent of the chocolate-bar wrapper was the 'dreck' of found-language and found-form.[102] It wasn't just a matter of 'gluing on' words and phrases from various sources – although he did that (for example, 'Paraguay' incorporates, and footnotes, bits of Le Corbusier) – or of appropriating characters and settings – although he did that also ('The Joker's Greatest Triumph' borrows from Batman, 'A Shower of Gold' from TV game shows). Other stories explore characteristically collage-linked situations ('The Viennese Opera Ball', 'The Party'), or psycho-logical experiences ('Brain Damage', 'City Life'), or satirise the piecing together of fragments involved in investigative journalism; for example, in 'Report' and 'Robert Kennedy Saved From Drowning', a 'pastiche of the slick magazine profile'.[103] And yet others describe collages. Consider the 'serape woven out of two hundred transistor radios like a large blaring building' which a 'son manqué' wears to disturb his parents in 'The Dolt', or the barricade constructed from bourgeois detritus with which the narrator of 'The Indian Uprising' tries to 'defend the city':

> I analyzed the composition of the barricade nearest me and found two ashtrays, ceramic, one dark brown and one dark brown with an orange blur at the lip; a tiny frying pan; two-liter bottles of red wine; three quarter-liter bottles of Black & White ... a hollow-core door in birch veneer on black wrought-iron legs ...[104]

The 'point of collage', Barthelme told an interviewer, is that 'unlike things are stuck together to make, in the best case, a new reality.'

This new reality, in the best case, may be or imply a commentary on the other reality from which it came, and may also be much else. It's an *itself*, if it's successful: Harold Rosenberg's 'anxious object', which doesn't know if it's a work of art or a pile of junk.[105]

But Barthelme did not see only the contemporary writer's task as analo-gous to that of the contemporary painter, he also admitted to being 'distracted by the things that painters can do' and 'maybe fiction can't do', that is, create 'an immediate impact – a beautifully realized whole that can be taken in at a glance and yet still be studied for a long time'.[106] This impulse – away from narrative towards a single controlling image – had long been a feature of the short story and accounts for the prevalence of analogies with various forms of visual art. The cultivation of what was sometimes called the 'spatial form' of the story was one of the ways in which it made itself into an autonomous 'literary object' rather than an 'authoritative account delivered by an expert'.[107] This formulation sounds like that of a New Critic, but it is Barthelme. But while in the stories of Cheever and O'Connor, a bit of real world (an enormous radio, a hat) is called into symbolic service, in Barthelme's fiction, the image intrudes upon the real world and imagines itself as something the reader can bump into, '*there*, like a rock or a refridgerator'.[108] 'The aim of literature', says a character in one story, 'is the creation of a strange object covered with fur which breaks your heart'; another ends when 'the doorway is suddenly blocked by the figure of an immense black bull. The bull begins to ring like a telephone.'[109] The narrator of 'See the Moon?' devotes a lengthy paragraph to comparing his unborn child to a battleship. This was an 'American surrealism' which owed as much to S. J. Perelman and John Ashbery as to Meret Oppenheim.[110]

Responding also to the 1960s impulse towards a public art that would both express the artist's vision and communicate with thousands, several of Barthelme's stories present large urban installations. In 'Return', an architect is commissioned to build a 'beautiful stainless steel azalea nine hundred feet high'; in 'I Bought a Little City', a man buys Galveston, Texas, and, despite his aim not to be 'too imaginative', rebuilds a housing scheme so that from the sky it resembles the Mona Lisa.[111] The discrepancy between these grandiose schemes and the modest space occupied by the short story is striking. The short story writer's job, rather, is to 'disenchant the symbol', as Barthelme put it in 'The Glass Mountain', a parodic quest tale about a man's attempt to scale a glass mountain at the corner of 13th Street and 8th Avenue in Manhattan. On the streets below, in vivid contrast to the 'enchanted' yet colourless mountain, are people, shooting up, walking dogs, shouting obscenities, and 'sidewalks ... full of dogshit in brilliant colors: ocher, umber, Mars yellow, sienna, viridian, ivory black, rose madder'.[112] A messy collage, 'exquisite mysterious muck', Barthelme implies, is the stuff of human life, and yet the story, like so much of his fiction, also acknowledges, as equally human, an unwillingness to give up the search for the 'ineffable' or at least 'another place, a place where *everything is different*'.[113]

'The Balloon' is another very short story about a very large 'anxious object' in downtown Manhattan.[114] The narrator, who has stage-managed its hanging, over forty-five blocks, struggles to describe the effect created by its blend of colours (muted heavy greys and browns for the most part, contrasting with walnut and soft yellows) and texture ('a deliberate lack of finish, enhanced by skillful installation, gave the surface a rough, forgotten quality').[115] He then observes the public's response. While children are the most fully alert to its 'possibilities', the narrator also notes approvingly that most New Yorkers have learned not to insist on, or even search for, meaning. Perhaps, like him, they had read Susan Sontag's 1964 essay 'Against Interpretation'. 'To interpret', Sontag wrote, 'is to impoverish, to deplete the world – in order to set up a shadow world of "meanings".'[116] Once again, this doesn't seem very different from the kind of argument put forward by O'Connor and the New Critics. But while writers such as O'Connor, Welty or Cheever had filled the gap left by interpretation with religious or secular revelation, Barthelme, like Sontag and Barth, favoured the kind of open-ended 'play' which guaranteed both 'eros' and 'seriousness'.[117] In all cases, however, the aim remained the creation of a 'new reality'.

'The Balloon' is very much a New York story. The shape-shifting, messy form derives its effect from its contrast to the 'hard, flat skin' of the city's distinctive Mondrian-like grid. Its playfully 'varied motions' stand out against the 'rigidly patterned' streets and, it is suggested, the rigidly patterned lives of New Yorkers. 'It is wrong to speak of "situations"', says the narrator, 'implying sets of circumstances leading to some resolution, some escape of tension; there were no situations, simply the balloon hanging there.' But the balloon cannot hang there forever or there would be no story, only a sketch, and so in the final paragraph, circumstance, situation and even 'autobiographical disclosure' are introduced.[118] The artist-narrator now addresses someone directly: his lover who, it turns out, has been away. On her return, the balloon is dismantled and packed off to West Virginia, 'awaiting some other time of unhappiness, sometime, perhaps, when we are angry with each other'. In this 'resolution' the balloon seems to perform a 'theatrical' and 'anthropomorphic' function: its breast-like, womb-like eroticism has not been public and impersonal after all, but an expression of individual desire and loneliness.[119] Charles Molesworth reads 'The Balloon' in the tradition of the Thurberesque farce of the 'little man', unlucky in love and, as Barthelme put it in another story, 'constantly being *overtaken* by events'.[120] But balloons do more than swell and heave erotically. They also deflate rapidly and, in this final image, he manages to use the short story's predisposition towards 'some escape of tension' even as he mocks it. As Alan Wilde points out, 'The Balloon' is finally 'an exercise not *in* but *about* play'.[121]

A great reader of cultural theorists (including Marshall McLuhan and Walter Benjamin), Barthelme described the 'rationalisation' of art under capitalism as a process of miniaturisation, because everyone would be given only 'as much art as his system can tolerate'. The artist's product is therefore simplified, 'minimized' and 'air-dried' and his or her role reduced to supplying 'variety' or 'distraction'.[122] Unfortunately, the 'development of new wonders is not like the production of canned goods,' noted the narrator of another story, before unveiling the latest wonder.[123] It is tempting to read these statements not simply as a statement of art's struggle against mass media entertainment, but more specifically in relation to Barthelme's situation as a prolific contributor of miniature 'strange ideas' to the *New Yorker*. The short story's capacity to provide just enough but not too much distraction, it had long been argued, made it the perfect form for modern readers. As we saw in the Introduction, from the end of the nineteenth century it had been suggested that readers 'educated upon the scraps into which newspapers are degrading' couldn't cope with any piece of prose that couldn't be 'be taken down with a gulp'.[124] By the late twentieth century, even Poe's single 'sitting' of between half an hour and two hours seemed a big commitment and some argued that 1,000- to 2,000-word 'flash fictions' or 'short shorts' had become 'symptomatic of an age where speed in everything'. In the 1960s, television's 'scenic blips' (stopping 'at twelve-minute intervals for commercial breaks') were held responsible for the appeal of short fiction's 'quick fix'.[125] In the 1980s, the 'ever dwindling readerly attention span' was blamed on MTV; today, computer games and Twitter stand accused.[126] As an argument about popular reading habits, this line doesn't really make sense; the bestseller lists from the 1890s to the present are filled with 400-page blockbusters not short story collections. Nevertheless, writers and critics have continually been drawn to make analogies between the modernity of the short story and that of new media.

From TV to Hypertext

Norman Mailer was one of many writers who drew attention to the effect of TV's production of interrupted narratives either through commercial breaks or by viewers switching channels. The minds of viewers, he said, are 'jabbed and poked and twitched and probed and finally galvanised into surrealistic modes of response' by these 'jumps and cracks and leaps and breaks'.[127] Mailer was speaking critically, but TV's surrealist collage was precisely the effect that Robert Coover's famous story 'The Babysitter' tried to capture. The story begins in Cheever territory – a couple leave a babysitter in charge of the children while they go out to a party – and rewrites it in the form of TV channel-hopping. There are 108 paragraphs, each separated from the next by a row of three dots and each offering a new perspective. We not only move between the points of view (and fantasies) of different characters and increasingly contradictory chronologies and plots, but the division between the living room and the TV screen also breaks down. What is imagined and what is reality? Has the babysitter suffocated the baby? Has she drowned? Or did she just do the dishes and fall asleep?[128]

Coover's interest in bifurcating narratives had been sparked by 'The Garden of the Forking Paths', one of Borges' most Poe-like fantasies, in which the labyrinthine fiction of Ts'ui Pên are described:

> In all fictional works, each time a man is confronted with several alternatives, he chooses one and eliminates the others; in the fiction of Ts'ui Pên, he chooses – simultaneously – all of them … He believed in an infinite series of times, in a growing, dizzying net of divergent, convergent and parallel times.[129]

If Borges is most interested in time, Coover investigates parallel spaces. Consider 'The Elevator'. The premise is simple – Martin rides the elevator to the 14th floor where he works – but each numbered segment provides an alternative narrative, one for each floor in the building, including the basement. Coover had fashioned a way out of the 'tight cell' of the short story just as Martin, eventually deciding to walk up the stairs, escapes 'small cage' of the elevator.[130] Later Coover became one of the first writers to recognise the possibilities for non-sequential writing offered by computers. The metaphor of a space within which other spaces can fit was the idea behind 'Storyspace', a software program developed by Michael Joyce and Jay David Bolter, which allowed the production of hyperfictions, notably Joyce's 'Afternoon, a Story' (1987), Stuart Moult-hrop's 'Victory Garden' (1991), Shelley Jackson's 'Patchwork Girl' (1995) and John McDaid's 'Uncle Buddy's Phantom Funhouse' (1992). Hypertext relies on the linking together of spaces and the creation of paths which take the reader from one to another. 'Usually a single space is linked to a number of others', explains Sarah Smith, 'for example the phrase "Ted took Terri to the movies" might have links on "Ted", "Terri" and "movies", each leading to a different writing space.'[131] By providing 'networks of alternative routes (as opposed to fiction's fixed unidirectional page-turning') hypertext, claimed Coover, freed the reader from 'domination by the author'. By providing 'a radically divergent technology, interactive and polyvocal, favouring a plurality of discourses over definitive utterances', hypertext fulfils and extends the utopian project of the 1960s short story.[132] Coover has not produced hypertexts himself, although he set up an 'online manifestation' called the Hypertext Hotel, to which any visitor could add a room.[133] Rather, his emphasis, in the course he still teaches at Brown University, has been on pedagogical liberation. Noting the reluctance of writing students to try out 'alternative or innovative forms', he argued that 'confronted with hyperspace, they have no choice':

> All the comforting structures have been erased. It's improvise or go home. Some frantically rebuild those old structures, some just get lost or drift out of sight, most leap in fearlessly without asking how deep it is (*infinitely* deep), admitting, even as they continue to paddle for dear life, that this new arena is indeed an exciting, provocative, if frequently frustrating medium for the creation of new narratives, a potentially revolutionary space, empowered, exactly as advertised, to transform the very art of fiction.[134]

In the early 1990s, hypertext's 'group fiction space' seemed to offer the ultimate open-ended answer to what in the 1960s seemed an urgent 'need to stretch, to step out' of the 'tiny enclave' of the short story. But try as they might to break the frame or find some 'elbow room' within it, short story writers seemed inevitably to come back to images – a closed-circuit, a hothouse, a funhouse, a straightjacket, a stone memorial – of controlled and exquisite entrapment. For Leonard Michaels, the 'story-of-stories' was told by Kafka in just eight words: 'A cage went in search of a bird.'[135]

Notes

1. Mailer, *Advertisements for Myself*, p. 99.
2. Mailer, *Advertisements for Myself*, pp. 141–3.
3. Mailer, *Advertisements for Myself*, p. 100.
4. Mailer, *Advertisements for Myself*, p. 182; Mailer, *Cannibals and Christians*, p. 152; Alfred Kazin described Flannery O'Connor's aesthetic as one of 'finality', which could be summed up in the word 'complete'. *Writing Was Everything*, pp. 139–40.
5. Trilling, *The Liberal Imagination*, p. 271.
6. Roth, *Letting Go*, pp. 239, 297.
7. See Roth, 'Iowa: A Very Far Country Indeed'.
8. Pynchon, *Slow Learner*, pp. 9, 11, 6.
9. Pynchon, *Slow Learner*, pp. 14, 17, 84, 88–9.
10. Pynchon, *Slow Learner*, pp. 78–9, 84.
11. Pynchon, *Slow Learner*, p. 16.
12. In 1960, the year in which 'Entropy' was published, Daniel Bell famously diagnosed a 'disconcerting caesura' between the older generation, for whom 'the old passions are spent' and the 'new generation', fuelled by a 'deep, desperate, almost pathetic anger'. *The End of Ideology*, p. 404.
13. Pynchon, *Slow Learner*, pp. 94, 92. Mulligan's choice is comparable with one which Pynchon later described as between anti-paranoia – 'where nothing is connected to anything, a condition not many of us can bear for long' – and paranoia, where everything connects. *Gravity's Rainbow*, pp. 434, 188.
14. Pynchon, *Slow Learner*, pp. 23–4.
15. Peden, *The American Short Story: Continuity and Change*, p. 12.
16. Introducing Hortense Calisher's 'The Seacoast of Bohemia' in an anthology, Robert Scholes advised readers that the 'aggressively *New Yorkerish* and very upper-middle class' setting 'should be seen as "regions" in the same way as Welty's Mississippi.' *Some Suggestions for Using Elements of Fiction*, p. 52.
17. Yagoda, *About Town*, p. 210.
18. Yagoda, *About Town*, p. 211
19. Yagoda, *About Town*, p. 226.
20. Travis, 'What We Talk About', p. 259.
21. Travis, 'What We Talk About', p. 260; Wolfe, *Hooking Up*, p. 280. On Barthelme's struggle with the magazine's punctuation conventions, and his success in retaining the word 'nipples', see Daugherty, *Hiding Man*, pp. 233, 257, 259–60.
22. Klinkowitz and Somer, *Innovative Fiction*, p. xvi.
23. Stevick, *Anti-Story*, p. xii.
24. Stegner and Scowcroft, *Twenty Years of Stanford Short Stories*, p. xiv.
25. Stevick, *Anti-Story*, p. xii.
26. Klinkowitz and Somer, *Innovative Fiction*, p. xix.
27. Barth, *Lost in the Funhouse*, p. ix.
28. Nadine Gordimer, 'The Flash of Fireflies', in May (ed.), *The New Short Story Theories*, p. 264.
29. Poe, *Essays and Reviews*, pp. 573, 577.
30. Barth, *The Friday Book*, p. 62.
31. Peden, *The American Short Story: Continuity and Change*, pp. 6–7.
32. Klinkowitz and Somer, *Innovative Fiction*, p. xxiv.

33. Garrett, 'Short Fiction Since 1950', p. 286.
34. Ronald Sukenick, 'What's Your Story?', in Bellamy (ed.), *Superfiction*, pp. 234–55; Brautigan, 'Ernest Hemingway's Typist', in *Revenge of the Lawn*, p. 46; Michaels, 'Storytellers, Liars and Bores', in *I Would Have Saved Them If I Could*, pp. 49–55.
35. Dixon, *The Stories*, pp. 469–72.
36. Brautigan, *Revenge of the Lawn*, p. 37.
37. Garrett, 'Short Fiction Since 1950', p. 298. Barthelme's 'Critique de la vie quotidienne' and 'At the End of the Mechanical Age' both parody and draw upon fashionable academic discourse. *Sixty Stories*, pp. 183–90, 272–9. Michaels argues with Borges in 'Literary Criticism', *I Would Have Saved Them*, p. 126.
38. Barthes, 'An Introduction to the Structural Analysis of Narrative', p. 241; Barthelme, *Forty Stories*, pp. 157–63.
39. The subtitle of Barth's *Lost in the Funhouse* is *Fiction for Print, Tape, Live Voice*.
40. Published in French in Paris in 1958, Beckett's *Stories and Texts for Nothing* appeared in America in 1967.
41. Anthony Kerrigan declared Borges's work to be a 'species of international literary metaphor'. *Ficciones*, p. 9. Translations of Borges's stories by Yates and Irby which had appeared in literary journals throughout the 1950s were collected in 1964 as *Labyrinths*. On the 'strong influence' of Borges on American fiction, see Tanner, *City of Words*, pp. 4–49, and Green, 'Postmodern Precursor'.
42. Barth, *Further Fridays*, p. 92
43. Barth, *The Friday Book*, p. 64.
44. Oates, *The Edge of Impossibility*, p. 7; Barth, *The Friday Book*, p. 64.
45. See Barth's 'mini-memoir', 'Borges and I', in *Further Fridays*, pp. 164–82.
46. Borges, *Labyrinths*, pp. 61–72.
47. Barth, *The Friday Book*, p. 69.
48. Eco, *Reflections on* The Name of the Rose, p. 66.
49. Brautigan, *Revenge of the Lawn*, p. 17.
50. Scholes, *Fabulation and Metafiction*, p. 114.
51. Todorov, *The Poetics of Prose*, p. 143.
52. Wolff, *The Stories*, pp. 35–52; Paley, *Collected Stories*, pp. 84–99; Davis, *Break It Down*, pp. 165–77.
53. Barth, *Lost in the Funhouse*, pp. 69–94.
54. Lodge, *The Art of Fiction*, p. 208. The story is also a footnote to stories of 'First Love' – a title used first by Turgenev and subsequently by Frank O'Connor, Eudora Welty and Vladimir Nabokov among others.
55. Barth, *Lost in the Funhouse*, pp. 164, 186.
56. Kermode, *The Sense of an Ending*, p. 41.
57. Lentricchia, *After the New Criticism*, pp. 53, 56.
58. Prince, 'An Interview with John Barth', p. 62.
59. McPherson, *Elbow Room*, pp. 256–86.
60. Tanner, *Scenes of Nature, Signs of Men*, p. 260.
61. Hemingway, *A Moveable Feast*, p. 70.
62. Gass, *In the Heart of the Heart of the Country*, pp. 172–206.
63. Gass, *Fiction and the Figures of Life*, pp. 282–3.
64. Davenport, *The Geography of the Imagination*, pp. 3–15.
65. Ammon (ed.), *Conversations with William H. Gass*, p. 52.
66. Hansen, 'The Celebration of Solipsism', p. 8; Stevick, *Alternative Pleasures*, p. 55.

67. Gass, *Willie Master's Lonesome Wife*, red section, pp. 12–13.
68. Gass, *Habitations of the Word*, p. 178.
69. Joyce, *Stephen Hero*, p. 216.
70. Yeats, *Collected Poems*, p. 199.
71. Eikhenbaum, 'The Structure of Gogol's "The Overcoat"', p. 380.
72. See, for example, Scholes and Kellogg, *The Nature of Narrative*, pp. 17–56. The trend is discussed in McGurl, *The Program Era*, pp. 230–6.
73. On technological 'secondary orality', see Ong, *Rhetoric, Romance and Technology*, ch. 12.
74. Barthelme's first *New Yorker* story was 'l'Lapse' in 1963.
75. Klinkowitz, *The American 1960s*, p. 58. Saunders's reading of 'The School' is in *The Brain-Dead Megaphone*; pp. 175–86. Antrim read 'I Bought a Little City' on the *New Yorker* podcast, 7 September 2009.
76. Daugherty, *Hiding Man*, p. 74. On Barthelme's career as an editor (of *Forum, Location* and *Fiction*), see *Hiding Man*, chs 18, 23, 26, 39.
77. Connolly, 'Fifty Years of Little Magazines', p. 95; Pleynet, 'An Experimental Reality', pp. 93–4.
78. Barthelme, *Sixty Stories*, pp. 44–52.
79. Lodge, *The Art of Fiction*, p. 187.
80. Lodge, *The Art of Fiction*, p. 188
81. Barthes, *Writing Degree Zero*, p. 16.
82. Ozick, *Collected Stories*, p. 285. The story begins with an account of listening to a 'famous writer' read 'The Magic Crown', a reference to Malamud's 'The Silver Crown'.
83. Gass's 'Order of Insects' also engages with 'Metamorphosis'. *In the Heart of the Heart of the Country*, pp. 163–71.
84. Milazzo (ed.), *Conversations with Joyce Carol Oates*, p. 39.
85. Barthelme, *The Dead Father*, p. 178. 'A Manual for Sons' is included in *Sixty Stories*, pp. 249–71.
86. Barthelme, *Forty Stories*, pp. 119–29. 'Eugénie Grandet' opens with a synopsis of Balzac's novel in the style of a book digest. *Sixty Stories*, pp. 236–44.
87. Wilde, *Middle Grounds*, p. 112.
88. Barthelme, 'After Joyce' (1964), in *Not-Knowing*, pp. 3–10.
89. Bellamy, *The New Fiction*, p. 51. Barthelme's thee novels – *Snow White* (1967), *The Dead Father* (1976) and *The King* (1990) – are in effect short story sequences.
90. Barthelme, *Not-Knowing*, p. 12. On the 'crucial problem posed for imaginative literature … by the widespread acceptance of the "new sciences" of sociology and psychology', see *Not-Knowing*, p. 99.
91. Barthelme, *Not-Knowing*, p. 12.
92. Barthelme, *Sixty Stories*, pp. 127–34.
93. Beckett, *Malloy, Malone Dies, The Unnameable*, p. 414. Barthelme said he was 'just overwhelmed by Beckett'. *Not-Knowing*, p. 226.
94. Barthelme, *Sixty Stories*, p. 161.
95. Barthelme, *Forty Stories*, pp. 186–7. On Barthelme's debt to the *Baltimore Catechism*, see Daugherty, *Hiding Man*, pp. 35–6. He became increasingly interested in dialogue stories. *Great Days* (1979) includes seven.
96. Barthelme, *Flying to America*, p. 272.
97. Barthelme, *Sixty Stories*, pp. 97–107

98. Asked if this last sentence represented an aesthetic statement, Barthelme produced a mock denial. *Not-Knowing*, pp. 205–6.

99. Lukács, *The Theory of the Novel*, p. 124. Beckett described the artist's task as finding a 'form that accommodates the mess'. Driver, 'Beckett by the Madeleine'.

100. On Rauschenberg's adeptness with 'that wonderful category, the messy', see Barthelme, *Not-Knowing*, p. 185

101. Barthelme, *Sixty Stories*, p. 98.

102. Barthelme's illustrated stories are collected in *The Teachings of Don B.*

103. Menand, 'Saved From Drowning', p. 76.

104. Barthelme, *Sixty Stories*, pp. 96, 109.

105. Bellamy, *The New Fiction*, pp. 51–2.

106. Barthelme, *Not-Knowing*, p. 268.

107. Barthelme, *Not-Knowing*, pp. 4–5. See Frank, 'Spatial Form in Modern Literature', in *The Widening Gyre*, pp. 3-62.

108. Barthelme, *Not-Knowing*, p. 4.

109. Barthelme, *Flying to America*, pp. 316–17; *Forty Stories*, p. 118.

110. Barthelme, *Not-Knowing*, p. 263. Woody Allen's humorous *New Yorker* 'casuals' – collected in *Getting Even* and *Without Feathers* – also followed Perelman. Yagoda, *About Town*, pp. 368–9.

111. Barthelme, *The Teachings of Don B.*, p. 57; *Sixty Stories*, pp. 296–7.

112. Barthelme, *Sixty Stories*, pp. 178–82

113. Barthelme, *Sixty Stories*, p. 15; Barthelme, *Not-Knowing*, p. 65; Barthelme, *Flying to America*, p. 318. See Giles, *American Catholic Arts and Fictions*, pp. 375–90.

114. On a possible allusion to Manet's 1862 *Le Ballon*, see Daugherty, *Hiding Man*, pp. 289–91.

115. Barthelme, *Sixty Stories*, pp. 53–8.

116. Sontag, 'Against Interpretation', pp. 98–9; Dougherty, *Hiding Man*, pp. 292, 294–5.

117. Barthelme, *Not-Knowing*, p. 10.

118. For Henry James, a short story can 'choose between being either an anecdote or a picture', although any 'given attempt may place itself near the dividing-line'. *Theory of Fiction*, p. 101.

119. In 1967, Michael Fried attacked the theatrical anthropomorphism of Rauschenberg, Oldenberg and, by implication, Harold Rosenberg. *Art and Objecthood*, pp. 157, 170. Daugherty, *Hiding Man*, p. 327.

120. Molesworth, *Donald Barthelme's Fiction*, pp. 22–3, 70; Barthelme, *Sixty Stories*, p. 85.

121. Wilde, 'Barthelme Unfair to Kierkegaard', in Patteson (ed.), *Critical Essays*, p. 106. On the difficulty of rendering 'messy' in prose, see *Not-Knowing*, p. 285.

122. Barthelme, *Sixty Stories*, p. 130.

123. Barthelme, *Forty Stories*, p. 140.

124. Ballou, *The Building of the House*, p. 444.

125. Aldridge, *Talents and Technicians*, p. 30; Charles Johnson, 'Afterword', in Shapard and Thomas (eds), *Sudden Fiction*, pp. 232–3.

126. Barth, *Further Fridays*, p. 71.

127. Mailer, *The Armies of the Night*, p. 98.

128. Coover, *Pricksongs and Descants*, pp. 165–93.

129. Borges, *Labyrinths*, pp. 51, 53.

130. Coover, *Pricksongs and Descants*, pp. 100–9.

131. Smith, 'Electronic Fictions', p. 8
132. Coover, 'The End of Books', p. 23.
133. Bolter, *Writing Space*, p. 122. In 2004 Coover described Hypertext Hotel as a failure because 'too many visitors vandalized the work of others'. Landow, *Hypertext 3.0*, p. 222. See www.hyperdis.de/hyphotel/1347.html.
134. Coover, 'The End of Books', p. 24.
135. Michaels, 'What's A Story', pp. 202–3; Kafka, *The Great Wall of China and Other Short Works*, p. 81.

CHAPTER 4

'Experiment is Out, Concern is In'[1]

In 1978, the novelist John Gardner published a fiercely polemical book called *On Moral Fiction* which, in arguing for a return to what he called 'life-giving' fiction, decried much of the experimental writing of the 1960s and 1970s as 'trivial' or 'false'.[2] The following year William Gass responded to the charge, and a debate on the nature and value of fiction between the two writers was published in the *New Republic*. 'I have very little to communicate,' said Gass, 'I want to plant some object in the world'. 'I think [fiction] helps you live,' said Gardner, 'I think with each book you write you become a better person.'[3] The argument encapsulated the decade's aesthetic disagreements, and by extension, some claimed, its political and cultural changes. And Gardner himself was a pivotal figure between generations of university-educated short story writers. Briefly Gass's student, he was also Raymond Carver's most important teacher. Carver acknowledged his influence in many places, most notably in 'The Writer as Teacher' which became the foreword to Gardner's 'how to' book, *On Becoming a Novelist* (1983). Whenever he wrote, Carver told one of his own students, he 'felt Gardner looking over his shoulder ... approving or disapproving of certain words, phrases and strategies'.[4] But it was not just a matter of certain words. Echoes of Gardner can also be heard in Carver's published views on the aims and purposes of fiction – in particular, his distrust of 'something that "looks funny" on the page' and his emphasis on a fiction of 'consequence' that combines 'values and craft', 'generosity' and 'seeing things clearly'.[5] This chapter will consider Carver's fiction, and that of some of his contemporaries, in the context of these ideas and as part of the 'renewal and revitalization of the realist mode' which began in the late 1970s, and which some argued was 'probably the most significant development in late twentieth-century American fiction'.[6]

The realist short story that emerged in the 1980s and which, said Carver, did 'nothing less than revitalize the national literature' was not quite the same as the realist short story as written by O'Connor, Welty, Updike or Cheever.[7] How to express the difference preoccupied critics and commentators as they struggled to outdo each other in the coinage of pithy names: 'neo-realism', 'catatonic realism', 'K-Mart realism', 'minimalism' and, most inventively, 'Post-Vietnam, post-literary, post-modernist blue-collar neo-early-Hemingwayism'.[8] This last, not pithy at all, pointed most directly to the style and feel of the new writing, in particular to its emphasis on what Edmund Wilson (speaking of Hemingway) had described as the 'ominous banality of human behaviour in situations of emotional strain'.[9]

Another popular term, 'dirty realism', was invented in 1983 by Bill Buford, the editor of the British literary journal, *Granta*, to frame a special issue of American fiction 'unlike what American fiction is usually understood to be'. Neither 'heroic or grand' nor 'self-consciously experimental', the new writing was, he claimed, as 'unadorned' and 'unfurnished' as the 'cheap hotels' or 'roadside cafés' of its setting.[10] Those included in the issue, among them Carver, Richard Ford, Bobbie Ann Mason, Tobias Wolff and Jayne Anne Phillips, benefited greatly from Buford's marketing of glimpses of the 'belly-side of contemporary life', although Ford later questioned the reality of 'the putative American short story renaissance, when Dirty Realists were riding imaginary Harleys all over Britain, gassing up at every Waterstone's'.[11]

As talk of K-Mart, dirt or belly-sides suggests, much of the discussion of the new fiction was couched in terms of the access it provided into 'low-rent' lives.[12] Many people seemed to find it 'news' that 'literature' could describe 'real life, wherever and however it was lived, even if it was lived with a bottle of Heinz ketchup on the table and the television set droning.'[13] When a reviewer noted of Mason's collection, *Shiloh and Other Stories* (1982), that 'the details of her characters' lives [in Western Kentucky] must seem as remote as Timbuktu to the readers of the *New Yorker* or the *Atlantic*' we might almost be back in the heyday of anthropological local colour.[14] But the yuppie taste for 'hick chic' (as another reviewer put it) was something that writers such as Mason and Carver seemed, in some degree, to accept and exploit.[15] Mason suffered nineteen rejections from the *New Yorker* before taking on board its fiction editor's suggestion that she offer readers some 'conclusions' about 'these people' beyond whatever it is that 'they themselves feel'.[16] The magazine finally accepted 'Offerings' in 1979 and, the following year, 'Shiloh', which was to become 'one of the most anthologized stories of the 1980s' and which ends with the narrator pointing out the protagonist's realisation that the 'inner workings' of history have 'escaped him'.[17] Carver's first *New Yorker* story (in 1981) was 'Chef's House', about a recovering alcoholic's summer sanctuary and 'the end of it'.[18] Carver later described his stories as 'bringing the news from one world to another', expressing a hope that they would 'allow certain areas of life to be understood a little better than they were understood before'.[19]

But to think of Carver in this way, simply as 'bringing the news', can, and did, result in a neglect of the artful ways in which he shaped that news. Consider, for example, the fact that his characters are often unable to 'talk and say what they really mean'.[20] 'I just want to say one more thing', declares a man whose wife has just asked him to leave in 'One More Thing'. The story ends: 'But then he could not think what it could possibly be'.[21] A man visits his ex-wife in 'A Serious Talk' and sits silently at the kitchen table drinking vodka. 'There were things he wanted to say, grieving things, consoling things, things like that', but instead he washes the carving knife and cuts the telephone cord while she is on the phone.[22] One critic described Carver's subject as 'the poetry of inarticulateness', but too often the poetry part of the formulation gets forgotten and it is assumed that the difficulty his characters have in communicating was actually his own.[23] Carver's remark that he stuck to the short story because 'to write a novel, it seemed to me, a writer should be living in a world that makes sense' is often cited as evidence that he himself was 'all out of words'.[24] While minimalism in the work of Brautigan or Barth or Barthelme was read as an intellectual comment on the exhaustion of literary genre, Carver's minimalism (and that of Mason and the others) was taken to be a kind of objective correlative of their 'dirty realist' subject matter.[25]

'Consoling Things, Things Like That': Raymond Carver

I have not included much biographical detail in my discussions of most of the writers in this book. Carver will be a partial and unavoidable exception, because the romance of his short life has become absorbed into readings of his work. The danger, however, is that so much energy is expended on speculation about Carver's life that little is left for a proper examination of his work. So I'll be brief.

Born into a working-class family in Washington State, Carver's education in the art of the short story famously began when, just a teenager, he enrolled in a correspondence course. By the time he was twenty (and married with children), he had become Gardner's student at Chico State College and his further education took him to the universities of Humboldt State, Iowa and Stanford. Richard Ford later recalled that he and Carver were 'typical' of postwar Americans 'seeking improvement through some form of pedagogy'; both were 'products of the environment that included college, writing workshops, sending stories to quarterlies, attending graduate school, having teachers who were writers'.[26] Carver's first major success – and, he said, 'a real turning point in my life' – came when 'Will You Please Be Quiet, Please?' was included in the *Best American Short Stories 1967*.[27] But the story – which borrowed more than its title from Hemingway's 'Hills Like White Elephants' – was out of tune with the mood of the 'High Sixties' discussed in the previous chapter, and it would be another nine years before his first collection of stories was published. During this time – and for the rest of his life – Carver was also writing and publishing poetry (indeed, he always thought of himself first and foremost as a poet).[28]

As is well-known, Carver's entry into the big time relied a great deal on the advocacy and blue pencil of his editor, Gordon Lish, first at *Esquire* magazine, and then at McGraw-Hill – which brought out *Will You Please Be Quiet, Please?* (1976) – and later at Knopf, the publisher of *What We Talk About When We Talk About Love* (1981), the book that made Carver's name and which quickly came to be seen as the seminal work of the new minimalism.

The author of several works of fiction himself, Lish is best known for his promotion of other writers, many of whom emerged through his fiction workshops. Other notable Lish–Knopf collections from this time include Barry Hannah's *Airships* (1978) and Mary Robison's *Days* (1979). (Robison, who studied at Johns Hopkins with Barth and Frederick Barthelme, is notable as the first 'regular fiction contributor' to the *New Yorker* to have a writing-school background.[29]) Amy Hempel – who studied with Lish at Columbia – praised him as 'the Lee Strasberg of American fiction', while for Joe David Bellamy, he became the 'cultural commissar' of anti-experimental 'literary republicanism'.[30] Whatever one thought of him, the self-styled 'Captain Fiction' was, for a time, at 'the epicenter of American literary publishing'.[31]

Although Lish had been editing Carver's stories since 'Neighbors' was first accepted for *Esquire* in 1971, controversy is largely confined to the work he did ten years later on *What We Talk About*. What had hitherto been a relatively light touch here became very heavy indeed. The effect was to give the collection a distinctive, unified voice which many found compelling. Tidy summations, such as David Newlove's 'Hopelessville … in prose as sparingly clear as a fifth of iced Smirnoff', turned Carver into a definable, and, hence, easily marketable, commodity.[32] (*Will You Please Be Quiet, Please?* and subsequent collections are more varied in tone.) In 2008, the unedited and much longer versions of the seventeen stories that appeared in *What We Talk About* were published under their original title, *Beginners*. There is no room here for a comparison of all the differences, so I'll restrict myself to a few general points, before concentrating on Carver's work as it was published in his lifetime.

Lish once said that Carver's 'value' lay in his 'sense of a particular bleakness'.[33] Most of his editing seems to have been an attempt to heighten this sense, by cutting introspection, description, explanation and anything he felt tended towards the sentimental or epiphanic. But he added as well as subtracted: paragraph breaks between lines of dialogue, a limited, repetitive vocabulary filled with indefinite signifiers ('thing', 'something') and memorably enigmatic titles which often picked up a phrase or image from the story, sometimes giving it a kind of ironic or symbolic resonance. He was also attracted to the cinematic quality afforded by the present tense – something that Ann Beattie's *New Yorker* stories had recently made popular and which became a signature of minimalism. 'Gazebo' memorably opens:

> That morning she pours Teacher's over my belly and licks it off. That afternoon she tries to jump out the window. I go, 'Holly, this can't continue. This has got to stop.'[34]

Carver's original was also in the first-person (the words Lish cut are italicised):

> That morning she pours Teacher's *scotch* over my belly and licks it off. In the afternoon she tries to jump out the window. *I can't stand this anymore, and I tell her so.* I go, 'Holly, this can't continue. *This is crazy.* This has got to stop.'[35]

Here Lish's editing seems to be driven by a desire not only to remove extraneous information, but also to speed up the pace of the sentences and pull the reader into the drama. A former student described him as practicing the 'cult of the sentence'.[36]

One of Lish's mottoes was 'Don't have stories, have sentences', and what sometimes became a kind of sentence-fetish marks out writers from his 'stable'. Amy Hempel's *Collected Stories* have recently been praised for 'trying to use sentences to save lives'.[37] Here are a couple of her openers with, to begin, a story that is sentence-long:

> Just once in my life – oh, when I have ever wanted anything just once in my life?
> ('Memoir')

> The year I began to say *vha** instead of *vase*, a man I barely knew nearly accidentally killed me. ('The Harvest')

> 'Tell me things I won't mind forgetting,' she said. 'Make it useless stuff or forget it.' ('In the Cemetery Where Al Jolson is Buried')[38]

'In the Cemetery', Hempel's first story for Lish's class, has since become one of the most frequently anthologised examples of the kind of minimalism that sees the creation of dazzling sentences not as a formalist good-in-itself, but as a type of moral behaviour, a way to provide 'consolation in small places, small packets'.[39] Lish, like Gardner, emphasised the 'huge utility of literature' as a 'human enterprise'.[40]

Carver never spoke openly about the extent of Lish's involvement, about which he clearly had mixed feelings.[41] Recent accounts, promoting *Beginners*, emphasise his unhappiness with the severely edited stories, but it should be remembered that Carver chose to include eight of them in *Where I'm Calling From*, the 'selected stories' that he prepared shortly before his death, and that he retained Lish as his editor for *Cathedral*. That said, he told interviewers that he felt he had 'gone as far' as he wanted in 'cutting everything down to the marrow, not just to the bone' and, with the help of a more powerful agent, ensured that Lish would henceforth be more restrained.[42] The stories in *Cathedral*, one of the books that established the Vintage Contemporaries series, like those in *Elephant* (1988), represented the development of what Carver (adopting one of Gardner's highest terms of approval) called a more 'generous' style.[43] Until recently, this account of a stylistic 'opening up' tended to be read in relation to the legend of Carver's 'two lives', as Bad Raymond and then Good Raymond. The first was marked by alcohol, financial struggle and marital turmoil; the second, alcohol-free, was 'redeemed by love and growing fame'.[44] What the discovery of the consequences of Lish's editing reveals is that Carver's style – for better or worse – was generous all along.

It is also worth recalling that a 'belief in revision' (and 'paring down') had been instilled in Carver from the start of his writing career with the force of a moral imperative. It was Gardner's 'basic tenet', he recalled, that 'a writer found what he wanted to say in the ongoing process of *seeing* what he'd said. And this seeing, or seeing more clearly, came about through revision.'[45] Carver never really lost the habit of revising, and his late poems and stories continually revisit earlier situations and 'obsessions'. 'The Kitchen', for example, recalls 'Nobody Said Anything'; 'Miracle' takes the couple from 'Intimacy' back to their origins; 'Elephant' dramatises 'The Mail'. As a teacher, too, Carver emphasised (quoting Chekhov) that 'what makes art' is a willingness to 'work on your sentences'.[46] Just as Gardner made his students spend a semester going over a single story – Carver reworked 'Furious Seasons' – Carver insisted that his students revise and then revise again.[47] Jay McInerney, whom he taught at Syracuse, recalled taking a story back to Carver seven times; 'he must have spent 14 or 20 hours on it'. 'Once we spent some 10 or 15 minutes debating my use of the word "earth". Carver felt it had to be "ground", and he felt it was worth the trouble of talking it through.'[48]

Seeing more clearly not only improved the story, however, it improved the writer. 'I believe that we revise our lives in our work', Gardner said, 'and with each revision we find a mistake we don't have to make again.'[49] This is an idea that motivates the many storytellers that populate Carver's work (as many as are to be found in the work of the so-called metafictionalists). Carver's narrators often feel as if they haven't said exactly what they wanted to, and therefore try telling the tale again, to find the mistake they don't have to make again. In 'Fat', a waitress tells her friend about an obese customer. Why was he important? She's not sure. His fatness is 'part of it' but 'not the whole story'.[50] In 'Why Don't You Dance?', a girl keeps retelling the story of a bizarre yard sale; 'there was more to it, and she was trying to get it talked out. After a time she quit trying.'[51] This failure to tell the whole story recalls the Romantic doctrine that literature's function is to strive, often knowingly in vain, to capture experience or understanding (Carver's 'it'). Recall Poe's admonition (in 'The Man of the Crowd') that 'some secrets … do not permit themselves to be told', or Kafka's cage forever in pursuit of a bird.[52]

Again and again Carver's work focuses on the relationship between the cage and the bird, between the shaping imagination and what he liked to call 'material' or 'the stuff that makes fiction'.[53] In 'Put Yourself in My

Shoes', Myers has quit his job in order to write full time. As the story begins, he is not writing, however, but 'running the vacuum cleaner'.[54] 'He had worked his way through the apartment and was doing the living room, using the nozzle attachment to get at the cat hairs between the cushions.' Carver shows a man at home doing woman's work of the most finicky kind. When Myers meets his wife later, the reversal of traditional husband and wife roles is emphasised.

> Paula sipped her drink. 'How was your day today?'
> Myers shrugged.
> 'What'd you do?' she said.
> 'Nothing,' he said. 'I vacuumed.'

But the vacuuming is also a metaphor for the process by which a writer gathers material. Driving to town to meet his wife, Myers looks around continually for something to write about:

> He looked at the people who hurried along the sidewalks with shopping bags. He glanced at the grey sky, filled with flakes, and at the tall buildings with snow in the crevices and on the window ledges. He tried to see everything, save it for later.

Myers and his wife then go to visit the Morgans, from whom they had sublet an apartment the previous year. On hearing that Myers is a writer, the couple start to tell anecdotes that they hope he will use. But they are the worst kind of storytellers, reliant on false suspense and clichéd summation: 'fate left her to die on the couch in our living room in Germany'. On the way home, Paula is eager to discuss the disastrous evening. But Myers remains detached as snow 'rushed at the windshield'. In the final line of the story, Myers and his creator merge: 'He was at the very end of a story.'

'The problem of storytelling', said Leonard Michaels, 'is how to make transitions into transformations.'[55] What has been transformed here is the way a writer might go about his business. Myers begins with a commitment to the hard work of the picturesque – the fastidious, slightly manic, gathering of small details (like cat hairs) – and ends with a conversion to a passive receptivity to the sublime. As soon as he stops striving after a story, it rushes at him like the snow. Carver may have been thinking of Joyce's 'The Dead' here – he certainly alludes to its final line in 'If It Please You' – or 'the first snow in a blizzard, which comes from nowhere', which another writer thinks about in Hemingway's 'The

Snows of Kilimanjaro'.[56] But Carver's protagonists needn't go to Africa to be scared by formlessness; what Frost called a 'blanker whiteness' is there at home.[57] In 'The Student's Wife', Nan, unable to sleep, looks out of the window at a 'terrible sunrise'. The sky grows 'whiter' and everything outside becomes 'very visible'. She turns her gaze to the room where her husband lies sleeping, jaws 'clenched' and with a 'desperate' look about him. 'As she looked, the room grew very light and the pale sheets whitened grossly before her eyes.'[58] She sinks to her knees and prays for help.

Such moments – not what we think of as 'Carveresque' – are in fact not that unusual in the stories (especially the unedited versions). Also common, though, are stories which rely instead on the more modest metaphor of writing as a version of tidying up; on transitions which are not transformations. 'Collectors' begins, like many of Carver's stories, with the intrusion of a stranger. One minute the narrator sees 'nothing' on the street, the next, an 'old guy, fat and bulky', is there at the door with 'something'. That 'something' – a special vacuum cleaner – is not for him but for Mrs Slater and he won't say whether he is Mr Slater. The salesman cuts a rather surreal figure, as he swaps his galoshes for carpet slippers, worries if he's getting a fever and drops references to Auden and Rilke in a 'churchly voice'. But mainly he goes 'about his business' – 'sweeping, sweeping' to 'collect' 'material' and 'stuff'. Much of that stuff is human. 'Every day, every night of our lives', he observes, 'we're leaving little bits of ourselves, flakes of this and that, left behind.' The 'out of work' narrator sits and watches 'him work', but that watching, too, becomes a kind of labour, a methodical collecting of human bits and pieces, such as the 'ring around his scalp where his hat had been' or the fat that 'hung over his belt'. The story ends simply, without any attempt to introduce another kind of literary work. Both men have completed their task.[59] In the words of another story, 'it's all work, one way or the other'.[60]

Carver returns to the subject of material and what to do with it in two late stories, 'Intimacy' and 'Menudo'. Many have read 'Intimacy' as a plea for forgiveness to his ex-wife for having allowed their lives to be used so freely in his stories. But, in an ironic twist, that very apology provides the impetus for yet another story. 'You know why you're here,' the 'former wife' says, 'You're on a fishing expedition. You're hunting for *material*'. The story is written in the present tense and its governing phrase – the opening of almost every paragraph – is 'she says'. The woman's voice dominates and her ex-husband is, he says, 'all ears'; and

yet the effect is not flattering to either. She comes across as linguisti-
cally incontinent – a bit like the nurse in Hemingway's 'A Very Short
Story' – and his lack of response, as she points out, makes him seem a
'coldhearted son of a bitch'. But the story does not end there. As in 'Put
Yourself in My Shoes', the narrator faces a choice between two ways of
dealing with material. First, here, is transcendence. His ex-wife opens
the front door and lets in 'light and fresh air' and the sounds of the street
– 'all of which we had ignored' – and then he looks up to see 'this white
moon hanging in the morning sky'. Carver is surely not wholly ironic
in allowing his narrator find the sight 'remarkable'.[61] The moon, for all
that we might see it as 'conventional' or a 'cliché', still has the power to
bring him to the brink of tears and reduce him to silence.[62] 'I'm afraid to
comment on it ... I might not understand a word I'd say.' So, instead, he
says goodbye and walks down the street through pile upon pile of leaves.
Kerry McSweeney maintains that this is simply another cliché, evoked
by Carver to suggest that the narrator is finally 'out of material and no
longer able to write a good story'.[63] But is he really out of material?
What about that phrase 'all of which we had ignored'?[64] Surely the
narrator's assertion that 'somebody ought to get a rake and take care of
this' suggests, more optimistically, that a man with the proper tools will
find material – that is, disorder – 'everywhere'. 'Make use of the things
around you,' admonishes Carver's poem 'Sunday Night'.[65]

Raking, or writing, in other words is inevitable or, suggests 'Menudo',
compulsive. 'Reviewing the mess of his life – his first marriage to Molly,
his unkindness to his now-dead mother, the ultimatum issued by his
across-the-road mistress Amanda – Hughes is 'keyed up'. He remembers
once believing that marriage represented some kind of 'destiny', but now
he views love as simply an ongoing process of 'compulsion and error'.
He wishes he could 'sleep and wake up and find everything ... different',
but instead he fidgets in his chair, fighting off an irresistible 'urge' to rake
the leaves in front of Amanda's window.[66] Eventually, feeling as if he
doesn't 'have a choice in the matter any more', he goes out and rakes his
yard: 'every inch of it', and 'done right'. 'It must feel to the grass like it
does when someone gives your hair a hard jerk,' he notes, along with the
fact that he's 'happy, raking' and packing the leaves into bags with 'tied
off tops'.[67] He moves on to the next door neighbours' yard and the story
ends as he prepares to cross the street.

Carver's characters are often presented, poised and ready for the
'next thing'. Stories begin and end as they hover on kerbs, porches and

landings, looking out of windows or across the streets; doors are left half open, half shut. And yet the abiding feeling is that if that 'thing' does happen, 'nothing will ever really be any different'.[68] 'We have made our lives', says the narrator of 'So Much Water So Close to Home', 'our lives have been set in motion, and they will go one and on until they stop.' [69] Hughes's raking – a compulsive and futile going on and on – is one of several compulsive and futile goings on and on in Carver's work; others include the compulsion to move (although 'there is never a place to go'), and an insatiable 'appetite' to eat and drink (even if you're not 'really hungry').[70] Wherever his characters happen to be they all come from 'someplace else' and they mostly talk about the next place they're thinking of, 'to try their luck'.[71] In 'Boxes', for example, the narrator's mother is always in the 'process of packing or unpacking':

> She talked bitterly about the place she was leaving and optimistically about the place she was going to … Sometimes she'd move out of an apartment house, move to another one a few blocks away, and then a month later, move back to the one she'd left, only to a different floor or different side of the building.[72]

The next place is always the one that will break the pattern of the life set in motion, just as the next snack is always the one that will satisfy its hunger:

> I put bread and lunchmeat on the table and I opened a can of soup. I got out crackers and peanut butter, cold meat loaf, pickles, olives, potato chips. I put everything on the table. Then I thought of the apple pie.[73]

This passage is from 'The Idea', in which a couple get 'hungry' from watching their neighbour watching his wife undress in front of him. Food and sex and the possibility of another life are also connected in 'What's in Alaska?' Mary and Carl go to the market to buy 'cream soda and potato chips and corn chips and onion-flavored snack crackers', before adding a 'handful of U-No bars to the order'. They will spend the evening at the house of another couple, Jack and Helen, eating their snacks, smoking pot and discussing Mary's job offer in Alaska. The conversation revolves around the question of what's in Alaska – another snowy blank – and through various slips Carl comes to see that, while for him 'there's nothing', for Mary, it offers the possibility of life and sex with Jack. Bathea notes the insistent phallic imagery of the water pipe,

Popsicles and spilled Cream Soda, but more than this, the story expresses a kind of emptiness that no amount of sex or beer or Alaska could fill: an emptiness made for a writer to vacuum up.[74]

Carver once described himself as drawn to 'traditional (some would call it old-fashioned) methods of storytelling', and one of the most traditional aspects of his stories is their reliance on encounters with strangers and doubles.[75] Often these encounters are voyeuristic: characters observe and then measure themselves against, or take sustenance from, other people who are either more 'normal' than themselves or much stranger. In the first category are the Millers longing for the 'fuller and brighter lives' of their next door neighbours in 'Neighbors' and Hughes admiring the 'decent ordinary guy' next door in 'Menudo'.[76] In the second, are the 'fattest person … ever seen' in 'Fat', the 'man without hands' in 'Viewfinder' or the blind man in 'Cathedral': mundane versions of Flannery O'Connor's grotesques.[77] The point about these people is what the protagonists seek from them. Whatever the situation, as the waitress in 'Fat' observes, Carver's protagonists are 'after something'.[78]

And 'something' – some kind of consolation – is what Carver inevitably gives them. That's what generosity means for the short story tradition into which he so consciously wrote himself – the tradition of Hemingway, O'Connor and Cheever.[79] The solace that O'Connor offers is absolute and enduring: the 'as if' leading to the certainty of God's love. For the others, consolation is more tenuous. For Cheever, the 'as if' of lyricism and 'calculated self-deception' could, momentarily, cheer things up. For Hemingway, consolation required strict adherence to codes and rituals of behaviour (on the part of the characters) and strict adherence to codes of writing (on the part of the author).

In Carver's work, no one kind of consolation prevails. There is release in hurling a rock ('Viewfinder') as well as in the 'human noise' of hearts beating ('What We Talk About').[80] At times, the best one can hope for is a momentary freeze-frame before the worst happens ('The Bath'); at others, we get close to Christian communion ('A Small Good Thing'). And yet even when employing the traditional trope of an insight that comes from blindness – the narrator's encounter with a blind man in 'Cathedral' – Carver tries hard to keep transcendence modest. Like many of his stories, 'Cathedral' tells a story of indefinite pronouns. The visit is 'not something' the narrator looks forward to, and yet, he finds the experience of having the blind man's fingers on his own while drawing the cathedral to be 'like nothing else in my life until now'.

My eyes were still closed. I was in my house. I knew that. But I didn't
feel I was inside anything.
    'It's really something,' I said.[81]

Minimalism, as Mars-Jones notes, 'always seems to play hide and seek
with sentimentality', and, we might add, with notions of transcendence.[82]
While the narrator feels a sense of liberation – he is no longer trapped
'inside' – all that has happened is that 'nothing' has been replaced by
'something'.[83] That's enough, however, for Gardner to choose the story
to 'lead-off' the *Best American Short Stories 1982*.

    In 'Cathedral', 'serious eating' ('as there was no tomorrow') gives
way to the serious work of empathetic art ('me and him are working
on it ... cooking with gas now'). It is the work that produces and earns
the epiphany, just as in 'A Small Good Thing', what's consoling is not
simply the shared hot bread, but the fact that it is the product of the
baker's 'sixteen hours a day' labour.[84] The Mexican tripe stew *menudo* –
with its promise to sooth the nerves – also requires considerable effort,
it's a dish of many stages and many ingredients, and Hughes watches
his friend 'very seriously' prepare it (just as the narrator of 'Collectors'
observed the vacuum cleaner man at work). Here, though, solace is not
his. Hughes sleeps through the meal and wakes to find the pot in the sink.
'I'll probably die without ever tasting *menudo*,' he thinks, before allowing
himself the small consolation of uncertainty: 'But who can say?'[85]

    Throughout his work Carver negotiated a path between two ideas
of what literature was for: one that relied on epiphany (the arrival of
something like snow on the windshield), and one that involved a particular kind of work comparable with vacuuming, cooking, raking and
bagging up, vacuuming, haircutting (in 'The Calm'), or picking up stray
champagne corks (as Chekhov's waiter does at the end of 'Errand').
These jobs (unlike epiphanies) are never completed once and for all.
Rather, they express the Sisyphean nature of the attempt to create order
in the face of the constant production of disorder – leaves keep falling,
dust keeps gathering, hair keeps growing, stuff keeps happening.

Notes

1. Spencer, 'Experiment is Out, Concern is In'.
2. Gardner, *On Moral Fiction*, pp. 15–16.
3. Ammon (ed.), *Conversations with William H. Gass*, pp. 47, 48, 52. For Barth's
   response, see *Further Fridays*, pp. 136–43.

4. Jay McInerney, 'Raymond Carver, Mentor', in Stull and Carroll (eds), *Remembering Ray*, p. 124
5. Carver, *The Best American Short Stories 1986*, p. xiv; Carver and Jenks, *American Short Story Masterpieces*, p. xiv; Carver, Foreword to Gardner, *On Becoming a Novelist*, p. xvii; Gardner, *On Becoming a Novelist*, pp. 47–50; Gardner, *The Art of Fiction*, pp. 8–9; Chavkin (ed.), *Conversations with John Gardner*, pp. 13, 262.
6. Stone, *The Best American Short Stories 1992*, p. xviii.
7. Carver, *No Heroics, Please*, p. 153.
8. Newman, *The Post-Modern Aura*, p. 93; Wilde, *Middle Grounds*, p. 119; Barth, *Further Fridays*, p. 65; Herzinger, 'Introduction: On the New Fiction', p. 8.
9. Wilson, *Axel's Castle*, p. 252.
10. Buford, 'Editorial', pp. 4–5. See also 'More Dirt', *Granta* (Summer 1986).
11. Richard Ford, 'Introduction', to Bausch, *Aren't You Happy for Me?*, p. x.
12. The phrase 'low-rent tragedies', ubiquitous in Carver reviews, comes from 'One More Thing'. *Collected Stories*, p. 323.
13. McInerney, 'Raymond Carver, Mentor', p. 120.
14. Levy, *The Culture and Commerce*, p. 111.
15. Yardley, 'Chic to Chic'. See also, Rebein, *Hicks, Tribes, and Dirty Realists*, ch. 4
16. Yagoda, *About Town*, p. 388.
17. Levy, *The Culture and Commerce*, p. 117; Mason, *Shiloh and Other Stories*, p. 24.
18. Carver, *Collected Stories*, p. 382.
19. Gentry and Stull (eds), *Conversations with Raymond Carver*, p. 52.
20. Gentry and Stull (eds), *Conversations with Raymond Carver*, p. 200.
21. Carver, *Collected Stories*, p. 326.
22. Carver, *Collected Stories*, pp. 295–6.
23. Mars-Jones, 'Words for the Walking Wounded', p. 76.
24. Carver, *Collected Stories*, pp. 741, 237.
25. Mullen, 'A Subtle Spectacle', p. 99.
26. Ford, 'Good Raymond', p. 70.
27. Gentry and Stull (eds), *Conversations with Raymond Carver*, p. 59.
28. Gentry and Stull (eds), *Conversations with Raymond Carver*, p. 197.
29. Yagoda, *About Town*, p. 388.
30. Hempel, 'Captain Fiction', p. 91; Bellamy, *Literary Luxuries*, p. 82.
31. Birkerts, *American Energies*, p. 156.
32. Newlove, 'Fiction Briefs'.
33. Gentry and Stull (eds), *Conversations with Raymond Carver*, p. 87.
34. Carver, *Collected Stories*, p. 234.
35. Carver, *Collected Stories*, p. 772.
36. Bowman, 'Lashed by Lish'.
37. Rick Moody, 'On Amy Hempel', in Hempel, *Collected Stories*, p. xii.
38. Hempel, *Collected Stories*, pp. 373, 103, 29.
39. Murphy, 'Sentence by Sentence'. See also, Hallett, *Minimalism and The Short Story*.
40. Lish, *All Our Secrets Are The Same*, p. ix.
41. For Carver on Lish, see *Collected Stories*, pp. 744–5. On their final break, see Sklenicka, *Raymond Carver*, pp. 410–13.
42. Gentry and Stull (eds), *Conversations with Raymond Carver*, p. 44; Sklenicka, *Raymond Carver*, p. 381.
43. Gentry and Stull (eds), *Conversations with Raymond Carver*. p. 199. On Vintage

Contemporaries, see Sklenicka, *Raymond Carver*, pp. 417, 423; Girard, '"Standing at the Corner"'.

44. Back cover, Stull and Carroll (eds), *Remembering Ray*.
45. Carver, Foreword to Gardner, *On Becoming a Novelist*, p. xiv.
46. Carver, *No Heroics, Please*, p. 146.
47. Carver, Maryann Burk, *What It Used to Be Like*, p. 236.
48. McInerney, 'Raymond Carver, Mentor', p. 124. On Carver's similar debate with Gardner, see *Collected Stories*, p. 744.
49. Chavkin (ed.), *Conversations with John Gardner*, p. 179.
50. Carver, *Collected Stories*, pp. 5–6.
51. Carver, *Collected Stories*, p. 227.
52. Poe, *Poetry and Tales*, p. 388.
53. Carver, *Collected Stories*, pp. 737–8.
54. Carver, *Collected Stories*, pp. 101–15.
55. Michaels, 'What's a Story', p. 201.
56. Joyce, *Dubliners*, p. 176; Carver, *Collected Stories*, p. 863; Hemingway, *The Complete Short Stories*, p. 56.
57. Frost, *The Poetry of Robert Frost*, p. 296.
58. Carver, *Collected Stories*, pp. 99–100.
59. Carver, *Collected Stories*, pp. 78–84.
60. Carver, *Collected Stories*, p. 92
61. Carver, *Collected Stories*, pp. 561–8.
62. McSweeney, *The Realist Short Story*, p. 104.
63. McSweeney, *The Realist Short Story*, p. 104.
64. 'Intimacy' reads like a response to 'I Could See the Smallest Things', which ends with the narrator thinking 'for a minute of the world outside my house', but unable to do more. Carver, *Collected Stories*, p. 243.
65. Carver, *A New Path to the Waterfall*, p. 87.
66. The story's trope of guilty raking recalls Cheever's 'The Heartbreaker of Shady Hill'. 'Late in the afternoon', the narrator notes, 'I raked leaves. What could be more contrite than cleaning the lawn of the autumn's dark rubbish under the streaked, pale skies of spring?' Cheever, *The Stories*, p. 264.
67. Carver, *Collected Stories*, pp. 569–82.
68. Carver, *Collected Stories*, p. 871.
69. Carver, *Collected Stories*, p. 872.
70. Carver, *Collected Stories*, pp. 56, 273.
71. Carver, *Collected Stories*, p. 512.
72. Carver, *Collected Stories*, p. 537.
73. Carver, *Collected Stories*, p. 16.
74. Carver, *Collected Stories*, pp. 60–71. Bethea, *Technique and Sensibility*, ch. 2
75. Carver, *The Best American Short Stories 1986*, p. xiv.
76. Carver, *Collected Stories*, pp. 8, 582.
77. Carver, *Collected Stories*, pp. 3, 228.
78. Carver, *Collected Stories*, p. 5.
79. Carver's work frequently, in his phrase, 'pays homage' to his mentors. 'The Aficionados' and 'Pastoral' (later revised as 'The Cabin') are most Hemingwayesque; 'Feathers' borrows O'Connor's key image, the peacock. 'The Train' is a sequel to Cheever's 'The Five Forty-Eight'; 'The Student's Wife' is modelled on Chekhov's

'The Chemist's Wife', while 'Errand' is about Chekhov. Discussions include Barbara C. Lonnquist, 'Narrative Displacement', in Logsdon and Mayer (eds), *Since Flannery O'Connor*, pp. 142–50; Facknitz, 'Missing the Train'; Boddy, 'Companion-Souls of the Short Story'; Sklenicka, *Raymond Carver*, pp. 77–8.
80. Carver, *Collected Stories*, p. 322. Compare the end of 'The Snows of Kilimanjaro'. Hemingway, *The Complete Short Stories*, p. 56.
81. Carver, *Collected Stories*, pp. 514–29.
82. Mars-Jones, 'Psycho Dramas'.
83. See McSweeney, *The Realist Short Story*, p. 99.
84. Carver, *Collected Stories*, p. 828.
85. Carver, *Collected Stories*, p. 580.

CHAPTER 5

Turning Points and the American Short Story Today

In 2006, Martin Scofield concluded *The Cambridge Introduction to the American Short Story* by defining the 'essential short story effect' as a 'focus on the most intense and life-changing experiences'. The short story, he argued, is 'perhaps the exemplary form for the perception of crisis, crux, turning point; and as such it has proved ideal for recording decisive moments, intimately private but often with broad social resonances'.[1] There is, of course, a long history to the association of the short story with the turning point, or more strongly (as here) to the sense that the formal *essence* of the short story is its staging of turning points. Frank O'Connor, in perhaps the most influential book on the genre, *The Lonely Voice*, puts it like this:

> The short story represents a struggle with Time – the novelist's Time: it is an attempt to reach some point of vantage from which past and future are equally visible. The crisis of the short story is the short story and not as in a novel the mere logical inescapable result of what preceded it. One might go further and say that in the story what precedes the crisis becomes a consequence of the crisis – *this* being what actually happened, *that* must necessarily be what preceded it.[2]

O'Connor's focus here is on the turning point as a narrative function – on the representation of time as turning point, as crisis. The effect of brevity on narrative, he suggests, is to allow a kind of panoramic perspective: 'some point of vantage from which past and future are equally visible'. The short story, being all crisis and nothing but crisis, turns on itself. But it's also worth noting an additional emphasis in O'Connor's book: the alignment of the short story's methods with those of lyric poetry. His description of the form as 'the nearest thing I know to lyric poetry' has been echoed by many other writers.[3] For Elizabeth Bowen, for example, the short story 'is at an advantage over the novel, and can claim its nearer kinship to poetry because it must be more concentrated, can be more visionary, and is not weighed down (as the novel is bound to be) by facts, explanation, or analysis.'[4] On this model, the turning point or crisis is a lyric rather than a narrative device. Both formulations recall those of the original theorist of the genre, Edgar Allan Poe. When Poe argued that the ideal short story should 'avail itself of the immense benefit of *totality*', he was thinking about the creation of lyric as well as narrative effects.[5] I'll come back to the difference between these two kinds of turning point at the end of this chapter.

Given its brevity, its formal constitution in and as crisis, the short story gravitates towards certain kinds of subject matter; in particular, towards the representation of moments of condensed significance, moments in time which allow or enforce a stepping out of routine, out of time. In nineteenth-century stories, unconcerned with strict probability, that step out of time was often considerable: twenty years in the case of Irving's 'Rip Van Winkle' and Hawthorne's 'Wakefield'. Hawthorne's narrator imagines that in retrospect Wakefield would look back on the two decades he had spent apart from his wife and home as 'no more than an interlude in the main business of his life'.[6] In modern naturalistic fiction, interruptions and dislocations are usually briefer and take place in the temporary hiatus of a railway station, a doctor's waiting room, a hotel lobby, a bar in the early hours of the morning – settings that, like the short story itself, suggest both impermanence and enclosure.

Birth and death are, of course, the ultimate 'borderlines' and, as the British writer Ali Smith recently noted, it's not surprising that the short story often alludes to one or the other, given that 'its nature concerns itself with the shortness of things; by its very brevity', she argues, the short story 'challenges aliveness with the certainty of mortality.'[7] Ann Beattie's 'Zalla' closes with an adult daughter sitting on her mother's bed, having just learned 'one of the Dark Secrets she'd never before revealed', and knowing that 'in a blink my mother would be dead'. 'That was the past. I imagined the future.'[8] In a very different tone and yet tending to the same conclusion, 'CivilWarLand in Bad Decline' by George Saunders ends with a man 'possessing perfect knowledge', while being 'hacked to bits': 'I see the man I could have been, and the man I was'.[9]

Thinking about oneself in relation to one's parents or children inevitably opens up time. When the teenage narrator of John Cheever's 'Reunion' meets his father for an hour-and-a-half and for the last time, at Grand Central Station 'between trains', he immediately recognises in him 'my future and my doom' : 'I knew that when I was grown I would be something like him; I have to plan my campaigns within his limitations.'[10] In Elizabeth Bishop's 'The Country Mouse', the protagonist experiences a similar, if more intense and uncertain, temporal confluence on returning to the house where her father had been born: 'it was a day that seemed to include months in it, or even years, a whole unknown past I was made to feel I should have known about, and a strange unpredictable future.'[11]

But more banal circumstances can also shake us up. Sometimes, it's just a matter of coming home a little earlier than usual (Edward P. Jones's 'A New Man') or picking up a hitchhiker (Sherman Alexie's 'The Toughest Indian in the World' or Maile Meloy's 'O Tannenbaum').[12] A break in the electricity supply has proved to be a surprisingly popular challenge to routine. 'What a happy time that was, when all the electricity went away! If only we could recreate that paradise!' says the narrator of Barthelme's 'City Life'.[13] In one of Updike's late stories, the 'Outage' simply provides a convenient excuse for sex with a neighbour, but for the estranged couple in Jhumpa Lahiri's story, the fact that 'for five days their electricity would be cut for one hour, beginning at eight P.M' proves to be more serious.[14] The lack of light, as the story's title points out, might be 'A Temporary Matter', but what is revealed during those dim, liminal hours has consequences both for their future lives and their understanding of the past.

While insights and overviews can come at any time, nevertheless there seems to be a period of life which has found persistent favour with short story writers because during it significance condenses unbearably: because it is *all* turning point. Adolescence is a point of vantage equally on childhood and on adult life, on innocence and on experience. The short story, a form constituted by and as crisis, well suits adolescence, a state of mind and body constituted by and as crisis:

Gazing up into the darkness I saw myself as a creature driven and derided by vanity; and my eyes burned with anguish and anger. (James Joyce, 'Araby', 1914)

Looking back in the big windows, over the bags of peat moss and aluminium lawn furniture stacked on the pavement, I could see Lengel in my place in the slot, checking the sheep through. His face was dark gray and his back stiff, as if he'd just had an injection of iron, and my stomach kind of fell as I felt how hard the world was going to be to me hereafter. (John Updike, 'A & P', 1961)[15]

While stories about such adolescent turning points – moments of seeing oneself in the process of turning – have existed as long as stories have existed, it would not be inaccurate to say that they are more common today than ever and that their number is a direct result of the trends in the teaching of literature and creative writing discussed in this book. Many college anthologists, keen to make accessible the work of 'classic' authors, tend to gravitate towards stories about young people. Thus, Hawthorne is frequently represented by 'Young Goodman Brown', and Hemingway by 'Indian Camp'. It is easy for students, unaware that these authors also wrote about adults, to develop a rather skewed view of American literature. Once again *Understanding Fiction* led the way. Two of the collection's stories – Hemingway's 'The Killers' and Anderson's 'I Want to Know Why' – were described as 'initiation' stories because, said Brooks and Penn Warren, they presented the 'discovery of evil'.[16] From a Christian point of view, evil is the ultimate discovery, the real in its most absolute guise, but the anthropological concept of initiation could also apply to other kinds of adolescent insight.[17] Joyce's 'Araby' was included in the anthology as a 'parable' of a universal problem: the recognition of 'the discrepancy between the real and the ideal'. This universality, said the editors, elevates the story from being 'merely an account of a stage in the process of growing up' (only of 'clinical interest') to a 'symbolic rendering of a central conflict in mature experience'.[18] Coming of age became an acceptable subject, in other words, at the moment at which the recognition of those new 'hard curled hairs around your privates' and a 'shiny face' became the gateway to an understanding of 'forever', of 'the vastness of the world, the strangeness of existence'.[19]

Since 1950, the association of the short story with adolescent initiation has become reinforced by the increasing influence of creative writing courses. This chapter will examine a phenomenon that has had consequences both for our understanding of adolescence and for the cultural status and literary vitality of the short story as a genre.

Writing Programmes Today

Today creative writing programmes are more fundamentally a part of the American writing scene than ever before, as the table overleaf, from the Association of Writers and Writing Programs (AWP), demonstrates.[20]

In 1983, John Barth 'did the numbers' and concluded that every year saw the arrival of '2,500 newly ordained fictionalists'.[21] Today's figure,

Growth of Creative Writing Programmes

Year	AA	BA/BS minor	BFA/BA major	MA	MFA	PhD	Total
2009	11	318	159	144	153	37	822
2004	7	320	86	154	109	39	715
1994	5	287	10	139	64	29	534
1984	0	155	10	99	31	20	315
1975	0	24	3	32	15	5	79

extrapolating simply from the fivefold increase in MFA programmes, seems more like 12,500. But, of course, there is more to writing programmes than producing writers. Within the confines of the university, the writing programme, which teaches 'reading as a writer', continues to see itself as an alternative to what the AWP executive director, David Fenza, describes as the English Department's insistence that 'only specialists who study, anatomize, deconstruct or systematically humiliate their subject should be allowed to teach it'.[22] Since 1950 there has been a mutual reinforcement of professionalisms. But more than this, Fenza claims, since it was founded in 1967, the AWP has helped to establish 'the largest system of literary patronage the world has ever seen'. Universities 'build audiences' but, Fenza estimates, they also spend around 'half a billion dollars annually' on a literary infrastructure of university presses, little magazines, reading series and conferences as well as, of course, salaries for writers.[23] In 1987, Rust Hills, then fiction editor of *Esquire*, argued that 'it is no longer the book publishers and magazines, but rather the colleges and universities that support the entire structure of the American literary establishment, – and moreover, essentially determine the nature and shape of that structure.'[24] Yet, inevitably, a certain defensiveness about the whole process remains. For every charge that writing programmes produce 'underdone', 'Type O' or 'assembly-line fiction' comes a demonstration of that fiction's 'complex and interesting and difficult and diverse' nature, or the claim that the Iowa MFA represents the 'closest American letters has yet advanced toward an American equivalent of Periclean Greece'.[25] 'It is my firm belief', Richard Bausch felt it necessary to declare in 2008, 'that future cultural historians will report that in one of the most heartening developments of the last sixty years of the twentieth century, American colleges and universities helped to establish an atmosphere for the release of literary talent, and for the support of literary art.'[26]

At the beginning of the twenty-first century, the short story has found itself in a rather strange position. On the one hand, as we have seen, universities like short stories. They are very teachable – short enough that a teacher can expect her students to have read to the end and to cover the relevant points in a single class; more immediately accessible than most poetry. As Deborah Eisenberg put it, in her pitch for a class she taught in 2008 at the University of Virginia, restricting the reading to 'short things' makes it possible for students 'to read a wide variety of work and to read with close attention'.[27] In teaching writing, the short story has the advantage of being faster to complete, and easier to discuss in class, than a novel. (At a 2005 *New Yorker* festival event, Chang-rae Lee and Lorrie Moore exchanged stories about their teaching experiences. 'You really don't want your students writing novels,' said Lee; 'Absolutely!' seconded Moore.[28]) Moreover, the short story is widely viewed in 'contradictory and yet complimentary' terms that make it perfect as a 'practice field'. As Andrew Levy has argued, short fiction has the advantage of being both formally easier than the novel – so that 'beginning authors, or authors whose ability to compose a sophisticated narrative was otherwise impaired' might be able to have a go – and formally more difficult, requiring 'greater discipline and skill'.[29]

Levy, like Fenza, argues that the workshop system (consisting of graduate programmes, conferences and small literary magazines) has developed as a kind of 'alternate economy, enclosed and complete'.[30] But if the economy was entirely enclosed, how could the workshop 'support the entire structure of the American literary establishment'? For many students, part of the point of attending a workshop is to make contacts and generate product – in college quarterlies and anthologies – to show to prospective commercial publishers.

Anthologies of writing school fiction are nothing new. In 1966, for example, Wallace Stegner and Richard Scowcroft published *Twenty Years of Stanford Short Stories* as evidence of the programme's success and to give readers a look at the early work of their favourite writers. The *Best of the Fiction Workshops*, which was launched in 1997 and which changed its name to the snappier *Best New American Voices* in 2000, has a different aim: to showcase 'tomorrow's literary stars'. 'Why organise a short story anthology around the workshop?' asks the preface to the 2007 edition: 'For the simple reason that the workshop has come to exert enormous influence on literary life and culture in North America.'[31] The anthology, which accepts submissions only from workshop directors and teachers, does not merely reflect that influence; it is itself the means to exert it. Agents and publishers are provided with an easy way of distinguishing among the 12,500-strong graduating class, while the following year's class can study and emulate work that has made the grade.

While 'a degree certainly doesn't guarantee publication', noted Alice Hoffman, 'one can be assured that a manuscript from a graduate of a writing program is taken more seriously that one that appears from out of the blue.'[32] A manuscript from a prize-winning graduate is, of course, taken even more seriously. When *Granta* published its second selection of the 'Best of Young American Novelists' in 2007, much was made of the multicultural background of the twenty-one authors included: a third were born or grew up outside America, in countries ranging from Peru to China. But as well as showcasing multiculturalism, the collection revealed the efficiency of assimilation – literary assimilation at least. The 'tremendous variety' of the authors' backgrounds, acknowledges the editor, Ian Jack, 'becomes less various when examined through the prism of class'.[33] When I interviewed Junot Díaz in 1996, just a year after he received his MFA from Cornell, he said that he thought writing programmes were 'problematic' because 'the people who go tend to be upper class so you're benefiting people who can stay at home and write anyway.'

> [Writing programmes] duplicate class structures in the United States. Rare is the person like me who's flat broke and ends up in a programme … The best schools in the country only want Ivy League students or top students. Ivy League students and top students tend to be rich.[34]

Two-thirds of the *Granta* 'Best' bunch attended Ivy League colleges. Most also graduated from prestigious writing schools; four from Iowa. What further unites them is their accumulation of prizes (more than forty-five awards and nominations between the twenty-one).

For those who don't make it into *Granta* (circulation 50,000) there are few other mainstream options. General magazines that used to be famous for their fiction, such as *Esquire*, *Harper's*, *Atlantic Monthly* and *Playboy*, now don't much bother. All that remains is 'the holy grail of the young fiction writer', the weekly *New Yorker*, with a circulation of just over a million (96 per cent by subscription).[35] Speaking of the effect on his career of the magazine's publication in 1995 of his story 'How To Date A Browngirl, Blackgirl, Whitegirl, or Halfie', Díaz said 'that did it all … Because you know people kill themselves to be in the *New Yorker*'.[36] If that doesn't work, they try fiction magazines such as *Zoetrope: All Story* (circulation 20,000), *Glimmer Train* (16,000) or *McSweeeney's Quarterly Concern* (17,000). More recently, online ventures such as *Narrative* or, on a smaller scale, *Flash Fiction* or *Five Chapters*, have, some claim, 'challenged' traditional publishing 'in ways that might benefit short fiction'.[37] On the whole, however, there is considerable overlap between the contributors to all these journals. 'There is nothing sadder, to me', said John Updike in 1995, 'in the situation of young American writers, as the colleges turn them out by the creative-writing classfuls, than the lack of a significantly paying market for short stories.'[38]

Most short fiction today appears in small literary journals, issues of which, Stephen King pointed out in a lively introduction to the *Best American Short Stories 2007*, are to be found only on the lowest shelves of the bookstore. As he handed over $80 for just six journals, he pondered the effect of the specialist market for short fiction on the form of that fiction:

> In 2006 I read scores of stories that felt ... not quite dead on the page, I won't go that far, but *airless*, somehow, and self-referring. These stories felt showy-offy rather than entertaining, self-important rather than interesting, guarded and self-conscious rather than gloriously open and – worst of all – written for editors and teachers rather than readers. [39]

Nevertheless, the anthology's appendix gave full contact details for all the journals to which such stories could be submitted.

King's point was hardly new. 'The suspicion exists', Updike said back in 1984, 'that short fiction, like poetry since Kipling and Bridges, has gone from being a popular to fine art, an art preserved in a kind of floating museum made up of many little superfluous magazines' and 'a kind of accreditation, a certificate of worthiness to teach the so-called art of fiction'.[40] 'I would not say the short story is exactly dead', echoed Mary Gaitskill, introducing the 2009 *Best New American Voices*, 'but it looks to me pallid and ill from neglect, volumes like this one to the contrary.'[41] Given such comments, why should educators and anthologists try so hard to preserve the short story?

First, as I've already discussed, there good pedagogic reasons why young writers are taught to write short stories: the form, as Levy said, is both easier (quicker) and more demanding (show-offy) than the novel; 'maximalism in a minimalist package' is how McGurl puts it.[42] But more than this, the short story is also generally thought to be suited to the kind of things young writers want to write about. Twelve out of the twenty-two short stories included in 1997's *Best of the Fiction Workshops* were from the point of view of a child or adolescent and about parent–child or sibling relationships. But to say that the adolescent form suits the adolescent sensibility is not just to say that 20-year-olds, instructed to 'write what you know', will write about family. What these stories inevitably seek is the turning point, the moment when everything changed and nothing would ever be the same again. The examples I gave earlier from Joyce and Updike suggest that the search for the moment before 'hereafter', before 'afterwards' kicks in, is nothing new. What is new is the ubiquity of these moments in short fiction, some forty years after Barth mocked the 'exhaustion' of the turning point in 'Lost in the Funhouse' and Coover 'sallied forth against adolescent thought-modes'.[43]

'That old insight train just comes chugging into the station, time after time'[44]

In 1997, Charles Baxter, the author of four collections of short fiction and director of the MFA programme at the University of Michigan, published an essay 'Against Epiphanies'. His first objection to 'insight endings' was simply boredom: 'in most anthologies of short stories published since the 1940s', he noted, 'insight endings or epiphanic endings account for approximately 50 to 85 per cent of all the climactic moments'. 'There is a smell about them of recently molded plastic.'[45] This was a view that Michael Chabon also, eventually, came to hold. Chabon had had an enviable post-writing school career. His first novel, *The Mysteries of Pittsburg* (1988), written for his Masters' thesis, became a bestseller, while nine of the twelve stories that made up his first collection, *A Model World* (1991), first appeared in the *New Yorker*. Half feature a boy called Nathan Shapiro as he reacts to his parents' divorce. This is the time-compressing ending of 'The Little Knife':

> As clearly as if he were remembering them, he foresaw his mother's accusation, his father's enraged denial, and with an unhappy chuckle he foresaw, recalled, and fondly began to preserve all the discord for which, in his wildly preserving imagination, he was and always would be responsible.[46]

I won't go into details of the plot, but simply present this passage as an example of the kind of writing Chabon subsequently renounced. The narrator of his second novel, *Wonder Boys* (1995), recalls his first weeks in his college short story class and the increasing burden imposed on his prose by 'all the inescapable shibboleths and bugbears of the trade of writing': 'knowing what was "at stake" in a story, where the mystical fairy-fire of epiphany ought to be set dancing above a character's head, the importance of what our teacher liked to call "spiritual danger" to good characterisation'. Writing school, in other words, meant turning a 'simple story' his grandmother had told him into a 'terrible symbolic mess'.[47] In 2003, after another novel and collection of stories saw his own work increasingly draw on genre fiction, Chabon launched a campaign against the 'contemporary, quotidian, plotless, moment-of-truth revelatory short story'.[48] The solution, he thought, might lie in the revival of 'ripping yarns' and so he commissioned a group of his peers to contribute to *McSweeney's Mammoth Treasury of Thrilling Tales*. Some fulfilled the brief, but many turned an encounter with a mummy or a sea monster or extreme poverty into an opportunity for their protagonists to learn about their own shame, responsibility, loss, or 'terrors of inadequacy'.[49] There was no lack of revelatory moments of truth.

Almost inescapably, the short story's turnings points had become those of self-improvement or psychotherapy, grounded in a 'flattery of the self as the axis of the world'.[50] For Baxter, the prevalence of 'insight-endings' is symptomatic of larger tendencies in modern American culture. Beginning with 'the assumption that the surface is false', he argues, epiphany encourages the 'vestigially religious' and conspiratorial conviction 'that what one sees – the evidence of one's eyes – is at best a partial truth. That almost everyone else has been mistaken.' 'The loss of innocence, and the arrival of knowingness' produced by the revelatory moment cannot be 'debated or contested'. It just is. 'Following the radiance comes the immobility,' says Baxter, recalling Mailer's complaint about the short story's insistence on 'one fatal point'.[51] How does this work in practice?

'Dance Cadaverous', by Uzodinma Iweala, one of *Granta*'s Best Young Americans, is about the repercussions felt by a teenage boy whose parents find a hidden photograph of him kissing another boy.

> Before this I was just a kid who drove Volvo, got good grades, got along with his parents. Now I'm gay.

If Joyce or Updike seemed comfortable about the dividing line between innocence and experience, Iweala is less sure. The sentences I quoted from the earlier writers come at the end of their stories. Iweala's narrator, Daven, follows up this seemingly stark announcement of a change of identity with a page-and-a-half of uncertainty: 'We only kissed – nothing more'; 'I want to tell him that I want my heterosexuality back, but I don't know if I ever lost it. And if I did, I don't know that I miss it so much.' The turning point of 'Dance Cadaverous' is not the discovery or repudiation of homosexuality; the important relationship in the story is between the son and his father. The site of the kiss turns out to be a place Daven used to go to with his father 'all the time'. The story ends when his parents drive there in the Mercedes and find him.

> I open the back door and a tinge of rose softens the inside of my nostrils. This isn't quite how I expected the answer to my prayers, but it's a start.

This characteristic short story ending allows me to return to two remarks I quoted previously: first, Stephen King's comment about stories being written for teachers (showing off their literariness, in other words); and, secondly, Frank O'Connor's claim that the short story is like a lyric poem.

Earlier, getting into the Merc, one of his father's 'particular spaces', Daven had observed that it 'smells of him. I haven't quite decided what the smell is, but it's something like a mixture of stress and new-car-scent.' This is seemingly a mere passing observation, and is followed by a matter of fact account of how they 'hit River Road and then veer off on to the Beltway to take George Washington Parkway directly downtown'.

The ending, however, asks that we revisit this 'particular space'. But what is the answer to Daven's prayers? Being picked up (and therefore presumably accepted) by his parents? Or the softening of the inside of his nostrils by 'a tinge of rose' (the active noun phrase in this sentence)? It's not, or not just, that stress + new-car-scent = rose. Daven, and Iweala, have achieved a kind of organic closure through a crystallising metaphor. The brash narrative turning point offered (good kid becomes gay kid) has been framed or set in context by a more subtle, lyrical turning point: the softening effect of a mere 'tinge of rose', which produces a new relation, not to sexual space, but to family space.[52]

The moment of crystallisation is a way to have a turning point without having to say 'I was never the same again'. It's also a way of eliciting book reviews which compare your stories to gems, 'flawless and brilliant'.[53] That is what the *Observer* said about *How to Breathe Underwater* (2003) by Iowa and Cornell graduate, Julie Orringer. A couple of her endings give a sense of what I mean by crystallisation through metaphor.

> When I think of Isabel this time it's not as a mermaid but as the living girlfriend of my brother, wearing blue jeans, playing bass in the garage, telling me to try singing. She would have liked to see us diving, Sage and me, going down into the richest blue of the bottom. We tread water, watching each other through our masks. I cannot see his eyes through the glass, but I can see, reflected small and blue, a girl wearing swim fins and a metal tank, self-contained and breathing underwater. ('The Isabel Fish')

> She turned down the covers of her bed, where Jack Jacob had touched her but would never touch her again. Then she went to the bathroom to take a shower, and when she took off her clothes she could still see the outline of the gun, plain as a photograph, against her skin. ('Stars of Motown Shining Bright')[54]

In fact, reading these endings without having read the story doesn't really make sense because the effect of the conclusion depends upon the withholding, until that moment, of metaphor. Metaphor's belated arrival marks a shift of gear, a rhetorical turning point. The first example is in the first-person narrative and the second in third-person, but there is very little difference between them. Isn't it the same voice?

A recent essay by Lucy Ferris offers a hypothesis about how and why this might be the case. Her subject is the disappearance of the 'Uncle Charles principle': Hugh Kenner's term for the technique he noted in *Portrait of the Artist as a Young Man* in which a word or two of a minor character's own language is used by the narrator, even when that character is not speaking or even thinking. In the phrase 'every morning … Uncle Charles repaired to his outhouse', the word 'repaired' belongs to Uncle Charles (although he need not utter it) instead of the narrator. It's a momentary effect: 'the normally neutral vocabulary pervaded by a little cloud of idioms which a character might use as if he were managing the narrative'.[55] Others have noticed the same technique in Hemingway, Malamud and others.

Looking at 144 stories published since 1982 (twelve stories by twelve different writers including Chabon, Sherman Alexie and Mary Gaitskill),

Ferris and her students could find no instance of the Uncle Charles Principle. 'Nowhere', she says, 'does a secondary character's dialect or diction exert such a pull on the narration that the story picks it up like lint. The UCP has vanished.'[56] In its place is what she calls the 'A&P Principle' or APP, named after the Updike story from which I quoted earlier. The story is written from the point of view of a 19-year-old checkout clerk, and Ferris notes a disjunction between its opening line:

> In walks these three girls in nothing but bathing suits.

And, a few paragraphs later:

> there was nothing between the top of the suit and the top of her head except just *her*; this, clean bar plane of the top of her chest down from the shoulder bones like a dented sheet of metal tilted in the light.[57]

'Hear the assonance?' Ferris asks, 'The internal half-rhyme? The iambs?' In the second instance, she concludes, 'the language intruding on the text belongs not to another character but to the author'.[58] Ferris's argument is complicated by the fact that this is a first-person not a third-person narrative. Moreover, Updike is more self-aware than she gives him credit for. The poetry is immediately followed by a disavowal: 'I mean, it was more than pretty ... She had sort of okay hair.' But Ferris's general point holds up, especially in stories published after 1961. Like the UCP, the APP occurs in brief snatches: it's (metaphorically) a little cloud, a gnat, a piece of lint. The difference concerns the relationship between who sees and who speaks. In the UCP, the narrative idiom momentarily belongs to the character (rather than the narrator); in the APP, the idiom momentarily belongs to the author (rather than the focalising character).

Ferris explains the shift from one mode to the other in terms of a parallel shift from theatre (Joyce, Kenner said, was interested in 'playing' parts[59]) to cinema, which she argues, presents everything from the author's point of view. I'm not convinced about this, however, as an explanation either of cinematic point of view or of the contemporary short story. Might the writing school culture instead have something to do with the contemporary story's tendency to augment the voices of its narrators with authorial lyricism?

Here is one last example, the title story of another successful recent collection, David Bezmozgis's *Natasha*.[60] The story begins by announcing its interest in the liminal:

When I was sixteen I was high most of the time. That year my parents
bought a new house at the edge of Toronto's sprawl. A few miles
north were cows; south the city. I spent most of my time in basements.
The suburbs offered nothing and so I lived a subterranean life. At
home, separated from my parents by door and stairs, I smoked hash,
watched television, read and masturbated.

The narrator, Mark Berman, is not only between country and city, he
is between school terms, between childhood and maturity, and neither
a Canadian nor a Russian. The exotic confronts him in the shape of
Natasha, the world-weary 14-year-old daughter of his uncle's new wife.
'Calibrated somewhere between resignation and joy', Natasha provides
him with an education, an initiation not just into the 'variations' possible
in sex, but also into the variations possible in life stories. While he's been
masturbating in the basement, she's been casually making porn movies
and sleeping with the crew: 'why not. At the end of the day everyone
got twenty-five dollars.' 'Russia's shit', she shrugs, 'but people enjoy
themselves.' Now that's nihilism.

The narrator carries 'all this information around like a prize'. He
thinks it is 'his connection to a larger darker world'. But what he's really
interested in is the value it has, the 'cool' capital it accrues, in the well-lit
suburban one – at parties, Mark can display Natasha and 'feel superior
to the other stoner acolytes comparing Nietzsche to Bob Marley'. But,
of course, Mark must undergo a moral as well as a sexual education. At
the crucial moment, he fails to take the necessary action to save Natasha
from his predatory uncle, and instead she finds refuge at the home of his
drug dealer, Rufus. He speaks of 'dread' and 'tragedy', but neither word
seems appropriate. After all that Natasha has gone through, Rufus – who
for all his drug dealing lives the suburban good life ('spotless kitchen',
'matching leather sofas', swimming pool) – does not represent 'tragedy'.

But the story is not really about Natasha, it's about Mark, and it ends
by offering two turning points:

In another country, under another code, it would have been my duty
to return to Rufus's with a gun. But in the suburbs, at the end of
my sixteenth summer, this was not an option. Instead I resorted to a
form of civilised murder. By the time I reached my house everyone
in Rufus's yard was dead. Rufus, Natasha, my stoner friends. I would
never see them again. By the time I got home I had already crafted
a new identity. I would switch schools, change my wardrobe, move

to another city. Later I would avenge myself with beautiful women, learn martial arts, and cultivate exotic experiences. I saw my future clearly. I had it all planned out.

The language in which Mark announces his turning point (with its talk of murder and revenge and 'craft') suggests that, contrary to what he says, he doesn't really see his future clearly. That is, he seems unchanged from the 16-year-old self-dramatist we encountered thirty pages earlier. But this is a mere dummy turning point. The paragraph continues:

> And yet, standing in our backyard, drawn by a strange impulse, I crouched and peered through the window into my basement. I had never seen it from this perspective. I saw what Natasha must have seen every time she came to the house. In the full light of summer, I looked into darkness. It was the end of my subterranean life.[61]

Once again, the narrative turning point has been framed by a rhetorical turning point, a return to, and poeticising of, a previously naturalistic space, a moment of crystallisation.

The story ends, as so many do, with a transition from sight to insight; that is, from literal, even empathetic, seeing ('I saw what Natasha must have seen') to metaphoric vision (light emerging from the darkness). This framing seems to suggest the onset of maturity, a passage beyond self-dramatisation. But does it work? Are Mark's metaphors, in fact, any less portentous than his now rejected fantasies of massacre?

The risk run by all short fiction that Frank O'Connor identified in 1963 – 'too much significance, not enough information' – becomes particularly risky in the story of the adolescent turning point written by an adolescent.[62] Perhaps that's because there has been no time for what Saul Bellow, in 'Something to Remember Me By', calls the 'hidden work of uneventful days' to take place.[63] Stories like Jhumpa Lahiri's 'Hell-Heaven' and Richard Ford's 'Communist' rely on a distance and a tension between what 'I did not know, back then' and 'what is clear to me now', or what 'I knew ... even then' and what 'I think now'.[64] In writing school fiction, metaphor tends to take the place of recollection and reassessment. Under such circumstances, 'it is only too easy', as O'Connor says, 'for a short-story writer to become a little too much of an artist'.[65]

Notes

1. Scofield, *The Cambridge Introduction to the American Short Story*, p. 238.
2. O'Connor, *The Lonely Voice*, p. 103.
3. Whittier, 'Frank O'Connor', p. 165.
4. Bowen, *The Mulberry Tree*, p. 128.
5. Poe, *Essays and Reviews*, p. 586.
6. Hawthorne, *Tales and Sketches*, p. 297.
7. Shaw, *The Short Story*, p. 192; Smith, *The Bridport Prize 2009*.
8. Beattie, *Park City*, pp. 78, 81.
9. Saunders, *CivilWarLand in Bad Decline*, p. 26.
10. Cheever, *The Stories*, p. 518. The story provoked a 'Reunion' from both Richard Ford – *A Multitude of Sins*, pp. 61–70 – and Jay McInerney – *How It Ended*, pp. 177–96.
11. Bishop, *Collected Prose*, p. 17.
12. Jones, *Lost in the City*, pp. 203–16; Alexie, *The Toughest Indian in the World*, pp. 21–34; Meloy, *Both Ways is the Only Way I Want It*, pp. 199–219.
13. Barthelme, *Sixty Stories*, p. 158.
14. Updike, *My Father's Tears*, pp. 264–75; Lahiri, *Interpreter of Maladies*, pp. 1–22.
15. Joyce, *Dubliners*, p. 24; Updike, *Forty Stories*, p. 322.
16. Brooks and Penn Warren, *Understanding Fiction*, pp. 317, 344.
17. See Mordecai Marcus, 'What is an Initiation Story?', in May (ed.), *Short Story Theories*, pp. 189–201.
18. Brooks and Penn Warren, *Understanding Fiction*, p. 423.
19. Foster Wallace, *Brief Interviews*, pp. 4, 13; Mason, *Shiloh and Other Stories*, p. 58.
20. Fenza, 'About AWP: The Growth of Creative Writing Programs'.
21. Barth, *The Friday Book*, pp. 106–9.
22. Fenza, 'Creative Writing and Its Discontents', p. 13.
23. Fenza, 'Who Keeps Killing Poetry?'. See also McGurl, *The Program Era*, pp. 23–4.
24. Hills, *Writing in General and the Short Story in Particular*, p. 184.
25. Aldridge, *Talents and Technicians*, p. 34; Frederick Barthelme, 'Editorial'; Bellamy, *Literary Luxuries*, p. 112.
26. Bausch, *Best New American Voices 2008*, pp. xvii–xviii.
27. Eisenberg, 'Form and Fiction'.
28. Moore and Lee, *New Yorker Festival*, 23 September 2005.
29. Levy, *The Culture and Commerce*, p. 8.
30. Levy, *The Culture and Commerce*, p. 3.
31. John Kulka and Natalie Danforth, preface to Miller (ed.), *Best New American Voices 2007*, p. viii.
32. Hoffman, *Best of the Fiction Workshops*, p. 11,
33. Jack, 'Introduction', p. 10.
34. Boddy, 'Unpublished Interview with Junot Díaz'.
35. King, *The Best American Short Stories 2007*, p. xvi.
36. Boddy, 'Unpublished Interview with Junot Díaz'.
37. Alter, 'When Brevity is a Virtue'. See also, O'Toole', 'Great Online Literary Magazines'.
38. Updike, *More Matter*, p. 763.
39. King, *The Best American Short Stories 2007*, p. xvi.

40. Updike, *The Best American Short Stories 1984*, pp. xiv–xv.
41. Gaitskill, *Best New American Voices 2009*, p. xiv.
42. McGurl, *The Program Era*, p. 375.
43. Coover, *Pricksongs*, p. 61.
44. Baxter, *Burning Down the House*, p. 67.
45. Baxter, *Burning Down the House*, pp. 67, 60.
46. Chabon, *A Model World*, pp. 138–9.
47. Chabon, *Wonder Boys*, p. 21.
48. Chabon, *McSweeney's Mammoth Treasury of Thrilling Tales*, p. 6.
49. Chabon, *McSweeney's Mammoth Treasury of Thrilling Tales*, p. 30.
50. Lohafer, *Coming to Terms with the Short Story*, p. 12.
51. Baxter, *Burning Down the House*, pp. 58–62.
52. Iweala, 'Dance Cadaverous', pp. 195–212.
53. *Observer* review, back cover of Orringer, *How to Breathe Underwater*.
54. Orringer, *How to Breathe Underwater*, pp. 75, 172.
55. Kenner, *Joyce's Voices*, p. 17.
56. Ferris, 'Uncle Charles Repairs to the A&P', p. 184.
57. Updike, *Forty Stories*, pp. 315–16.
58. Ferris, 'Uncle Charles Repairs to the A&P', p. 185.
59. Kenner, *Joyce's Voices*, p. 21.
60. Although *Natasha* was very well received, one reviewer noted 'a whiff of the creative writing course – a hint that these neat tales have been crafted to please a teacher rather than to delight a reader'. Lacey, 'Home and Away'.
61. Bezmozgis, *Natasha*, pp. 81–110.
62. O'Connor, *The Lonely Voice*, p. 23.
63. Bellow, *Collected Stories*, p. 414.
64. Lahiri, *Unaccustomed Earth*, pp. 63, 67; Ford, *Rock Springs*, pp. 226, 229.
65. O'Connor, *The Lonely Voice*, p. 23.

CHAPTER 6

Sequences and Accumulations

Throughout this book, I've suggested that when reading a short story we tend to take account, consciously or unconsciously, of the context in which it appears: whether in a magazine, surrounded by a variety of other kinds of writing, in a volume of stories 'selected' by single author, in a multi-authored collection arranged around a common theme, or in an anthology labelled 'the best' (of one category or another). Where we read the story shapes the expectations we bring to our reading of it, and thus the effect it has on us. It was not the same experience to encounter a Barthelme story in the little magazine *Art and Literature*, sandwiched between Jean Genet and spatial theory, as it was to read one in the *New Yorker*, with cartoons and light verse cutting into its three-column layout. More recently, Joyce Carol Oates, reviewing George Saunders's *Pastoralia*, noted how different his 'goofy riffs on the travails of freaks and losers who sometimes manage to rise, only just barely, to the human' seemed when collected between hard covers and in their 'original settings in the columns of the *New Yorker*, amid glossy advertisements for high-priced merchandise'. In the magazine setting, she argued, the stories recall the 'spectacle' of lunatics provided for the 'voyeuristic fascination/revulsion of those eighteenth-century European aristocrats who visited asylums'.[1] Short stories appear in many places and thus gain, or lose, from many contexts. Susan Minot's 'Thanksgiving Day', for example, which was written for her creative writing class at Columbia, was first published in the little magazine *Grand Street* and then in an anthology of 'best' new stories by 'young writers', and finally in what her publishers suggested she call a novel, *Monkeys*, as one of six chronologically arranged stories about a single family.[2] Another story that ended up in *Monkeys*, 'The Navigator', also appeared first in *Grand Street*, then in volume of women's writing, in a collection of stories about alcoholism and in a book of stories set on beaches.[3]

Only when writers put together their own collections can they hope to control the resonances that might be produced by the juxtaposition of separate individual pieces.[4] Some are happy to leave the connections between stories loose and more or less to chance, but most of the time the construction of a book (either retrospectively or from the outset) leads to thoughts of some kind of deliberate arrangement: a 'sequence', 'cycle', 'composite' or 'cluster'.[5] The uncertainty among critics about what to call collections of linked stories is matched only by that of writers, who often draw analogies with other (usually visual) art forms. The short story collection has been compared to a sketchbook,[6] exhibition,[7] quilt[8] or, what some regard as the quilt's modern equivalent, MTV.[9] Each of these terms suggests a different degree, and kind, of organisation between the part and whole.

A sort of sliding scale of orchestration seems to operate. Some writers carefully arrange progression according to such factors as the chronological development of a single place, milieu or protagonist (Cisneros's *The House on Mango Street*, Ozick's *The Puttermesser Papers*, Danticat's *The Dew Breaker*); the passing of a day, from dawn to dusk (Naylor's *Women of Brewster Place*); or the passing of a generation (Jones's *Lost in the City*). Some rely on intricate networks of mythic allusion (Welty's *The Golden Apples*), and many sustain some kind of symbolism (Moore's *Birds of America*). It is also possible to 'integrate' or 'interlock' (to use two common terms for the process) different parts of a book in different ways. Jumpa Lahiri's *Unaccustomed Earth*, for example, has two parts: the first contains five distinct, if thematically related, stories, while the second, 'Hema and Kaushik', consists of three stories about two overlapping lives. In each case, however, the discontinuities inherent in the idea of a collection produce an effect as decisive as any pattern arising out of it. If Salinger's Zen epigraph pointed to a common theme between his tales, his title, *Nine Stories*, highlighted their original lack of relation and apparently arbitrary bringing together. Introducing *Shakespeare's Kitchen*, Lore Segal also emphasises a pull in both directions. The book's thirteen stories 'take place in a particular situation', with a 'protagonist, some main characters and a chorus of minor ones'. The collection has 'a theme' and it 'may have a chronology'. And yet, she observes, 'each story created its own choreography, became fixed in shape and would not always attach to what happened before and what was going to happen next'.[10] And, of course, a collection of stories, like a collection of poems, can be read in different ways. In the note with which he introduces the fifty-three vignettes that make up *The Atlas*, William Vollmann both informs his readers that his book is arranged 'palindromically: the motif in the first story is taken up again in the last; the second story finds its echo in the second to last, and so on', and disavows the significance of pattern. In the 'five minutes between lying down and turning off the light', he recognises, readers might simply prefer to dip in and out of the volume 'in no particular order'.[11]

Linked Excitements and Book-unity

> A collection of short stories, not a novel. This in itself is a disappoint-ment. It seems to diminish the book's authority, making the author seem like somebody who is just hanging on to the gates of Literature, rather than safely settled inside.[12]

The common feature of all collections and anthologies is that they are books, and books have always been valued for their capacity to save the ephemeral story from oblivion. Many collections are linked by a character whose adventures formed the basis of a newspaper, magazine or radio serial. In 1901 Arnold Bennett noted that the 'connected series of short stories ... in which the same characters ... pass again and again' was better suited to magazines than a serialised novel, because it 'enables the reader to enjoy the linked excitements of a serial tale with binding him to peruse every instalment'.[13] Langston Hughes's Simple stories – featuring conversations in a Harlem bar between a middle-class narrator, Boyd, and Jesse B. Semple or Simple, a working-class 'race man' – were syndicated in black newspapers from 1943 to 1965, while Armistead Maupin's *Tales of the City* (1978) and the volumes that followed it gathered together the daily pieces about a boarding-house community that had first appeared in the *San Francisco Chronicle*. Garrison Keillor's *Lake Wobegon Days* (1985) and its sequels originated, and continue, on National Public Radio and in the *New Yorker*.[14] Other notable works that began as *New Yorker* serials include Leo Rosten's *Education of H*y*m*a*n K*a*p*l*a*n* (1937), Nabokov's *Pnin* (1957), Renata Adler's *Speedboat* (1976), Updike's Bech books (1970, 1982 and 1998) and Jamaica Kincaid's *Annie John* (1985).[15]

From Poe onwards, short story writers have often tried to meet the requirement of specific magazines while keeping 'book-unity always in mind'. Every one of his tales, Poe recalled, had 'been composed with reference to its effect as part of *a whole*', something Duyckinck, the editor of *Tales* (1845), did not take into account.[16] 'To a collection of short stories', wrote William Faulkner, 'form, integration, is as important as to a novel – an entity of its own, single, set for one pitch, contrapunctal in integration, toward one end, one finale – the uplifting of men's hearts.'[17] Faulkner both wrote stories with a book in mind (for example, *The Unvanquished*) and arranged existing stories to create a new 'book-unity' according to patterns of geography, theme and chronology (*Collected Stories*). More recent writers have also aimed for overall 'form' and 'integration'. John Barth introduced *Lost in the Funhouse* as 'neither a collection, nor a selection, but a series … meant to be received "all at once" and as here arranged'.[18] Readers now largely encounter Coover's 'The Babysitter' in anthologies, but he intended it to be read as the penultimate story in *Pricksongs and Descants*, a book that was carefully constructed to have 'a beginning, a middle and an end', and a pattern of musical motifs.[19] Jayne Anne Phillips insisted that *Black Tickets* 'wasn't just put together in any order': 'the short pieces introduced the long ones and taught the reader how to read the book'.[20]

For Joyce Carol Oates, the true test of a 'distinguished short story collection' is that it is 'greater than the sum of its disparate parts'.[21] After publishing two collections in which she simply gathered together all the stories she had at that point, Oates decided to shape her books 'deliberately' according to particular themes. Her books would no longer be mere 'assemblages of disparate material but wholes, with unifying strategies of organization'.[22] Once his career became established, and book publication more or less guaranteed, Charles Baxter also tended to think more in terms of 'book-unity'. 'Now', he told an interviewer in 2003, 'I'm more likely, if I write a short story, to think, *What other short stories could I write that would have something to do with the story I've just written?* I never used to think that way, but I do now.'[23] Thinking in terms of books can be a mixed blessing. On the one hand, by planning integrated volumes from the start, Oates and Baxter are able to lift the short story above its station as 'minor literature'; on the other hand, Oates noted that in compiling collections she was 'forced to omit more and more stories' she would 'otherwise have wished to preserve'.[24]

If integrated short story collections are more distinguished than assemblages, then perhaps it follows that the most distinguished of all have the 'makings of a novel' in them.[25] This is certainly the view of publishers, for the simple reason that a novel or, at the very least, a 'novel in stories' will sell better. When Gloria Naylor presented her publishers with *The Women of Brewster Place*, a collection of stories about a group of women who live in the same housing project, they quickly added the subtitle 'A Novel in Seven Stories'; 'it was just a publishing thing', she later recalled.[26]

But it is not only publishers who value the novel. As we've already seen, writers like Pynchon, Mailer and Roth were anxiously aware that novels were 'major league'.[27] Barthelme and Cheever agreed.[28] When Raymond Carver died in 1988, it was not unusual for his obituarists to point out the fact of his 'failure' to write the novel which 'was to decide how important a writer he might be'.[29] For much of his career, Carver claimed to be working on a novel (the posthumous collection *No Heroics, Please* contains an eight-page 'fragment'); when he became successful, he declared himself 'happy doing what I'm doing'.[30] After Carver's death, some of his critics also took it upon themselves to suggest that his achievement was no mere accumulation of fine discrete stories 'best read one at a time, inching along the prose in order to take its exact measurement', but rather a 'cohesive body of work'.[31] J. Gerald Kennedy, for example, praises *Cathedral* for allowing readers to imagine possible encounters between its various characters. 'Although the textual autonomy of each story precludes such interactions', Kennedy concedes, 'the recent Robert Altman film, *Short Cuts*, captures just this potentiality in the tangential encounters that connect the multiple story lines developed there.'[32] Altman, it is implied, was doing Carver the favour of putting in the 'interstices *between the stories*' and thus writing the novel that he himself 'never had time to write'.[33] Carver's stories were really 'just one story', said Altman, a kind of 'Carver soup' that 'could go on for ever'.[34]

All these pressures towards book-unity raise the stakes for the short story as a genre in ways which it will be the aim of this chapter to explore.

Pattern in the Short Story Sequence

'One of the most amusing questions concerning the short story', declared William Dean Howells in 1901, 'is why a form which is singly so attractive' is 'collectively so repellent'. Howells thought the problem was that in demanding that readers 'subjectively fill in the details and carry out the scheme which in its small dimensions the story can only suggest', their 'feeble powers' were over-stretched.[35] But perhaps the problem is not that readers do too much work, but that they do too much of the same work. Introducing her *Collected Stories*, Hortense Calisher worried that the shock-effect of an individual story – its 'apocalypse served in a very small cup' – would spill out or spill over when set in series. 'Worlds meant to be compacted only to themselves, bump. Their very sequence can do them violence. Even when all the stories are by the same hand.'[36] Shock-effects, whether of horror or epiphany, suffer from repetition. 'How many epiphanies can a reader take in succession', asks Valerie Shaw, 'without feeling they are merely literary tricks with little bearing on actual experience?'[37] A succession of turning points (thwarted or not) can be hard to take. Moreover, as the narrator of John Barth's collection of nine interlinked stories, *The Development*, reminds himself, 'much as we may be programmed by evolution to see patterns in things, and significance in patterns', 'a Pattern – of last names, happenings, whatever – doth not in itself a Meaning make'.[38]

Many short story collections, however, suggest that meaning can be created, not through the insistent repetition of one revelatory effect, but through the juxtaposition of different views. 'Every arrangement in life', thinks Lorrie Moore's 'Agnes of Iowa', 'carried with it the sadness, the sentimental shadow, of its not being something else, but only itself.'[39] The short story sequence can give expression to those shadows, most strikingly in Moore's own book, *Anagrams*, which, as its title suggests, rearranges the protagonist's life in various combinations or, as she puts it, 'parallel universes'.[40] Others use sequence to explore the contrasts and contradictions of a particular place, situation or concept. Susan Minot said that the stories in *Lust* were 'grouped together to reflect that they are all basically about the same thing – each one a different version, at a different stage, as if a different colour of wash was over it. Let's see how this looks in blue, how it looks in green.'[41] Charles Baxter said that in writing *Believers* he was 'very conscious of working on a group of stories that were more or less about a similar theme, that is: people who are choosing to believe something or not, and whose belief would change the direction of the narrative.'[42] Often the effect, and the philosophy, of the short story collection is less the relativistic *One Way or Another* (Peter Cameron) than the greedy *Both Ways is the Only Way I Want It* (Maile Meloy).

The juxtaposition of perspectives might seem a particularly modern or even modernist ambition – thirteen ways of looking at a blackbird becomes eleven kinds of loneliness – but it was a feature of the short story collection from its Romantic start.[43] Washington Irving's *Sketch-Book*

(1820) places his indictment of 'shrews at home' in 'Rip Van Winkle' immediately after the celebration of wifely virtues in 'The Wife', while a hundred years later, Hemingway arranged *In Our Time* so that 'The Doctor and the Doctor's Wife' qualifies and replies to 'Indian Camp'.[44] Both, one might argue, were simply updating the 'marriage debate' of Chaucer's *Canterbury Tales*.

Hemingway was also interested in showing 'all the different sides' of war. 'Never think one story represents my viewpoint', he told a critic, 'because it is much too complicated for that.'[45] A sense of multiple and 'contradictory' 'angles of vision' also informs Tim O'Brien's *The Things They Carried* (1990), one of the most celebrated short story sequences of recent years.[46] The book suggests that stories of the Vietnam war, like days spent in the war, consist of 'odd little fragments' that gradually accrue, over a long period of time, in 'layers' upon each other. The fragments of war not only include 'bloody stories', but also love stories, 'peace stories', stories about beauty and about 'the kind of boredom that causes stomach disorders'. The point is that one can never pin down 'the final and definitive truth'. 'You can tell a true war story by the way it never seems to end', says the narrator; an idea that finds expression in the collection's mode of mere accumulation, its promise that further stories can always be added, that you have to 'just keep on telling it'.[47] The title story, which opens the book, suggests that among the many things that soldiers carry (weapons, machetes, letters, love, shame) is the trauma that leads to retelling. 'The bad stuff never stops happening: it lives its own dimension, replaying itself over and over again.' The story circles around a single event, the death of Ted Lavander and Jimmy Cross's guilt. 'He tried not to think about it': but of course 'it' keeps coming back. As in Hemingway's *In Our Time*, simple words repeated assume a kind of incantatory power that builds to something almost like prayer. 'There it is, they'd say. Over and over – there it is, my friend, there it is – as if the repetition itself were an act of poise ... there it is, there it absolutely and positively and fucking well *is*.'[48]

The feeling that 'you can't change what can't be changed' is particularly well expressed by an accumulation of short stories.[49] By presenting repetition or juxtaposition (that is, something static, like an exhibition or a quilt) rather than development, a collection of linked stories can be used to depict unsolvable situations and to convey experiences that are habitual, monotonous or compulsive. The title of *The Development*, Barth's nine interlinked tales of the Oyster Cove retirement community, is, of course, a pun. These stories don't add up to a 'duly gratifying resolution nor end a capital-E ending, really, just a sort of petering out, like most folks' lives'.[50]

John Updike used an accumulation, rather than a sequence, of stories to describe the 'quarrels and reunions' of suburban married life. Over twenty-three years, beginning in 1956, resuming in 1963 and continuing intermittently until 1976, he published seventeen stories about a couple called Richard and Joan Maple, mainly in the *New Yorker*, later including these, among other stories, in individual collections. In 1979, he gathered all the Maples stories together in a collection called *Too Far to Go* to coincide with a 'made-for-television movie' of the same title.[51] He later added another piece about the couple's post-divorce reunion, when their daughter has a baby. If the effect of each story is to 'click shut' (to borrow Updike's favourite photographic analogy), its closure is nevertheless not final.[52] Another instalment could always be added. In other words, the accumulative short story collection enabled Updike to make his point that marriage – through children, adultery, separation, divorce and the arrival of 'wife-substitutes' and grandchildren – is never finished.[53] By the fourth story in the collection, the Maples have already 'talked and thought about separation' for a long time – they're on their tenth 'kill or cure' trip – but again 'accusation, retraction, blow, and caress alternated and cancelled'. Updike described the collection as a 'duet', a repeated 'musical pattern of advance and retreat' to the 'rhythm of apathy and renewal'. Even a 'Pattern' without 'Meaning' is surely preferable, he suggests, to the 'human mess' that the Maples both create and struggle to put right. 'He wondered if he could punch her in the face and at the same time grab the glass in her hand so it wouldn't break.' If the collection has a moral, it emerges in Richard's plea, 'Help me clean up this mess.'[54]

Of course, it is not only married couples who repeat themselves, 'making the same mistake' and then 'coming back' to make it again.[55] The pattern of life with a more obvious addiction – to hard drugs – is something which Denis Johnson captured in *Jesus' Son*. The title comes from Lou Reed's song 'Heroin' – 'when I'm rushing on my run/I feel just like Jesus' Son' – and the stories detail the moments of almost religious transcendence which the narrator, Fuckhead, experiences when high. These interrupt his confused and confusing 'dirty realist' daily life, spent in motels and bars 'where you might think today was yesterday and yesterday was tomorrow, and so on'. Work, meanwhile, is the place to which, when you return from being away, it is 'as if it had never stopped happening' and you'd 'never been anywhere else'. Of course, chronology is hard to ascertain when 'certain important connections have been burned through'. In Fuckhead's narratives, characters leave at the end of one paragraph and then come back at the beginning of the next. He doesn't know why. The second story 'Two Men' begins 'I met the first man'; the eighth, 'The Other Man' begins 'But I never finished telling you about the two men'.[56]

The real problem for Fuckhead, however, is the fact that we are 'just meat' and that at any moment the 'goop inside of us' might escape and make us dead 'forever'. The tone is set by the first story, 'Car Crash While Hitchhiking'. After the crash, Fuckhead is impressed by the scream emitted by the driver's wife on realising he has been killed. 'She shrieked as I imagined an eagle would shriek. It felt wonderful to be alive to hear it! I've gone looking for that feeling anywhere.' This startling response is only the beginning and, as we read further into the collection, we start to appreciate just how odd and disjointed his picaresque adventures are. In one story he thinks he's gone 300 miles – 'a long way from home' – but he's just outside town having driven 'around and around'.[57] In some ways *Jesus' Son* is a kind of anti-*On the Road*.

Critics have drawn admiring attention to Fuckhead's epiphanies, but their status as epiphany is rather compromised by the fact that they depend on pills and mushrooms and that they happen continuously and with little variation. Fuckhead might concur with Sherwood Anderson's sense that the 'true history of life is but a history of moments'. Only in 'rare moments', Anderson said, do 'we live'.[58] But the effect of Johnson's collection, for all the lyricism of its sunlit moments, is to suggest that Fuckhead's insights are the spiritual, and literary, equivalent of two-for-the-price-of-one drinks at Happy Hour (which, further evoking the method of the short story, is 'also Rush Hour').[59]

Narratives of Community

I say, Rocío, just write about this little street of ours, it's only one block long, but there's so many stories. Too many stories! ... Why not just write about 325? That's our house! Write about 325 and that will take the rest of your life.[60]

The form of the linked story collection is both ancient and modern. Long before there were novels to aspire to or revolt against, writers grouped stories by supplying some excuse for their telling; consider, for example, the 'framed miscellanies' of Boccaccio's *Decameron*, Chaucer's *Canter-bury Tales* or the Arabian *Thousand and One Nights*.[61] Within American literature, however, the idea of grouped stories really took off as part of the fashion for 'local colour' fiction that emerged after the Civil War, which I discussed in the Introduction. 'By the turn of the century', notes James Nagel, 'nearly a hundred volumes of interrelated stories had been published in America.'[62] Collections such as George Washington Cable's *Old Creole Days*, Kate Chopin's *Bayou Folk*, Hamlin Garland's *Main-Travelled Roads*, Sarah Orne Jewett's *The Country of the Pointed Fires* and Sui Sin Far's *Mrs Spring Fragrance* were organised around parti-cular small communities and suggested that the relationship between the community and its inhabitants was in some ways analogous to that between a collection and individual tales.[63] These collections were less interested in the progress of the individual or the family – the great subjects of the nineteenth-century bourgeois novel – than in the endur-ance of a group. Their emphasis tended to be conservative; that is, they were often concerned with conserving the rituals, and the stories, that bind and sustain communities, often in response to some external moder-nising threat. 'Narratives of community' (as Sandra Zagarell calls them) appealed particularly to the ever-increasing numbers of migrant and immigrant city-dwellers nostalgic for the worlds they had left behind.[64] This is not the place to provide a history of the form, merely to draw attention, as James Nagel has done, to a revival of narratives of commu-nity since the 1980s. The short story cycle, he argues, became the 'genre of choice for emerging writers from a variety of ethnic and economic backgrounds' whose concern was with the 'situation of the ethnic commu-nity as a whole'.[65] Among the works he discusses is Louise Erdrich's *Love Medicine*, whose structure he links to 'traditional narratives among Native Americans', and Amy Tan's *The Joy Luck Club*, which alternates stories of mothers and daughters.[66] Both books collect together previ-ously published stories. Tan admitted to feeling guilty when reading a review praising 'the clever and innovative structure of "a novel with eight voices, mysteriously interlocked like a Chinese puzzle box".'[67]

Many short story sequences – in the 1990s as well as in the 1890s – explore a tension between a sense of the 'coherent multiplicity of commu-nity' and feelings of isolation or confinement within it.[68] The effect partly depends on whether the community is viewed and described from the inside, from the outside, or, as is often the case, from some half-way position. The urban writer-narrator who visits Maine in Jewett's *The*

Country Firs learns from her experience of Dunnet Landing both that 'in each of us there is a place remote and islanded' and that a communal 'gayety and determined floweriness' can go some way to counteracting loneliness.[69] Viewed from inside, as it is in Sherwood Anderson's *Winesburg, Ohio*, small town life offers very little communal comfort; the townsfolk look at each other only through the closed windows of their confined rooms or creep around the back streets to avoid being seen. The stagnant atrophy of Winesburg is contrasted to the fast-moving trains which leave from its station, eventually allowing its restless observing protagonist (that is, a 'familiar novelistic character') to escape from its provincial confines into the big city and the 'adventure of his life'.[70] Trains also play an important part in *The Heartbreaker of Shady Hill*, Cheever's collection of eight stories about couples who live in a suburb within commuting distance of New York. But there, the train does not lead to liberation, first, because it only takes commuters from the claustrophobia of their identikit suburban homes to the claustrophobia of their identikit office 'cubicles', and, secondly, because, every evening, it comes back again. The trains themselves are just 'lighted aquarium tanks'.[71]

I want now to look at three narratives of community in more detail: two tightly structured sequences, both first books – Edward P. Jones's *Lost in the City* (1992) and Junot Díaz's *Drown* (1996) – then the ongoing New York stories of Grace Paley, which accumulated gradually from the late 1950s to her death in 2007.

Making Room: *Lost in the City* and *Drown*

Lost in the City is not about 'the Washington they put on postcards and in the pages of expensive magazines' or indeed very much about 'the land of white people' at all, although occasionally 'the city people' issue letters in what seems like a 'foreign language'. Instead, it's about 'real people' who pass their lives in the confines of a specific neighbourhood – Northwest, Northeast, Southwest, Southeast – within the city and who, if they venture further afield, find themselves lost.[72]

The collection is carefully constructed. 'It was always as if I was writing one book', said Jones, 'I never wrote a story here and a story there.'[73] The first story is about a child and is set in 1957; the last features an octogenarian and takes place in the 1970s, during the Carter presidency. Most importantly, however, the book begins 'before the community was obliterated', when the sidewalks were filled with children

playing, and ends when 'the colored people and their homes are gone,
with an elderly woman living alone in a 'senior citizen building', her
door firmly locked and a serrated knife ready in case of intruders.
Marie looks back, before the 1950s, to the time when her Southern
mother thought of Washington as the place 'up there', where 'things
can be made right'. Of course, Washington was never 'heaven without
dyin'', and while Jones's book is undoubtedly a story of decline and
loss, it nevertheless enacts a kind of back and forth between a sense of
the neighbourhood as a refuge and as a prison.[74] From the start, many
of the characters live narrowly confined lives, rarely 'venturing out'
beyond their immediate locality for fear of getting 'lost'. Some yearn
for escape, for more space. 'The Girl Who Raised Pigeons' watches as
her last bird flies away, 'following him her eyes, with her heart, as far as
she could', while adults fantasise about lives in other neighbourhoods,
if not beyond, while riding in the subway or in a taxi or a borrowed car.
So far, so *Winesburg*. But looked at another way, confinement is safety
and home is the place where you are 'known by all the world'. The line
between safety and danger is so precise that Jones maps the city street by
street. All it takes are a few wrong turnings to be 'in a different country'
('white folks' neighbourhood') where 'the laws might be different'. In
'The Store', a boy is caught jaywalking on 5th Street by a white cop
and made to go 'all the way back to 7th Street and cross again on the
green light', and then do it all again three more times. Waiting for the
light to change after the fourth time, he begins to pray, 'Just let me come
back to one fifteen New York Avenue safely and I'll never come to their
world again.' But then he gets a job running a store a little way away and
realises that his 'allegiances were expanding'; he was 'making room in
[his] soul for more than one neighbourhood'.[75]

    The protagonists of Junot Díaz's *Drown* need room for more than
one country and more than one language. *Drown* is a collection of ten
stories, some of which are set in the Dominican Republic, some of which
take place in Manhattan's Washington Heights or New Jersey, and others
which move between the two. Most feature a recurrent set of characters: two brothers, Yunior, the narrator, and Rafa, and their mother and
father. The father is absent for most of the collection – first in New York,
while they are in Santo Domingo (Rafa dreams that he will 'come in the
night, like Jesus'), and then off with another woman. We hear about him
mainly from the mother and from Yunior whose teacher can't believe
that his essay 'My Father The Torturer' is not a joke. In the final story,

however, Yunior retells the story from his father's point of view, ending with his 'flying south to get us'.[76]

Because of these continuities, reviewers tended to see the collection as something approaching (but falling short of) a novel. One described the book as 'more like a loosened, shuffled novel than a book of stories'; another declared it to be 'a whisker away from being a coherent narrative in its own right' (and looked forward to 'a fully-fledged novel').[77] But such comments miss the point of the book's structure. Díaz described the collection as a 'tapestry', and the stories he has published since *Drown* have, in featuring some of the same characters, added further to its texture.[78] The absence of a 'coherent narrative' is crucial to a book which is all about living in gaps and fissures, between childhood and adulthood, between countries and between languages.[79]

Stories of 'becoming American' have traditionally taken the form of conversion narratives, describing the slow but one-directional process of leaving behind the ways of the old country and adopting those of the new.[80] But today's patterns of migration often involve moving backwards and forwards between cultures and languages. We can see this process at work in the highly-educated, middle-class world described by Jhumpa Lahiri. Many of her characters belong to what Rubén Rumbaut calls the 'one-and-a-half' generation, that is, they were born in one country and then moved and grew up in another, both of which seem strange to them, like 'unaccustomed earth'.[81] 'Although it is true enough that the 1.5 generation is "marginal" to both its native and adopted cultures', argues Gustavo Pérez Firmat, 'the inverse may be equally accurate: only the 1.5 generation is marginal to *neither* culture.'

> The 1.5 individual is unique in that, unlike younger and older compatriots, he or she may actually find it possible to circulate within and throughout both the old and new cultures. While one-and-a-halfers may never feel entirely at ease in either one, they are capable of availing themselves of the resources – linguistic, artistic, commercial – that both cultures have to offer. In some ways they are *both* first and second generation ... One-and-a-halfers are translation artists.[82]

The structure, as well as the content, of *Drown* reflects the position of 'one-and-a-halfers'. Wherever they are, the characters seem to be thinking of the other place (and, indeed, the other generation). In the Dominican Republic, they fantasise about the United States: it's what 'folks planned on'. The brothers try to imagine their father's life in the

States, adopt American names (Sinbad and Muhammad Ali one summer) and notice who has clothes or toys sent from the United States. In the New Jersey cold, however, they dream of jacarandas and console themselves with Dominican food. 'In [Mami's] mind, American things – appliances, mouth wash, funny-looking upholstery – all seemed to have an intrinsic badness about them.'[83] The 'gaps' between stories interrupt both the assimilation narrative and the coming-of-age story in a way that the gaps between the chapters of a novel couldn't do. 'It's speaking about some events and it's being silent about others,' says Diaz. 'With stories, you're allowed to be silent.'[84]

Thinking about the way that short story collections exploit gaps, we might recall Washington Irving's *Sketch-Book*, and, in particular, the negotiation between British and American subjects and forms represented in 'The Voyage'. When travelling by land within Europe, Irving says, 'the features and populations of one country blend almost imperceptibly with those of another'. Travelling by sea from America to Europe, however, there is no such 'gradual transition':

> The vast space of waters that separates the two hemispheres is like a blank page in existence ... It seemed as if I had closed one volume of the world and its concerns, and had time for meditation before I opened another.[85]

Although the distance between Santo Domingo and New Jersey is much shorter, and travel today much faster, blank pages in existence nevertheless still inform *Drown*, particularly in the gap between Spanish and English. In the book's epigraph, Pérez Firmat writes that the problem is 'how to explain to you that I/don't belong to English/though I belong nowhere else'. Díaz wants to highlight what can and cannot be expressed in each language – his narrator is always 'looking for' words – but he is also concerned to dramatise, through structure, the abruptness with which Spanish gives way to English. The form of the short story sequence allows him to avoid a 'gradual transition', the sense, cultivated by so many writers, that the 'language of *outside the house*' slowly 'seeps' inside.[86] In the early Dominican stories, the conversation between the boys is rendered in English (which we assume represents Spanish), while the narrator speaks an English that incorporates Spanish words. In the later US stories, however, there is no gap between the Spanish-inflected English of the narrator and that of the characters. By the time the boys are old enough to think about 'How to Date a Browngirl', the narrator instructs that 'if the girl's from around the way', they must return to their 'busted-up Spanish. Let her correct you if she's Latina'.[87] Diaz neither italicises nor translates the Spanish words, although in preparing the British edition of *Drown* he conceded to pressure to include a short glossary. What he didn't want to be, he said, was 'a narrative informant': 'I hate them ... 'the people who are writing the exotic. And you know who their audience is because they're translating everything, translating for the mainstream.'[88]

One of the main differences between *Lost in the City* and *Drown* is that of narrative perspective. Apart from two first-person narratives, Jones sticks to a detached 'God-like' third-person.[89] Apart from one story in the third-person ('No Face') and one in the second-person, 'How to Date a Browngirl, Blackgirl, Whitegirl, or Halfie' – his breakthrough *New Yorker* publication – Díaz sticks to a forceful, intimate first-person ('you know the sort of photograph I'm talking about') and, mostly, to a 'non-literary vernacular'.[90] It was because of this voice that he was heavily marketed as 'authentic', a 'natural', and that his fictions were seen as providing a window onto immigrant life in America in general, and his own life in particular. He certainly attracted unusual attention. The press loved the story of Díaz's advance 'in the mid-six figures' on the strength of just five stories. And what added bite to the story was the often-repeated assertion that with the publication of *Drown*, he had been 'literally freed ... from the ghetto'.[91] But Díaz was unhappy with the idea that what Latino authors 'have to offer is our experience and not our talent. I don't think my experience is anything special.'[92]

Díaz's talent was to create the impression of being the 'authentic voice of his community', while simultaneously drawing, and reflecting, on the skills that he had learned as a writing school student at Cornell.[93] In one story, the narrator praises the honest labour behind a well-made pool table. The 'precision of their construction' is, he says, 'the sort of thing I can believe in'.[94]

In many ways, *Drown* resembles *Lost in the City* in its emulation of a kind of Joycean naturalism. Díaz writes about the confinement of urban poverty, about people whose names are usually found on convicts' uniforms or 'coupled together on boxing cards', and whose lives are 'going nowhere'.[95] More than Jones or Joyce, he writes about work and the fine line between anger and exhaustion that comes from nineteen-hour days. One man works so much that 'he had to bite his lip to stay awake', but often 'tired's the best way to be'. Another thinks, 'when I'm

fifty this is how I'll remember my friends: tired and yellow and drunk'.
Escape from the world of work is found in the fleeting pleasures of drink,
drugs, sex, TV, movies, parties and, occasionally, in the dreaminess of
a new romance. In 'Aurora', the narrator's girlfriend recalls how, while
in the 'Quiet Room' at juvenile detention, she liked to draw pictures of
a 'whole new life': 'The two of us had kids, big blue house, hobbies,
the whole fucking thing.' He listens to her as they hole up in an empty
apartment – both a sanctuary from, and a duplicate of, Aurora's prison
confinement. He ends by saying that within a week their fights would
start up again, and that he would hit her to make 'the blood come out of
her ear like a worm'; but then circles back to 'right then, in that apartment' when 'we seemed like we were normal folks. Like maybe everything was better.'[96] Such moments of fantasised escape – in which people
feel that they 'could do anything … It's all possible' – are rare and brief,
for, whatever the occasion, 'the moment closes and we're back in the
world we've always known.'[97] Díaz fluctuates between naturalism and
symbolism, between an inventory of a life filled with 'cold and greasy
pizza' and kisses that end when you find a sanitary pad in the girl's under-
wear – and a lyricism that transcends all of those things.[98] *Drown* may not
strive for 'stylistic lavishness' but nor is it consistently 'stripped down'.[99]
Every now and again Díaz tries to suggest that authenticity does not
preclude poetry, for example, in the observation that 'pollutants have
made Jersey sunsets one of the wonders of the world'. But the observation of harsh reality and the enactment of its transcendence don't always
fit together so neatly. In 'Arguantando', Yunior recalls:

> On the ride to Boca Chica I was always too depressed to notice the
> ocean, the young boys fishing and selling cocos by the side of the
> road, the surf exploding into the air like a cloud of shredded silver.[100]

If Yunior is too depressed, who did notice the ocean? And then formed
the simile? To the various schizophrenic impulses which *Drown* explores
and dramatises, we might add the familiar gap between 'escape from the
world' lyrical insight and 'back in the world' tale-telling.

'I couldn't have done it any other way': Grace Paley

Grace Paley's first collection of stories, *The Little Disturbances of Man*,
was published in 1959, around the same time as Philip Roth's collection,
Goodbye, Columbus, and the books were reviewed and praised together.

'Then', Paley recalled, 'we were told to write novels. And he wrote novels. And I tried for two years to write a novel but I failed. So.'[101] When Paley's three volumes of stories – *Enormous Changes at the Last Minute* was published in 1974 and *Later the Same Day* in 1985 – were collected, she was faintly praised as having in her the 'makings' of a novelist – largely because her stories are largely set within the same small close-knit community and feature a recurrent set of characters. 'Put it all together, and maybe you've got a novel,' she said, 'But I couldn't have done it any other way.'[102]

Paley's New York was the Lower East Side 'before urban renewal', and her community that of women, with children, with men and with each other.[103] With each story, we become acquainted with another member of a loose community of family, friends and neighbours. The narrator of one story is likely to turn up in another as a character. The stories have no clear temporal relationship with each other, they do not build upon one another and there is no suggestion of progress towards some final revelation or understanding. Like Gass and Barthelme, contemporaries with whom she often shared a platform, Paley foregrounds the strategies of fiction, often presenting a 'narrative act within a narrative act'.[104] As we have seen, in what we might call the Romantic–through-modernist tradition of the short story – from Poe to Anderson to Carver – the point of such embedding is to emphasise that some stories cannot be told, that mystery remains. Gass is sceptical of even finding an 'other pair of ears' to hear his words.[105] Paley, however, retained a belief in the combined power of 'listening ears' and 'a few hot human truthful words' in the creation and maintenance of community.[106] If her stories are about one thing it is the 'great' and unending 'social task' of 'speaking for others'.[107]

In order to understand what she means by this it is useful to look at Walter Benjamin's 1936 essay 'The Storyteller'. Benjamin thought that storytelling was a dying art, and that the literary 'short story' had 'removed itself' completely from the oral tradition. He does not say much more about the short story other than that it is a kind of 'abbreviated' storytelling, reliant, like the novel, on the solitary individual passing on 'information'. Of course, as we've seen most commentators on the short story want to distinguish between the kind of information provided by the empirically-driven novel and that provided by the symbolically transcendent short story. For Benjamin, however, both forms are connected by their attention to the 'pure essence of the thing'. Storytelling, on the other hand, he argues, is fluid and communal;

its purpose is neither information nor revelation, but rather the giving and receiving of 'counsel' or 'wisdom'. The storyteller, says Benjamin, is a kind of 'teacher or sage', but the 'useful' lessons that he or she offers are 'less an answer to a question than a proposal concerning the continuation of a story which is just unfolding'.[108] That emphasis on continuation and lack of resolution is what modern story collections like Leskov's (which Benjamin discusses) or Paley's try to reproduce.

The idea of a story continuing ('later the same day') means various different things to Paley. On the most obvious level – one that recalls O'Brien and others – it implies that no story is complete, for there are always other parts or points of view to be taken into account. Every truth is a 'floating truth'.[109] But the role she imagines for her storyteller-sage – which perhaps Benjamin shares – is part rabbinical narrator of parables and part Marxist dialectician. Her stories don't add to each other, they argue with each other without arriving at an answer. Ceasing is not an option, something that Paley emphasises in the surname of her recurrent narrator, Faith Darwin. Individual stories also stage arguments, not just between men and women, fathers and daughters, mothers and sons, friends, but also between comedy and tragedy, open form and closure, 'rotten rosy' optimism and 'gloomy gray' pessimism.[110] In approaching these matters, everyone speaks from their 'particular historical moment' as well as from their experience as a woman or a man and so, in Benjamin's terms, there is no answer beyond a proposal to continue the conversation.[111]

The narrator often gives her antagonist the more powerful argument, or finds herself chastised by another narrator, in another story. In 'A Conversation with My Father' the storyteller-daughter refuses to tell her father the tidily finished Maupassant-style story he desires. Her 'responsibility', she says firmly, is to her 'invention', and 'everyone, real or invented, deserves the open destiny of life'. Reading the story we incline to her point of view – that tightly closed form 'takes away all hope' – but then we notice that the conversation is set in a hospital room, that the father's lecture on writing is 'last-minute advice', and that his daughter lets him have the last word. Inserting oxygen tubes into his nose, as if to emphasise the point, he asks, 'How long will it be? ... Tragedy! You too. When will you look it in the face?'[112]

The title of Paley's second collection, *Enormous Changes at the Last Minute*, is partly a joke at the expense of the short story's characteristic reliance on revelation and epiphany. Raymond Carver pinned to his wall a three-by-five card inscribed with Chekhov's line, 'and suddenly every-thing became clear to him'.[113] For Paley, however, it is not consciousness that changes but life. Consider an example. 'Wants' is a very simple story, a single scene narrated with a spontaneous, anecdotal feel. A woman meets her ex-husband while she's sitting on the library steps about to return some books. He follows her inside and, while she's paying her fines, presents his theories about the 'dissolution' of their marriage. She decides to check out the books she'd just brought back and they leave. She sits back down on the library steps and he goes away. But there is more going on.

Paley once said that every story consists of at least two stories ('bumping into', and arguing with, each other).[114] 'Wants' is the story of three encounters – with the ex-husband, with the librarian and with the library books – and a number of contrasts are made. With the librarian, the transaction is simple, financial. Her books are eighteen years overdue so she owes $32 ($16 each). 'Immediately she trusted me, put my past behind her, wiped the record clean.' The ex-husband is not so easy to deal with. They had been married for twenty-seven years 'once' and she feels 'justified' in addressing him as 'my life'. The past that was behind her is now standing next to her on the street. His response is both to deny their history – 'no life of mine' – and to locate its turning point. 'In many ways, he said, as I look back, I attribute the dissolution of our marriage to the fact that you never invited the Bertrams to dinner.' The story does not pause to consider why he makes this claim. It doesn't matter even if, as the narrator concedes, it's 'possible'. But there are other possibilities too:

> ... really, if you remember: first my father was sick that Friday, then the children were born, then I had those Tuesday-night meetings, then the war began. Then we didn't seem to know them anymore. But you're right. I should have had them to dinner.

The turning point is over-determined to the point of absurdity. Did the marriage end because of a single Friday when the Bertrams would have been invited to dinner? And how does that one moment relate to events that take place over a longer span of time – having children, meetings on numerous Tuesdays, the Vietnam war?

The conversation slides easily from the past to the future: his second complaint about his ex-wife is that she 'didn't want anything'. He had 'wanted a sailboat' and he still 'may' get one; in fact, he has 'money down on an eighteen-foot two-rigger'. The eighteen, of course, recalls how long she had kept her library books, while the novels themselves (Edith Wharton's 1905 *The House of Mirth* and her 1928 *The Children*) suggest how the world, and a person's view of it, might change over the course of twenty-plus years.

The narrator, feeling accused, now enumerates her wants; not 'requests' or 'absolute requirements' but 'something'. 'Something', of course, turns out to be much more than a mere sailboat. She wants, 'for instance, to be a different person' (the kind that returns library books in two weeks, changes the school system and stops the war), but the 'for instance' undermines the desire from the start. And her wants even extend to the past conditional, to fantasy. 'I wanted to have been married forever to one person', she says, 'my ex-husband or my present one.'

The story ends by circling back to the moment before its beginning – to explain what took her to the library that morning after only eighteen years.

> Just this morning I looked out the window to watch the street for a while and saw that the little sycamores the city had dreamily planted a couple of years before the kids were born that day to the prime of their lives.
>
> Well! I decided to bring those two books back to the library. Which proves that when a person or an event comes along to jolt or appraise me I *can* take some appropriate action, although I am better known for my hospitable remarks.[115]

If Paley's narrators don't experience turning points at which everything becomes clear, they do have jolting points to move them along. But the appraisal which results can be understood to arise out of, or co-exist with, rather than to supersede, the hospitable remarks.

Endings

Like the patterned story, the patterned short story collection, as Faulkner noted, moves towards one end, one finale, a Meaning. Only when the sequence is complete can it be apprehended as a unified entity. Many short story sequences therefore conclude with a tale which reflects back on what came before and asks that its pattern be observed, even as the protagonists escape from its power. The final story in *The Things They Carried* is about how 'stories can save us', while *Jesus' Son* ends with

Fuckhead in rehab, smoking low-tar cigarettes and drinking instant coffee with low-fat milk.[116] He takes a break from AA to spy on a Mennonite couple, hoping, he says, to see them having sex. But what he really enjoys is 'seeing them in their living room' reading the Bible. One evening they quarrel until the man 'put an end to the argument by getting down before her and washing her feet'. From Jesus' Son to Jesus in eleven stories. He is learning to 'live sober' and so is the prose.[117]

But what if salvation just isn't possible? If writers can't imagine escape as possible, they sometimes entertain its possibility in the realm of fantasy or dream (analogues, of course, for fiction itself). Joyce's Dubliners look for 'doors of escape', but they remain thwarted by a sense of paralysis until, that is, the epiphany of the 'solid world' dissolving into the 'other world' that comes to Gabriel Conroy at the end of the concluding story, 'The Dead'.[118] The final story of Naylor's *The Women of Brewster Place* dissolves into a dream of liberation, in which the violent disjunctures of the previous six stories are repaired and resolved. The women come together to destroy the wall that had made their street and their lives a 'dead-end'. The sun breaks through, 'just like a miracle', and, in the dreamworld at least, the possibilities of collective action seem endless. 'Today Brewster – Tomorrow America' reads the banner.[119]

Drown and *Lost in the City* both end with stories that highlight the fact that stories inevitably select and distort reality. In 'Negocios', Yunior goes to a restaurant run by Nilda, the woman with whom his father had a second family while his first waited in Santo Domingo. Looking through the window, though, he realises that his father's alternative life was little different from the one had he left behind and, moreover, that his view of the situation was distorted by his own reflection:

> when I got there and stared through my reflection in the glass at the people inside, all of them versions of people I already knew, I decided to go home.[120]

This is the kind of embedded, allusive metafiction on which the realist short story relies. Looking through the glass at the autobiographical subject matter he is about to turn into fiction, Yunior recalls George Willard, looking out of the train window as he prepares to leave Winesburg and thinking that 'his life there had become but a background on which to paint the dreams of his manhood'.[121] The process is not identical – Yunior decides to go home not away – but like Willard, he recognises that projection and wish-fulfilment will play a part in his narrative. At the story's end, the collection's end, Yunior acknowledges that what he 'would like to think' happened is not the same as what he senses 'was more likely true'.[122]

Meanwhile, Marie, the protagonist of the final story in *Lost in the City*, is visited by a student who records her life story on a series of audio cassettes: 'Husband No. 1', 'Children', 'Working', 'Husband No. 2', 'Race Relations' and so on. Although she is charmed by the young man, she finds the experience 'stunning' for 'she had never in her whole life heard her own voice' and 'for a few moments before she found herself, her world turned upside down'. Like Díaz's mirroring window, the tape alters as it records. But while Díaz considers the implications of this for the artist, Jones explores what the combination of 'familiar and yet unfamiliar' might mean for 'the people inside'. Marie puts the tapes in a drawer. She knew 'that however long she lived, she would not ever again listen to them, for in the end, despite all that was on the tapes, she could not stand the sound of her own voice'.[123]

Paley's *Collected Stories* also ends self-reflexively, but her emphasis is not on the stories that have been told as much as those that remain to be told. The story is called 'Listening'. Rather a lot happens but finally, 'as often happens in stories, it was several years later'. Faith is driving in her car, eying up a handsome man as he crosses the street, when her friend Cassie turns to her and asks 'why don't you tell my story?' But Faith has no answer to the charge that she had neglected the 'woman-loving life', and can only ask Cassie to forgive her. The story, and the collection, ends with Cassie's accusatory reply: 'From now on, I'll watch you like a hawk. I do not forgive you.'[124] For a dialectician, failure is not sad but provocative.

Notes

1. Oates, 'An Endangered Species', p. 41.
2. Minot, 'Thanksgiving Day'; Spark (ed.), *20 Under 30*, pp. 259–69; Minot, *Monkeys*, pp. 23–39.
3. Minot, 'The Navigator', pp. 90–100; Walker (ed.), *The Graywolf Annual Two*, pp. 3–14; Dow and Regan (eds), *The Invisible Enemy*, pp. 3–14; Shirley (ed.), *The Beach Book*, pp. 198–211; Minot, *Monkeys*, pp. 91–108.
4. Editors also create collections. Philip Young arranged Hemingway's stories about Nick Adams chronologically in order to construct a 'meaningful narrative … closely paralleling the events of Hemingway's own life', ignoring the fact that such a narrative was exactly what Hemingway had tried to avoid. *The Nick Adams Stories*, pp. 5–6.

5. On the 'cycle', see discussions by Davis, Ingram, Mann and Nagel; on the 'composite', see Dunn and Morris, and Lundén. Reid talks about 'clusters' in *The Short Story*, p. 46. On 'sequences', see Kennedy, Nagel and Robert M. Luscher, 'The Short Story Sequence', in Lohafer and Clarey (eds), *Short Story Theory at a Crossroads*, pp. 148–67.

6. For example, Washington Irving's *The Sketch-Book of Geoffrey Crayon, Gent* (1820).

7. For example, Bernard Malamud's *Pictures of Fidelman: An Exhibition* (1969).

8. For example, Whitney Otto, *How to Make an American Quilt* (1992); Sylvia Watanbe, *Talking to the Dead* (1993). Critical discussions include Showalter, 'Piecing and Writing'; Dunn and Morris, *The Composite Novel*, pp. 23–5.

9. On MTV as modern quilting, see Mason, *Love Life*, pp. 1–18.

10. Segal, *Shakespeare's Kitchen*, pp. ix, xi. See also Ian Reid, 'Destabilizing Frames for Story', in Lohafer and Clarey (eds), *Short Story Theory at a Crossroads*, p. 301.

11. Vollmann, *The Atlas*, pp. xv–xvi

12. Munro, *Too Much Happiness*, pp. 49–50.

13. Winnie Chan, 'The Linked Excitements of L. T. Meade', in Harrington (ed.), *Scribbling Women*, p. 71.

14. Yagoda, *About Town*, pp. 374–6.

15. Yagoda, *About Town*, pp. 105–6, 227.

16. Charvat, *The Profession of Authorship*, pp. 90–1.

17. Faulkner, *The Faulkner–Cowley Files*, pp. 15–16.

18. Barth, *Lost in the Funhouse*, p. xi.

19. Gado, *Conversations with Writers*, p. 151.

20. Boddy, 'Unpublished Interview with Jayne Anne Phillips'.

21. Oates, 'An Endangered Species', p. 29.

22. Oates, *Where Are You Going, Where Have You Been?*, p. 521.

23. Weich, 'Charles Baxter Visits Old Friends'.

24. Oates, *Where Are You Going, Where Have You Been?*, p. 521. Hunter applies Deleuze and Guattari's concept of 'minor literature' to the short story. *The Cambridge Introduction to the Short Story in English*, p. 139.

25. Ross, 'Interview with Grace Paley', pp. 399–400.

26. Boddy, 'Unpublished Interview with Gloria Naylor'. See also Margot Kelley, 'Gender and Genre', in Brown (ed.), *American Women Short Story Writers*, pp. 295–310.

27. Plath (ed.), *Conversations with John Updike*, p. 193.

28. Bellamy, *The New Fiction*, p. 51; Barthelme, *Not-Knowing*, pp. 287, 224; Cheever, *Journals*, p. 13 and passim.

29. Weatherby, 'Turning Life Into Great Literature', p. 33. Miriam Marty Clark cited Carver's 'failure to write a novel' as evidence of his 'monological imagination'. 'Raymond Carver's Monological Imagination', p. 246.

30. Carver, *No Heroics, Please*, pp. 65–72; Gentry and Stull (eds), *Conversations with Raymond Carver*, p. 12 and passim; Sklenicka, *Raymond Carver*, pp. 163–4, 215, 339–40.

31. Clarke, 'Investing the Glimpse', p. 120; *Choice* review of Runyon, *Reading Raymond Carver*, quoted on cover.

32. J. Gerard Kennedy, 'From Anderson's *Winesburg* to Carver's *Cathedral*', in Kennedy (ed.), *Modern American Short Story Sequences*, p. 213.

33. Runyon, *Reading Raymond Carver*, p. 1; Kaplan and Dorr, *Luck Trust and Ketchup*.

34. Robert Altman, 'Corroborating with Carver', in Carver, *Short Cuts*, p. 7. Individual stories been adapted for films, notably 'So Much Water So Close to Home' (also part of *Short Cuts*) which formed the basis of *Jindabyne* (2006), dir. Ray Lawrence. See also Boddy, '*Short Cuts* and Long Shots'.

35. William Dean Howells, 'Some Anomalies of the Short Story', in Bungert (ed.), *Die Amerikanische Short Story: Theorie und Entwicklung*, p. 40.

36. Calisher, *Collected Stories*, p. ix.

37. Shaw, *The Short Story*, p. 200.

38. Barth, *The Development*, p. 7.

39. Moore, *Collected Stories*, p. 135.

40. Although *Anagrams* was originally sold as a novel, four of its component stories are included in Moore's *Collected Stories*; the fifth – a novella – is not.

41. Boddy, 'Unpublished Interview with Susan Minot'.

42. Weich, 'Charles Baxter Visits Old Friends'.

43. I am referring to the poem 'Thirteen Ways of Looking at a Blackbird' (1917) by Wallace Stevens and to Richard Yates's 1962 story collection, *Eleven Kinds of Loneliness*.

44. Irving, *The Sketch-Book*, p. 25.

45. Hemingway, *Selected Letters*, p. 480.

46. O'Brien, *The Things They Carried*, pp. 70, 77.

47. O'Brien, *The Things They Carried*, pp. 34, 20, 77, 33, 73, 80. A similar dynamic informs Thom Jones's Vietnam stories, although for him war functions largely as a metaphor for a more widespread violence. 'Roadrunner' and 'A Run Through the Jungle' (in *Sonny Liston Was a Friend of Mine*) revisit and revise our understanding of the recon unit described in 'Break on Through' and the title story of *The Pugilist at Rest*. The governing perspective of these stories is that of an ex-boxer called Hollywood. 'Fields of Purple Forever' allows one of the men he describes, Ondine, to give his own version of things.

48. O'Brien, *The Things They Carried*, pp. 15, 17.

49. O'Brien, *The Things They Carried*, p. 17.

50. Barth, *The Development*, p. 22.

51. Updike, *The Maples Stories*, p. 12.

52. Plath (ed.), *Conversations with John Updike*, p. 193. See Updike's 'The Day of Dying Rabbit', *Forty Stories*, pp. 267–76.

53. Updike, *The Maples Stories*, p. 201.

54. Updike, *The Maples Stories*, pp. 55, 57, 11, 68, 48, 158, 147.

55. Johnson, *Jesus' Son*, p. 37.

56. Johnson, *Jesus' Son*, pp. 39, 84, 51, 15, 105.

57. Johnson, *Jesus' Son*, pp. 133, 70, 3, 11.

58. Anderson, *The Story Teller's Story*, p. 309.

59. Johnson, *Jesus' Son*, p. 121.

60. Chávez, *The Last of the Menu Girls*, p. 190.

61. Reid, *The Short Story*, p. 50.

62. James Nagel, 'The American Short Story Cycle', in Gelfant (ed.), *The Columbia Companion*, p. 10.

63. An early British precedent for this kind of collection, itself influenced by Irving's *Sketch-Book*, is Mary Russell Mitford's *Our Village* (1824).

64. Zagarell, 'Narratives of Community', p. 513.

65. Nagel, *The Contemporary American Short-Story Cycle*, p. 255.
66. Nagel, *The Contemporary American Short-Story Cycle*, p. 21.
67. Tan, *The Opposite of Fate*, p. 304.
68. Hertha Wong, 'Louise Erdrich's *Love Medicine*', in Kennedy (ed.), *Modern American Short Story Sequences*, p. 174.
69. Jewett, *Novels and Stories*, pp. 444, 377.
70. Zagarell, 'Narratives of Community', p. 513.
71. Cheever, *The Stories*, p. 215.
72. Jones, *Lost in the City*, pp. 66, 104, 136, 229, 134.
73. Johnson, *The Very Telling*, p. 84.
74. Jones, *Lost in the City*, pp. 8, 11–12, 232, 241.
75. Jones, *Lost in the City*, pp. 79, 9, 25, 4, 45, 79, 93.
76. Díaz, *Drown*, pp. 23, 68, 164.
77. Hofmann, 'Sex, Drugs and Rotten Roles', p. 38; Reid, 'On the Move', p. 23.
78. Zeledón, 'Dominican Dominion'
79. Reid, 'On the Move', p. 23.
80. See Stavans (ed.), *Becoming American*.
81. Rumbaut, 'The Agony of Exile', p. 61.
82. Pérez Firmat, *Life on the Hyphen*, pp. 4–5.
83. Díaz, *Drown*, pp. 56, 61, 20.
84. Boddy, 'Unpublished interview with Junot Díaz'.
85. Irving, *The Sketch-Book*, pp. 14–15.
86. Jen, *Typical American* p. 124.
87. Díaz, *Drown*, p. 113.
88. Boddy, 'Unpublished interview with Junot Díaz'.
89. Wood, 'Metaphysical Parenting', p. 21.
90. Díaz, *Drown*, p. 53; Wood, Review of *Drown*, p. 39.
91. Wroe, 'Breached Barrios', p. 55.
92. Boddy, 'Unpublished interview with Junot Díaz'.
93. Stanton, 'Junot Díaz', pp. 26–38.
94. Díaz, *Drown*, p. 99.
95. Díaz, *Drown*, pp. 101, 84.
96. Díaz, *Drown*, pp. 45, 52.
97. Díaz, 'Nilda', p. 97.
98. Díaz, *Drown*, pp. 46–7.
99. Wood, Review of *Drown*, p. 39.
100. Díaz, *Drown*, pp. 114, 58.
101. Bach and Hall (eds), *Conversations with Grace Paley*, p. 217.
102. Paley, quoted in Nasso (ed.), *Contemporary Authors*, p. 533.
103. Paley, *Collected Stories*, p. 248.
104. Chambers, *Story and Situation*, p. 33. See Barthelme, *Not-Knowing*, pp. 52–92; Wilde, *Middle Ground*, pp. 173–87.
105. Gass, *In the Heart of the Heart of the Country*, p. xiii.
106. Paley, *Collected Stories*, pp. 17, 313.
107. Bach and Hall (eds), *Conversations with Grace Paley*, p. 35.
108. Benjamin, 'The Storyteller', pp. 83–109.
109. Paley, *Collected Stories*, pp. 119–30.
110. Paley, *Collected Stories*, pp. 245–6.

111. Bach and Hall (eds), *Conversations with Grace Paley*, p. 87.
112. Paley, *Collected Stories*, pp. 237–43.
113. Carver, *Collected Stories*, p. 729.
114. Bach and Hall (eds), *Conversations with Grace Paley*, pp. 169, 85–6.
115. Paley, *Collected Stories*, pp. 133–5.
116. O'Brien, *The Things They Carried*, p. 221.
117. Johnson, *Jesus' Son*, pp. 154, 158.
118. Joyce, *Dubliners*, pp. 11, 176.
119. Naylor, *The Women of Brewster Place*, pp. 188, 186.
120. Díaz, *Drown*, p. 163.
121. Anderson, *Winesburg, Ohio*, p. 138.
122. Díaz, *Drown*, p. 164.
123. Jones, *Lost in the City*, pp. 238, 243.
124. Paley, *Collected Stories*, p. 398.

Conclusion

The short story often begins with 'familiar material':

> Oh yes, the reader says: a couple quarrelling in a sidewalk restaurant, a nine-year-old boy stealing a Scripto in Woolworth's, a woman crying in the bathtub. We've seen that before. We know where we are. Don't give us details; we don't need them. What we need is surprise, a quick turning of the wrist toward texture, or wisdom, something suddenly broken or quickly repaired. Yes, we know these people. Now just tell us what they do.[1]

Since 1950 the American short story has worked on many different kinds of familiar material and in a variety of ways, 'violating' expectations and undermining 'stock scenes', demanding that its readers question ideas and situations that might otherwise be 'taken for granted'.[2]

Satire's fondness for surprise violation, which attracted it to the short story from the outset, is a recurrent note in contemporary fiction. T. C. Boyle often begins with a recognisable type ('The Hit Man' or 'The Love of My Life') or a topical received opinion, such as that abortion is 'Killing Babies', and reduces it to violent absurdity.[3] In 'My Amendment', George Saunders uses a pun to expose the assumptions that lie behind objections to same-sex marriage. What if, instead of the law making an amendment to suit people, people amended themselves to suit the law? Otherwise, asks his narrator, 'what will we have?'

> A nation ruled by the anarchy of unconstrained desire. A nation of wilful human hearts, each lurching this way and that, reaching out for whatever it spontaneously desires, totally unconcerned about the external form in which that desired thing is embodied.
>
> That is not the kind of world in which I wish to live.[4]

Saunders's stories tend to exaggerate to the point of dystopia some familiar aspect of our late capitalist world before introducing a character who voices, either sincerely or in horror, an alternative vision of enlightened (or at least 'light-craving') individuality.[5] In this way, he presents the kind of world in which he wishes to live: a liberal democracy characterised by 'a bunch of shouting voices, most of them wrong' and the 'radical spreading-around of our good fortune'.[6] Like Flannery O'Connor, he is keen to distinguish between 'twisted, false' gods and the 'true God', but that's where the similarity ends. O'Connor would surely not have had much truck with the 'gentler and more generous GOD within us' that Saunders hopes to release.[7]

The suburban world of A. M. Homes is also shot in vivid and gaudy colours. Developing Cheever's surrealist side, she is less concerned with the 'reticence' of suburban sadness (for that, see Jhumpa Lahiri) than with the sexual fantasies it conceals.[8] Her first collection, *The Safety of Objects* (1991), took the enduring dream of American suburbia – 'the whole family is always in the car together, going places, singing songs, eating McDonald's' – and gave it a quick turn of the wrist.[9] With their children away, feeling like 'off-duty parole officers', the parents in 'Adults Alone' go wild, only to be 'relieved' when the kids come home. In 'Jim Train', a man who is forced to stay home from work for two days, finds himself 'not himself' and decides that 'if they cancel it again tomorrow he will go in anyway'. To 'anchor' themselves, Homes's characters rely on tiny rituals – a daily pee in the boss's plant pot, walking home a certain way, 'suspending' life by hiding in the linen closet – and the confining yet comforting 'safety' of their relationships with objects. Elaine, who 'feels like she's been having an extramarital relationship with their house', leaves her children in Florida ('like they're dry cleaning'), flying home with oranges instead. Cheryl is nicknamed 'Chunky' after her favourite chocolate bar. Jenny's brother loses his virginity to her Barbie doll, and then, more satisfyingly, to Ken. Esther dreams of a burglar who will 'take the things that make me who I am, and then I would be able to be someone else'.[10] Yet, more often than not, life returns to 'normal', to what it was before and perhaps will always be. The kids come home, the job is still there, Barbie keeps smiling, Chunky stops masturbating in the garden and goes to help her mother unpack the groceries.

In recent years, partly in response to the 'linguistic turn' of deconstruction and identity politics (the short story's university base means that it is never far away from academic trends), writers have used its constricted form to uncover and undermine the constrictions imposed by particular identities and discourses. Toni Morrison's only published short story, 'Recitatif', was 'an experiment', she said, 'in the removal of all racial codes from a narrative about two characters of different races for whom racial identity is crucial.'[11] Twyla tells the tale of her relationship with Roberta, whom she met when both girls were eight and temporary residents at a children's home. They look 'like salt and pepper', but we are never told which is which.[12] The aim of the story is not so much to remove racial codes as to expose the 'lazy' and 'predictable' ways in which readers locate and interpret those codes.[13] Twyla and Roberta meet five times (according to the story's musical pattern) and on each occasion, Morrison tempts us to fall into the trap of stereotype, to characterise a 'whole other race' rather than an individual. Finally, their conversation turns to an incident from their time at the home, when some girls kicked the 'kitchen woman', Maggie, down the stairs. They can't agree about 'what happened' to Maggie nor to what race the mute and 'sandy-coloured' woman' with 'legs like parentheses' belonged. But Maggie exists as more than a 'floating signifier'; she silently demands that Morrison's readers, like Roberta and Twyla, think about her as a person.[14]

The problem of naming and reading identity is also the subject of Andrea Lee's 'Anthropology'. The story is narrated by a woman writer with interruptions from her academic anthropologist cousin. He is cross because she published a magazine article 'about quilts and superstitions' and their family in North Carolina. Moreover, she 'called them black'. To her retort – 'they *are* black' – he lectures her that 'they don't choose to define themselves that way'. 'It's not your place to tell them who they are.' She smiles because the phrase he uses – 'not your place' – is a family 'heirloom', a sign of how difficult it is to escape the terms (and the places) which formed you. When she challenges him – 'what would you have called them?' – he responds with an 'exasperated laugh', for there is no way of talking about race in America that doesn't, in some way or other, keep people in 'their own niches'. In the shadow of this debate is the question of how these 'always travelling' young people can talk about places and identities they have left behind. 'Roots' is a 'shameful' and 'spurious seventies term', evoking 'fat black American tourists in Alex Haley tour buses'; 'folkways' brings on an ironic recital of Jean Toomer. The parenthesised rhetorical question with which the story ends – 'it doesn't make a damn bit of difference, does it?' – invites us to ask what might make a difference.[15]

The anthropological questions that preoccupied the short story at the turn of the twentieth century – who is speaking? in whose language? for whom? – returned with force at the turn of the twenty-first. What, for instance, did it mean for Sherman Alexie to publish a story in the *New Yorker* whose opening sentence announced that 'Indians have to work hard to keep secrets from hungry white folks'? The narrator of 'What You Pawn I Will Redeem', a Spokane Indian living rough on the streets of Seattle, begins aggressively by challenging his audience – 'I probably don't interest you' – and telling them just what he is not going to talk about. 'I'm not going to let you know', for example, 'how scared I get sometimes of history and its ways.' Of course, in the act of denying he'll 'let you know', Jackson Jackson does let 'you' know. He then proceeds to tell a 'whole story' about his quest to retrieve his grandmother's powwow-dance regalia from a pawnshop. The shop keeper gives him twenty-four hours to come up with $999. Alexie then switches to countdown mode as Jackson rushes around, spending, on others, exactly as much as he accumulates ('it's an Indian thing'). What can happen now? The story's answer is to shift into magical realism. Jackson can't find the pawnshop until it emerges before him 'like a ghostship'. He has entered an alternative (better) world in which the pawnbroker, who now looks 'a little younger than he had', agrees to sell him the regalia for $5. Jackson wraps himself in its folds and steps off the pavement. Pedestrians and cars stop and so does time, as he becomes his 'grandmother, dancing'.[16] Jackson may not have given the 'hungry white folks' the secrets of history, but he is willing to share with them his dream of redemption from history.

By the late 1990s, 'thanks to multiculturalism', Gish Jen noted, 'the laundry list of topics a story could be about – man versus nature, coming of age, et cetera' expanded 'to include "being between worlds".' Very quickly, however, 'multiculturalism-as-publishing-phenomenon' became a 'pigeon-hole and albatross'. 'Minority writers like me, once marooned by prejudice, now find ourselves marooned again by identity politics'.[17] Against this, Jen's fiction explores the way that 'all the groups in America have rubbed off on each other'.[18] In 'Who's Irish?' a Chinese woman struggles to understand her daughter's lazy Irish husband and wild granddaughter. When her daughter complains that she is not supportive, she is bamboozled: 'we do not have this word in Chinese, *supportive*'.[19] The story enacts a 'boundary crossing' in which the question of who's Irish or Chinese collapses in the face of the shared generational identity of grandmothers.[20]

The discourses of race and ethnicity are not, of course, the only constrictions that the short story tries to expose or transcend. Annie Proulx's 'Brokeback Mountain' asks what it might have been like to be a cowboy in love with another cowboy in 1960s Wyoming. It's not about embracing a 'gay' or 'queer' identity (as one might have done at that time in San Francisco or New York), it's about recognising that 'if you can't fix it you've got to stand it'. Like 'What You Pawn', the story was published in the *New Yorker*, and like Alexie, Proulx offers the magazine's readers a case study of both illiberal provincialism and utopian compensation (in Proulx's case, a 'moment' of 'artless charmed happiness' in an almost 'pretend' pastoral haven).[21]

Psychiatric categories can be just as claustrophobic. In Z. Z. Packer's 'Drinking Coffee Elsewhere', when Dr Raeburn tells Dina that she's suffering from a 'crisis of identity', she responds 'Oh, is that what this is?' Her first-person narrative takes us beyond the label.[22] No such liberation is possible in David Foster Wallace's 'The Depressed Person'. The eponymous protagonist remains a prisoner of a psychotherapeutic discourse which tries to explain away her suffering in terms of the 'Blame Game' she plays, or the 'Healthy Eating Lifestyles' camp, 'Quiet Time' and 'Support System' she requires.[23] But for 'all that is said about her', 'the depressed person' cannot be contained in these terms – something Foster Wallace formally suggests in the way the story overflows into footnotes. Form is the only way in which depression can be expressed, however; neither she nor the narrator can 'articulate' her 'terrible and unceasing pain'. Like 'Bartleby', and so many other stories, this is a tale about a tale that can't be told.

For Lorrie Moore, the problem with language is not so much that it is inadequate or coercive as that it won't hold still. That, of course, is also its great liberating power. 'People Like That Are The Only People Here' is about the way in which 'The Mother', who is also 'The Writer', responds to the cancer diagnosis and treatment of 'The Baby'. Wit is always the first weapon that Moore's characters deploy in times of trouble and The Mother/Writer is an expert at slips of sound and sense. 'Goodbye' becomes 'could cry', while 'paediatric oncology' is easier as 'Peed Onk'. But it's not only bad puns that allow the writer to escape from the hospital. What the doctors call 'blood in the diaper' is for her something 'like tiny mouse heart packed in snow'. Such similes are rare and fleeting as Moore holds off sentimentality, framing and interrupting the tale with the constant admonition of 'The Husband' to 'take notes' for they are going to 'need the money'.[24]

Like Homes and Foster Wallace, Moore targets the promises of the self-improvement industry – exemplified by books with titles such as *Get Real, Smarting Cookie, Get Real* and *Why I Hate Myself*.[25] Her early stories offered 'guides' to divorce or 'the tenor of love' and advised on such matters as 'How to Talk to Your Mother (Notes)', 'How to be a Writer' ('First, try to be something, anything, else.') and 'How to be Another Woman'. A story called 'How' offers alternatives at every stage in its account of a woman's restless romance, but they exist simply to show how little – after 'a week, a month, a year' – 'choices' really matter. You might 'begin by meeting him in a class, in a bar' or 'at a rummage sale', and you might end by never seeing him again or 'perhaps' you will. You might feel 'sadness' or 'indifference'. 'One of those endings', the story wearily concludes.[26] Human vulnerability does not conform to self-help's optimistically linear narrative. But Moore's jokes, comparisons and aphorisms rely as much on the reader recognising herself as do the self-help books they supplant. Stories, she suggests, are the 'lozenge of pretend' we allow ourselves when faced with pain, disappointment, and, so often in her work, the immanence of disease and death.[27]

For all that Moore and Foster Wallace's smart-alecky 'jazzing around' is seen as an alternative to the 'grim' taciturnity offered by the 'Resurrection of Realism', both remain committed to what Foster Wallace calls 'passionately moral fiction' and what for Moore are 'those moments in which we help each other out'.[28] Homes, too, was only partly joking when she entitled a collection of stories, *Things You Should Know*. The difference is perhaps more one of tone than of ideology. The 'small joys' that Moore's stories provide are often 'theatrical' or 'possessed of great silliness', especially when women get together with each other.[29] If Carver's characters compulsively rake leaves and Foster Wallace's compulsively digress, Moore's can't stop telling jokes or breaking into show tunes. 'Dance in America' begins with a paragraph describing the capacity of dance to be, among other things, 'life flipping death the bird'. Lest we are too easily convinced, the next paragraph begins, 'I make this stuff up'. But the sentence that follows then qualifies that debunking as the narrator confesses that she sometimes believes her own 'rented charisma' and 'jerry-rigged authority'.[30] The story – about a dance teacher's visit to an old friend whose son has cystic fibrosis – is all about negotiating what Foster Wallace called the risk of 'the yawn, the rolled eyes, the cool smile, the nudged ribs, the parody of gifted ironists, the "Oh how *banal*".'³¹ By the end of the story she is not only 'telling' others about the 'dancing body's magnificent and ostentatious scorn', she is enacting it herself as she and the boy 'dip-glide-slide' to the suitably banal and perfectly-titled Kenny Loggins hit, 'This Is It'. The charisma is genuine. Moore's characters are not consoled by insights, but by actions (life lived 'from the neck down').³² In 'The Juniper Tree', a ghost called Robin pushes a lemon meringue pie into her own face and then tastes it. 'I've always wanted to do that', she says, 'and now I have.' She waves goodbye to her friend with her 'one pie-free hand' and tells her 'Onward'.³³

Again and again, we've seen the short story stage a struggle between familiar discourse and itself. That discourse may be that of stereotype or social control, or it may just be the clichéd language in which we generally conduct our lives – whether in the form of sociological 'distortions' (O'Connor), 'statistical reports' (Cheever), 'authorative accounts delivered by an expert' (Barthelme), the 'sort of words used on TV shows' (Carver) or self-help (Moore *et al.*). The short story tells us how powerful and pervasive such discourses are, but it also, usually, suggests that it can help us break free, if only for a moment.

The protagonist of Deborah Eisenberg's 'Some Other, Better Otto' is an acerbic, middle-class, middle-aged man who displaces his unhappiness into a pedantic distress at the misuse of language. William, his loving and extremely tolerant partner, drives him particularly crazy by uttering banal phrases such as 'everyone is so alone'. 'This is unbearable', he screeches at one point before collapsing into guilt at his pettiness, 'I've spent the best years of my life with a man who doesn't know how to use the word "and".' Otto is proudly if unhappily 'literal minded', unlike his schizophrenic sister, Sharon. She has a 'tremendous capacity for metaphor', that is, he says, 'a tremendous sensitivity to the deeper structures of the universe'. Over the course of forty-three pages, Otto approaches and shies away from the kind of sensitivity that would let him experience life as not merely 'arbitrary' and 'cruel'. Might a 'monumental effort' allow his 'errant and enslaved' self to be 'purified to an unmarked essence' and bring 'true freedom'? He tries to catch the eye of an 'actually attractive' baby and to signal 'let's you and I communicate in a manner far superior to the verbal one'. But the 'baby ignored him ... see if he cared'. Eisenberg presents a moving picture of 'life with its humorous theatricality', but finally she, too, seems to think that this is not quite enough. The story ends with William coming to find Otto, who

has been brooding in the 'clean, dim kitchen'. But then, a full moon rises
and it becomes a clean, well-lighted place.

> He blinked up at William, whose face, shadowed against the night
> sky, was as inflected, as ample in mystery as the face in the moon.
> 'It's late, my darling,' Otto said, 'I'm tired. What are we doing down
> here?'[34]

As in the case of Carver's 'Intimacy', the introduction of the moon is
a knowing trick, an example of the have-your-cake-and-eat-it attitude
we have come to call post-modern. At first Otto's epiphany seems to be
anti-transcendent, if no longer literal-minded – there is 'ample mystery'
in daily life. But the introduction of ambiguity into his final question – is
he talking about being in the kitchen or being in the world? – allows us,
if we're that way inclined, to glimpse transcendence.

The challenge to the short story is whether it can do without the
resonance and 'ramified implications' of such moments – what Moore
calls the 'makeshift construction of holiness' – and still retain what Poe
called an 'air of consequence'.[35] One writer who takes up that challenge
– perhaps because she's looking to Kafka and the meditative essay rather
than to Poe – is Lydia Davis. Davis's stories rarely offer any distraction from a witty yet rigorous investigation of the ways in which words
constrain and confuse. What is it, they ask, to be 'the mother' or 'the
daughter', 'the husband' or 'the wife', or even 'wife one' or 'wife two'?[36]
How might one distinguish between 'two types', 'excitable' and 'phleg-
matic'?[37] What does it mean to be 'Right and Wrong', 'Interesting', or
'Selfish'?[38] Can 'the angry man' really be the same person as 'the playful
man', 'the serious man' and 'the patient man'?[39]

A recurring concern for Davis is the difference between how one
appears to oneself and to others. One narrator realises that the gap
between the way 'A Friend of Mine' sees herself and how others see
her also applies to herself; another, with 'Almost No Memory', reads
old notebooks and wonders 'how much they were of her and how much
they were outside her'.[40] The protagonist of 'Five Signs of Disturbance'
distinguishes herself from 'her voice', which she fears 'will communicate something no one will want to listen to'.[41] What 'if I were not me
and overheard me from below, as a neighbor,' thinks one narrator, while
another worries that someone learning that she has 'A Position at the
University' will think she is 'the sort of person who has a position at the
university', whereas 'a complete description of me would include truths

that seem quite incompatible with the fact that I have a position at the university.'[42] Identities are the slipperiest of things and the process of 'breaking it down' leads to no turning or end-point; not even a 'small release' is offered.[43] Life is always 'unfinished business'.[44]

Supremely self-conscious, Davis's work is most moving when, like Moore's, it reveals the cost of that self-consciousness. What a relief it would be, thinks one character, if, after all, 'what I feel is not very important'. 'The Professor' dreams of marrying a cowboy because she is 'tired of so much thinking'. 'I thought that when my mind, always so busy, always going around in circles, always having an idea and then an idea about an idea, reached out to his mind, it would meet something quieter ...' She says this on the third page of her story; by page 9, after many 'ideas about ideas', the 'daydream' collapses. The story must either 'end, or begin' (and that very ambiguity opens up a whole other series of questions about questions) with her husband and herself 'standing awkwardly there in front of the ranch house, waiting while the cowboy prepared our room'.[45] In 'Getting Better', a mother smacks her child, puts him to bed, reads a magazine, has a nap, goes to the bathroom where she can't look at herself in the mirror, does the dishes and sits for a bit before going to bed, telling herself that perhaps things were getting better. Brooks and Penn Warren wouldn't have recognised this as a story for there is no 'denouement' (the 'point at which the fate of the character is clear ... or, perhaps, the moment when the character comprehends his own final position'), and no moment of 'illumination' which 'brings into focus all previous events and interprets all previous events' and 'contains within itself, by implication at least, the total meaning of the story'.[46] And yet something of consequence is achieved, through rhythm as well as sense. By witnessing the 'writer's stutter', says Davis, the reader becomes 'witness' to her emotions and to her 'process', the workings of her mind and finally, to 'what we might think of as the origin', if not the end, of her writing.[46] Her story closes with the narrator's reflection that 'this day had been better than the day before, and the day before had been better than most of last week, though not much better'.[48] The next day awaits and, with it, the next story.

Notes

1. Charles Baxter, 'Afterword', in Shapard and Thomas (eds), *Sudden Fiction*, p. 229.
2. Lahiri, *Unaccustomed Earth*, pp. 27, 273; Lethem, *Men and Cartoons*, p. 2.
3. Boyle, *Stories*, pp. 365–9; Boyle, *After the Plague*, pp. 43–65; 121–39
4. Saunders, *In Persuasion Nation*, in *The Brief and Frightening Reign of Phil*, pp. 176, 178.
5. Saunders, *In Persuasion Nation*, in *The Brief and Frightening Reign of Phil*, p. 358.
6. Saunders, *In Persuasion Nation*, in *The Brief and Frightening Reign of Phil*, pp. 120, 261.
7. Saunders, *CivilWarLand in Bad Decline*, p. 64; Saunders, *In Persuasion Nation*, in *The Brief and Frightening Reign of Phil*, p. 302.
8. Lahiri, *Unaccustomed Earth*, p. 23.
9. Homes, *The Safety of Objects*, p. 18.
10. Homes, *The Safety of Objects*, pp. 19, 33, 85, 59, 111, 16, 15, 117.
11. Morrison, *Playing in the Dark*, p. xi.
12. Toni Morrison, 'Recitatif', in Major (ed.), *Calling the Wind*, pp. 438–53.
13. Morrison, *Playing in the Dark*, p. xi.
14. Abel, 'Black Writing, White Reading', p. 103.
15. Lee, *Interesting Women*, pp. 68–84.
16. Alexie, *Ten Little Indians*, pp. 169–94.
17. Jen, 'Who's to Judge?', pp. 18–19.
18. Partridge, *Beyond Literary Chinatown*, p. 170.
19. Jen, *Who's Irish?*, pp. 3–16.
20. Lee, 'Gish Jen', p. 229. See Prasad (ed.), *Mixed* for more boundary 'blurring'.
21. Proulx, *Close Range*, pp. 311–12.
22. Packer, *Drinking Coffee Elsewhere*, p. 117.
23. Foster Wallace, *Brief Interviews with Hideous Men*, pp. 31–58.
24. Moore, *Collected Stories*, pp. 239–71.
25. Moore, *Collected Stories*, p. 436.
26. Moore, *Collected Stories*, pp. 565–73.
27. Moore, *Anagrams*, p. 225.
28. Foster Wallace, *Girl with Curious Hair*, pp. 267, 265; Foster Wallace, *Consider the Lobster*, p. 274; Gardner, 'Moore's Better Blues'.
29. Moore, *Collected Stories*, p. 356; Gardner, 'Moore's Better Blues'.
30. Moore, *Collected Stories*, p. 93.
31. Foster Wallace, *A Supposedly Fun Thing*, p. 81.
32. Moore, *Collected Stories*, p. 423.
33. Moore, *Collected Stories*, p. 22
34. Eisenberg, *Twilight of the Superheroes*, pp. 43–88.
35. Lohafer, *Coming to Terms with the Short Story*, p. 97; Moore, *Collected Stories*, p. 246; Poe, *Essays and Reviews*, p. 13.
36. Davis, *Break It Down*, pp. 79, 82–3, 119; Davis, *Almost No Memory*, p. 32.
37. Davis, *Varieties of Disturbance*, p. 25.
38. Davis, *Samuel Johnson is Indignant*, pp. 129, 48, 138.
39. Davis, *Almost No Memory*, p. 82.
40. Davis, *Almost No Memory*, pp. 116, 134.
41. Davis, *Break It Down*, p. 167.

42. Davis, *Almost No Memory*, pp. 167, 180.
43. Davis, *Break It Down*, p. 20; Ford, *A Multitude of Sins*, p. 30.
44. Davis, *Break It Down*, p. 18.
45. Davis, *Almost No Memory*, pp. 150, 17–26.
46. Brooks and Penn Warren, *Understanding Fiction*, pp. 583, 577.
47. Davis, 'Form as Response to Doubt'.
48. Davis, *Varieties of Disturbance*, p. 190.

Bibliography

Primary Sources

Alexie, Sherman, *The Toughest Indian in the World* (London: Vintage, 1991).
Alexie, Sherman, *Ten Little Indians* (London: Vintage, 2005).
Anderson, Sherwood, *Winesburg, Ohio* (New York: Norton, 1996).
Barth, John, *Lost in the Funhouse* (New York: Bantam Books, 1969).
Barth, John, *The Development* (Boston, MA: Houghton Mifflin, 2008).
Barthelme, Donald, *The Dead Father* (New York: Pocket Books, 1976).
Barthelme, Donald, *Sixty Stories* (London: Secker and Warburg, 1989).
Barthelme, Donald, *Forty Stories* (London: Futura, 1989).
Barthelme, Donald, *The Teachings of Don B.* (Berkeley, CA: Counterpoint, 1992).
Barthelme, Donald, *Flying to America* (Berkeley, CA: Counterpoint, 2007).
Bausch, Richard, *Aren't You Happy for Me?* (London: Macmillan 1995).
Bausch, Richard (ed.), *Best New American Voices 2008* (Boston, MA: Houghton Mifflin, 2008).
Beattie, Ann, *Park City* (New York: Vintage, 1999).
Bellow, Saul, *Collected Stories* (London: Penguin, 2001).
Bellamy, Joe David (ed.), *Superfiction* (New York: Vintage, 1975).
Bezmozgis, David, *Natasha* (London: Jonathan Cape, 2004).
Bishop, Elizabeth, *Collected Prose* (New York: Farrar, Straus & Giroux, 1984).
Boyle, T. C., *Stories* (New York: Penguin, 1999).
Boyle, T. C., *After the Plague* (New York: Penguin, 2001).
Brautigan, Richard, *Revenge of the Lawn* (Edinburgh: Canongate, 2006).
Brooks, Cleanth and Penn Warren, R. (eds), *Understanding Fiction* (New York: F. S. Crofts, 1943).
Brooks, Cleanth and Penn Warren, R. (eds), *Understanding Fiction*, 2nd edn (New York: Appleton-Century-Crofts, 1959).
Cable, George W., *Old Creole Days* (London: Hodder and Stoughton, 1943).
Calisher, Hortense, *Collected Stories* (New York: Arbor House, 1975).
Carver, Raymond (ed.), *The Best American Short Stories 1986* (Boston, MA: Houghton Mifflin, 1986).

Carver, Raymond and Jenks, Tom (eds), *American Short Story Masterpieces* (New York: Doubleday, 1987).

Carver, Raymond, *A New Path to the Waterfall* (London: Collins Harvill, 1989).

Carver, Raymond, *No Heroics, Please* (London: Collins Harvill, 1991).

Carver, Raymond, *Short Cuts* (London: Harvill Press, 1993).

Carver, Raymond, *Collected Stories* (New York: Library of America, 2009).

Chabon, Michael, *A Model World* (London: Hodder and Stoughton, 1991).

Chabon, Michael (ed.), *McSweeney's Mammoth Treasury of Thrilling Tales* (London: Hamish Hamilton, 2003).

Chabon, Michael, *Wonder Boys* (London: Harper Perennial, 2006).

Chávez, Denise, *The Last of the Menu Girls* (Houston, TX: Arte Público Press, 1986).

Cheever, John, *The Stories* (Harmondsworth: Penguin, 1982).

Coover, Robert, *Pricksongs and Descants* (London: Picador, 1973).

Coover, Robert (ed.), 'Minute Stories', *TriQuarterly*, 35 (Winter 1976).

Davis, Lydia, *Break It Down* (New York: Farrar, Straus & Giroux, 1996).

Davis, Lydia, *Almost No Memory* (New York: Farrar, Straus & Giroux, 1997).

Davis, Lydia, *Samuel Johnson is Indignant* (New York: McSweeney's, 2001).

Davis, Lydia, *Varieties of Disturbance* (New York: Farrar, Straus & Giroux, 2007).

Díaz, Junot, *Drown* (London: Faber, 1996).

Díaz, Junot, 'Nilda', *New Yorker*, 4 October 1999, pp. 92–7.

Dixon, Stephen, *The Stories* (New York: Henry Holt, 1994).

Dolmetch, Carl R. (ed.), *The Smart Set* (New York: The Dial Press, 1966).

Dow, Miriam and Regan, Jennifer (eds), *The Invisible Enemy* (Saint Paul, MN: Graywolf, 1989).

Eisenberg, Deborah, *Twilight of the Superheroes* (New York: Farrar, Straus & Giroux, 2006).

Farrell, James T., *The Short Stories* (New York: The Universal Library, 1962).

Ford, Richard, *Rock Springs* (London: Flamingo, 1989).

Ford, Richard (ed.), *The Granta Book of the American Short Story* (London: Granta, 1992).

Ford, Richard, *A Multitude of Sins* (London: Harvill, 2001).

Ford, Richard (ed.), *The New Granta Book of the American Short Story* (London: Granta, 2007).

Foster Wallace, David, *Girl with Curious Hair* (London: Abacus, 1997).

Foster Wallace, David, *Brief Interviews with Hideous Men* (London: Abacus, 2000).

Gaitskill, Mary (ed.), *Best New American Voices 2009* (Boston, MA: Houghton Mifflin, 2009).

Gass, William H., *Willie Master's Lonesome Wife*, *TriQuarterly Supplement*, 2 (1968).

Gass, William H., *In the Heart of the Heart of the Country* (Boston, MA: Nonpareil Books, 1981).

Harte, Bret, *Barker's Luck* (Cambridge, MA: Riverside Press, 1896).

Harte, Bret, *The Luck of Roaring Camp* (London: Penguin, 2001).

Hawthorne, Nathaniel, *Tales and Sketches* (New York: Library of America, 1982).

Hemingway, Ernest, *The Nick Adams Stories* (New York: Scribner, 1972).

Hemingway, Ernest, *The Complete Short Stories* (New York: Scribner, 1998).

Hempel, Amy, *Collected Stories* (New York: Scribner, 2006).

Hoffman, Alice (ed.), *Best of the Fiction Workshops 1997* (New York: Scribner, 1997).

Homes, A. M., *The Safety of Objects* (New York: Vintage, 1991).

Irving, Washington, *The Sketch-Book of Geoffrey Crayon, Gent* (Oxford: Oxford University Press, 2009).

Iweala, Uzodinma, 'Dance Cadaverous', *Granta*, 97 (2007), 195–212.

Jen, Gish, *Who's Irish?* (London: Granta, 1999).

Jewett, Sarah Orne, *Novels and Stories* (New York: The Library of America, 1994).

Johnson, Denis, *Jesus' Son* (London: Methuen, 2004).

Jones, Edward P., *Lost in the City* (New York: Amistad, 2003).

Jones, Thom, *The Pugilist at Rest* (London: Faber, 1994).

Jones, Thom, *Sonny Liston was a Friend of Mine* (London: Faber, 1999).

King, Stephen (ed.), *The Best American Short Stories 2007* (Boston, MA: Houghton Mifflin, 2007).

Klinkowitz, Jerome and Somer, John (eds), *Innovative Fiction* (New York: Dell, 1972).

Lahiri, Jhumpa, *Interpreter of Maladies* (London: Flamingo, 1999).

Lahiri, Jhumpa, *Unaccustomed Earth* (London: Bloomsbury, 2009).

Lee, Andrea, *Interesting Women* (London: Fourth Estate, 2002).

Lethem, Jonathan, *Men and Cartoons* (London: Faber, 2005).

Lish, Gordon (ed.), *All Our Secrets Are the Same* (New York: Norton, 1976).

Major, Clarence (ed.), *Calling the Wind: Twentieth-Century African-American Short Stories* (New York: HarperCollins, 1993).

Malamud, Bernard, *Complete Stories* (New York: Farrar, Straus & Giroux, 1997).

Mason, Bobbie Ann, *Shiloh* (London: Flamingo, 1988).

Mason, Bobbie Ann, *Love Life* (London: Chatto and Windus, 1989).

McCullers, Carson, *The Mortgaged Heart* (Harmondsworth: Penguin, 1975).

McInerney, Jay, *How It Ended* (London: Bloomsbury, 2007).

McPherson, James Alan, *Elbow Room* (New York: Fawcett Books, 1979).

Meloy, Maile, *Both Ways is the Only Way I Want It* (New York: Riverhead Books, 2009).

Melville, Herman, *Short Novels* (New York: Norton, 2002).

Michaels, Leonard, *I Would Have Saved Them If I Could* (New York: Farrar, Straus & Giroux, 1982).

Miller, Sue (ed.), *Best New American Voices 2007* (New York: Harcourt, 2006).

Minot, Susan, 'Thanksgiving Day', *Grand Street*, 3 (1984), 44–53.

Minot, Susan, 'The Navigator', *Grand Street*, 4 (1985), 90–100.

Minot, Susan, *Monkeys* (London: Flamingo, 1987).

Moore, Lorrie, *Anagrams* (London: Faber, 1987).

Moore, Lorrie, *Collected Stories* (London: Faber, 2008).

Naylor, Gloria, *The Women of Brewster Place* (New York: Penguin, 1983).

Oates, Joyce Carol, *Marriages and Infidelities* (New York: Vanguard, 1972).

Oates, Joyce Carol (ed.), *The Oxford Book of American Short Stories* (Oxford: Oxford University Press, 1992).

Oates, Joyce Carol, *Where Are You Going, Where Have You Been?* (Princeton, NJ: Ontario Review Press 1993).

O'Brien, Edward J. (ed.), *The Best Short Stories of 1915* (Boston, MA: Small, Maynard, 1916).

O'Brien, Edward J. (ed.), *The Best Short Stories of 1917* (Boston, MA: Small, Maynard, 1918).

O'Brien, Edward J. (ed.), *The Best Short Stories of 1920* (Boston, MA: Small, Maynard, 1921).

O'Brien, Edward J. (ed.), *The Best Short Stories 1934* (Boston, MA: Houghton Mifflin, 1934).

O'Brien, Tim, *The Things They Carried* (London: Flamingo, 1991).

O'Connor, Flannery, *Collected Stories* (London: Faber, 1990).

O'Hara, John, *Collected Stories* (London: Pan Books, 1984).

Orringer, Julie, *How to Breathe Underwater* (London: Penguin, 2005).

Ozick, Cynthia, *Collected Stories* (London: Phoenix, 2007).

Packer, Z. Z., *Drinking Coffee Elsewhere* (Edinburgh: Canongate, 2004).

Paley, Grace, *Collected Stories* (New York: Farrar, Straus & Giroux, 1994).

Poe, Edgar Allan, *Poetry and Tales* (New York: Library of America, 1984).

Prasad, Chandra (ed.), *Mixed: Short Fiction on the Multiracial Experience* (New York: Norton, 2006).

Proulx, Annie, *Close Range* (London: Fourth Estate, 1999).

Pynchon, Thomas, *Slow Learner* (London: Picador, 1985).

Remnick, David (ed.), *Wonderful Town: New York Stories from The New Yorker* (London: Pavilion, 2000).

Roth, Philip, *Letting Go* (London: Corgi, 1964).

Roth, Philip, *Goodbye, Columbus* (Harmondsworth: Penguin, 1986).

Salinger, J. D., *Franny and Zooey* (Harmondsworth: Penguin, 1964).

Salinger, J. D., *For Esmé – with Love and Squalor* (Harmondsworth: Penguin, 1986).

Saunders, George, *CivilWarLand in Bad Decline* (London: Jonathan Cape, 1996).

Saunders, George, *The Brief and Frightening Reign of Phil* (London: Bloomsbury, 2007).

Segal, Lore, *Shakespeare's Kitchen* (New York: The New Press, 2007).

Shapard, Robert and Thomas, J. (eds), *Sudden Fiction* (Salt Lake City, UT: Peregrine Smith, 1986).

Shirley, Aleda (ed.), *The Beach Book* (Louisville, KY: Sarabande Books, 1999).

Spark, Debra (ed.), *20 Under 30* (Harmondsworth: Penguin, 1988).

Stavans, Ilan (ed.), *Becoming Americans* (New York: Library of America, 2009).

Stegner, Wallace and Scowcroft, Richard (eds), *Twenty Years of Stanford Short Stories* (Stanford, CA: Stanford University Press, 1966).

Stevick, Philip (ed.), *Anti-Story* (New York: The Free Press, 1971).

Stone, Robert (ed.), *The Best American Short Stories 1992* (Boston, MA: Houghton Mifflin, 1992).

Sui Sin Far, *Mrs Spring Fragrance* (Urbana, IL: University of Illinois Press, 1995).

Thurber, James, *Writings and Drawings* (New York: The Library of America, 1996).

Twain, Mark, *The Complete Stories*, ed. Charles Neider (London: Bantam, 1958).

Updike, John (ed.) *The Best American Short Stories 1984* (Boston, MA: Houghton Mifflin, 1984).

Updike, John, *Forty Stories* (Harmondsworth: Penguin, 1987).

Updike, John, *The Maples Stories* (London: Everyman, 2009).

Updike, John, *My Father's Tears* (London: Hamish Hamilton, 2009).

Vollmann, William T., *The Atlas* (New York: Penguin, 1997).

Walker, Scott (ed.), *The Graywolf Annual Two* (Saint Paul, MN: Graywolf Press, 1986).

Welty, Eudora, *Collected Stories* (London: Penguin, 1983).

Wolff, Tobias, *The Stories* (London: Picador, 1988).

Secondary Sources

Abel, Elizabeth, 'Black Writing, White Reading', in E. Abel, B. Christian and H. Moglen (eds), *Female Subjects in Black and White* (Berkeley, CA: University of California Press, 1997), pp. 102–31.

Adler, Renata, *Gone: The Last Days of The New Yorker* (New York: Simon and Schuster, 1999).

Aldridge, John W., *Talents and Technicians* (New York: Scribner, 1992).

Alter, Alexandra, 'When Brevity is a Virtue', *Wall Street Journal*, 20 November 2009.

Ammon, Theodore G. (ed.), *Conversations with William H. Gass* (Jackson, MS: University Press of Mississippi, 2003).

Anderson, Elliott and Kinzie, Mary, *The Little Magazine in America* (Yonkers, NY: Pushcart Press, 1978).

Anderson, Sherwood, *The Story Teller's Story* (Ann Arbor, MI: University of Michigan Press, 2005).

Arac, Jonathan, *The Emergence of American Literary Narrative, 1820–1860* (Cambridge, MA: Harvard University Press, 2005).

Asals, Frederick, *Flannery O'Connor: The Imagination of Extremity* (Athens, GA: University of Georgia Press, 1982).

Bach, Gerhard and Hall, Blaine (eds), *Conversations with Grace Paley* (Jackson, MS: University Press of Mississippi, 1997).

Bacon, Jon Lance, *Flannery O'Connor and Cold War Culture* (Cambridge: Cambridge University Press, 1997).

Bailey, Blake, *Cheever: A Life* (New York: Alfred A. Knopf, 2009).

Ballou, Ellen B., *The Building of the House: Houghton Mifflin's Formative Years* (Boston, MA: Houghton Mifflin, 1970).

Barth, John, *The Friday Book* (Baltimore, MD: Johns Hopkins University Press, 1984).

Barth, John, *Further Fridays* (Boston, MA: Back Bay Books, 1995).

Barthelme, Donald, *Not-Knowing* (Berkeley, CA: Counterpoint, 1997).

Barthelme, Frederick, 'Editorial', *Mississippi Review*, 19:1–2 (1990), 8.

Barthes, Roland, *Writing Degree Zero*, trans. Annette Lavers (New York: Hill and Wang, 1968).

Barthes, Roland, 'An Introduction to the Structural Analysis of Narrative', trans. Lionel Duisit, *New Literary History*, 6 (1975), 237–72.

Baxter, Charles, *Burning Down the House: Essays on Fiction* (Saint Paul, MN: Graywolf Press, 1997).

Beck, Warren, 'The Real Language of Men: A Note on An Aspect of the Short Story', *The English Journal* (November 1934), pp. 731–9.

Beckett, Samuel, *Malloy, Malone Dies, The Unnameable* (New York: Grove, 1965).

Bell, Daniel, *The End of Ideology* (Cambridge, MA: Harvard University Press, 2000).

Bellamy, Joe David, *The New Fiction* (Urbana, IL: University of Illinois Press, 1974).

Bellamy, Joe David, *Literary Luxuries* (Columbia, MO: University of Missouri Press, 1995).

Benjamin, Walter, 'The Storyteller', in *Illuminations*, ed. Hannah Arendt, trans. Harry Zohn (London: Fontana 1973), pp. 83–109.

Bethea, Arthur F., *Technique and Sensibility in the Fiction and Poetry of Raymond Carver* (New York: Routledge, 2001).

Birkerts, Sven, *American Energies* (New York: William Morrow, 1992).

Boddy, Kasia, 'Unpublished Interview with Susan Minot', London, 1990.

Boddy, Kasia, 'Unpublished Interview with Gloria Naylor', Brooklyn, 1994.

Boddy, Kasia, 'Unpublished Interview with Jayne Anne Phillips', London, 1995.

Boddy, Kasia, 'Unpublished Interview with Junot Díaz', London, 1996.

Boddy, Kasia, 'Companion-Souls of the Short Story', *Scottish Slavonic Review*, 18 (September 1992), 105–12.

Boddy, Kasia, '*Short Cuts* and Long Shots: Raymond Carver's Stories and Robert Altman's Film', *British Journal of American Studies*, 34:1 (2000), 1–22.

Boddy, Kasia (ed.), 'The Short Story', special issue, *Critical Quarterly*, 52:2 (2010).

Bolter, J. D, *Writing Space: Computers, Hypertext and the Remediation of Print*, 2nd edn (London: Routledge, 2001).

Borges, Jorge Luis, *Ficciones*, trans. Anthony Kerrigan (New York: Grove Press, 1962).

Borges, Jorge Luis, *Labyrinths*, trans. Donald Yates and James E. Irby (Harmondsworth: Penguin, 1970).

Bowen, Elizabeth, *The Mulberry Tree* (London: Virago, 1986).

Bowman, David, 'Lashed by Lish', *Salon*, 1 September 1998, available at: www.salon.com/media/1998/09/01media.html.

Bradbury, Nicola (ed.), 'North American Short Stories and Short Fictions', *The Yearbook of English Studies*, 31 (2001).

Brinkmeyer, Jr., Robert H., *The Art and Vision of Flannery O'Connor* (Baton Rouge, LA: Louisiana State University Press, 1989).

Brooks, Cleanth, *The Well Wrought Urn* (London: Denis Dobson, 1949).

Brooks, Cleanth and Wimsatt, W. K., *Literary Criticism* (London: Routledge and Kegan Paul, 1970).

Brown, Julie (ed.), *Ethnicity and the American Short Story* (New York: Garland, 1997).

Brown, Julie (ed.), *American Women Short Story Writers* (New York: Routledge, 2000).

Buford, Bill, 'Editorial', 'Dirty Realism', *Granta*, 8 (1983), 4–5.

Bungert, Hans (ed.), *Die Amerikanische Short Story: Theorie und Entwicklung* (Darmstadt: Wissenschaftliche Buchgesellschaft, 1972).

Carver, Maryann Burk, *What It Used to Be Like* (New York: St. Martin's Griffin, 2006).

Chambers, Ross, *Story and Situation* (Manchester: Manchester University Press, 1984).

Charvat, William, *The Profession of Authorship in America, 1800–1870* (Columbus, OH: Ohio State University Press, 1968).

Chavkin, Allan (ed.), *Conversations with John Gardner* (Jackson, MS: University Press of Mississippi, 1990).

Cheever, John, *Journals* (London: Vintage, 1993).

Clark, Miriam Marty, 'Raymond Carver's Monological Imagination', *Modern Fiction Studies*, 37:2 (Summer 1991), 240–7.

Clarke, Graham, 'Investing the Glimpse: Raymond Carver and the Syntax of Silence', in Graham Clarke (ed.), *The New American Writing* (New York: St. Martin's Press, 1990), pp. 99–122.

Coleridge, Samuel Taylor, *Biographia Literaria*, 2 vols., ed. J. Shawcross (Oxford: Oxford University Press, 1909).

Connolly, Cyril, 'Fifty Years of Little Magazines', *Art and Literature* (March 1964), 95–109.

Coover, Robert, 'The End of Books', *New York Times*, 21 June 1992, p. 23.

Corey, Mary F., *The World Through a Monocle: The New Yorker at Midcentury* (Cambridge, MA: Harvard University Press, 1999).

Crews, Frederick, *The Critics Bear It Away: American Fiction and the Academy* (New York: Random House, 1992).

Curnutt, Kirk, *Wise Economies: Brevity and Storytelling in American Short Stories* (Moscow, ID: University of Idaho Press, 1997)

Damon-Moore, Helen, *Magazines for the Millions* (Albany, NY: State University of New York Press, 1994).

Dana, Robert (ed.), *A Community of Writers: Paul Engle and the Iowa Writers' Workshop* (Iowa City, IA: Iowa University Press, 1999).

Daugherty, Tracy, *Hiding Man: A Biography of Donald Barthelme* (New York: St. Martin's Press, 2009).

Davenport, Guy, *The Geography of the Imagination* (San Francisco, CA: North Point Press, 1981).

Davis, Lydia, 'Form as Response to Doubt', HOW(ever), 4:2 (October 1987), available at: www.asu.edu/pipercwcenter/how2journal/archive/print_archive/alerts1087.html.

Davis, Philip, *Bernard Malamud* (Oxford: Oxford University Press, 2007).

Davis, Rocío G., *Transcultural Reinventions: Asian American and Asian Canadian Short-story Cycles* (Toronto: Tsar, 2001).

Denning, Michael, *The Cultural Front* (London: Verso, 1998).

Donaldson, Scott, *John Cheever* (New York: Random House, 1988).

Douglas, George H., *The Smart Magazines* (New York: Archon Books, 1991).

Driver, Tom, 'Beckett by the Madeleine', *Columbia University Forum*, 4 (Summer 1961), 21.

Dunn, Maggie and Morris, Ann, *The Composite Novel* (New York: Twayne, 1995).

Eco, Umberto, *Reflections on* The Name of the Rose, trans. William Weaver (London: Secker and Warburg, 1985).

Eikhenbaum, Boris, 'The Structure of Gogol's "The Overcoat"' [1918], trans. Beth Paul and Muriel Nesbitt, *The Russian Review*, 22:4 (October 1963), 377–99.

Eisenberg, Deborah, 'Form and Fiction', ENSP 551, University of Virginia, Fall 2007.

Facknitz, Mark A. R., 'Missing the Train: Raymond Carver's Sequel to John Cheever's "The Five-Forty-Eight"', *Studies in Short Fiction*, 22:4 (Autumn 1985), 345–7.

Faulkner, William and Cowley, Malcolm, *The Faulkner–Cowley Files* (New York: Viking, 1966).

Fenza, David, 'Creative Writing and Its Discontents', *Writing in Education*, 22 (Spring 2000), 8–18.

Fenza, David, 'Who Keeps Killing Poetry?' AWP, December 2006, available at: www.awpwriter.org/magazine/writers/fenza02.htm.

Fenza, David, 'About AWP: The Growth of Creative Writing Programs', AWP, April 2009, available at: www.awpwriter.org/aboutawp/index.htm.

Ferris, Lucy, 'Uncle Charles Repairs to the A&P: Changes in Voice in the Recent American Short Story', *Narrative*, 16:2 (May 2008), 178–92.

Fitzgerald, F. Scott, *The Great Gatsby* (London: Penguin, 1990).

Foley, Martha (ed.), *The Best American Short Stories 1942* (Boston, MA: Houghton Mifflin, 1942).

Foley, Martha, *The Story of STORY Magazine* (New York: W. W. Norton, 1980).

Ford, Richard, 'Good Raymond', *New Yorker*, 5 October 1998, pp. 70–9.

Foster Wallace, David, *A Supposedly Fun Thing I'll Never Do Again* (London: Abacus, 1998).

Foster Wallace, David , *Consider the Lobster* (London: Abacus, 2005).

Frank, Joseph, *The Widening Gyre* (New Brunswick, NJ: Rutgers University Press, 1963).

Fried, Michael, *Art and Objecthood* (Chicago, IL: Chicago University Press, 1998).

Frost, Robert, *The Poetry of Robert Frost* (New York: Henry Holt, 2002).

Frye, Northrop, *Anatomy of Criticism* (Princeton, NJ: Princeton University Press, 1957).

Gado, Frank, *Conversations with Writers* (Schenectady, NY: Union College, 1973).

Gardner, Dwight, 'Moore's Better Blues', *Salon*, 27 October 1998, available at: www.salon.com/books/int/1998/10/cov_27int.html.

Gardner, John, *On Becoming a Novelist* (New York: Harper and Row, 1983).

Gardener, John, *The Art of Fiction* (New York: Vintage, 1991).

Gardner, John, *On Moral Fiction* (New York: Basic Books, 2000).

Garrett, George, 'Short Fiction Since 1950', in Fred Magill (ed.), *Critical Survey of Short Fiction* (Englewood Cliffs, NJ: Salem Press, 1981), vol. 1, pp. 278–322.

Gass, William H., *Fiction and the Figures of Life* (Boston, MA: Nonpareil Books, 1971).

Gass, William H., *Habitations of the Word* (New York: Touchstone, 1986).

Gelfant, Blanche (ed.), *The Columbia Companion to the Twentieth-Century Short Story* (New York: Columbia University Press, 2000).

Gentry, Marshall Bruce and Stull, William L. (eds), *Conversations with Raymond Carver* (Jackson, MS: University Press of Mississippi, 1990).

Giles, Paul, *American Catholic Arts and Fictions* (Cambridge: Cambridge University Press, 1992).

Girard, Stephanie, '"Standing at the Corner of Walk and Don't Walk": *Bright Lights, Big City*, Vintage Contemporaries and the Problem of Betweenness', *American Literature*, 68:1 (March 1986), 161–85.

Gooch, Brad, *Flannery* (New York: Little, Brown, 2009).

Gordon, Sarah, *Flannery O'Connor: The Obedient Imagination* (Athens, GA: University of Georgia Press, 2000).

Gray, Richard and Robinson, O. (eds), *A Companion to the Literature and Culture of the American South* (Oxford: Blackwell, 2004).

Green, Geoffrey, 'Postmodern Precursor: The Borgesian Image in Innovative American Writing', in Edna Aizenburg (ed.), *Borges and His Successors* (Columbia, MO: University of Missouri Press, 1990), pp. 200–13.

Hallett, Cynthia Whitney, *Minimalism and the Short Story* (Lewiston, NY: Edwin Mellen Press, 1999).

Hansen, Arlen, 'The Celebration of Solipsism', *Modern Fiction Studies*, 19 (Spring 1973), 5–15.

Hargrove, Nancy D., 'Portrait of an Assassin: Eudora Welty's "Where is the Voice Coming From?"', *The Southern Literary Journal*, 20:1 (Fall 1987), 74–88.

Harrington, Ellen Burton (ed.), *Scribbling Women and the Short Story Form* (New York: Peter Lang, 2008).

Hawkes, John, 'Flannery O'Connor's Devil', *Sewanee Review*, 70 (Summer 1962), 396–407.

Hawthorne, Julian, *Confessions and Criticism* (Boston, MA: Ticknor, 1887).

Hayes, Kevin J. (ed.), *The Cambridge Companion to Edgar Allan Poe* (Cambridge: Cambridge University Press, 2002).

Heller, Joseph, *Now and Then* (London: Scribner, 1999).

Hemingway, Ernest, *A Moveable Feast* (London: Jonathan Cape, 1964).

Hemingway, Ernest, *Selected Letters* (New York: Scribner, 1981).

Hempel, Amy, 'Captain Fiction', *Vanity Fair* (December 1984), pp. 91–3, 126.

Herzinger, Kim A., 'Introduction: On the New Fiction', *Mississippi Review*, 40/41 (Winter 1985), 7–22.

Hills, Rust, *Writing in General and the Short Story in Particular* (Boston, MA: Houghton Mifflin, 1987).

Hofmann, Michael 'Sex, Drugs and Rotten Roles', *Esquire* (November 1996), p. 38.

Horne, Philip, 'Henry James and the Economy of the Short Story', in Ian Willison, W. Gould and W. Chernaik (eds), *Modernist Writers and the Marketplace* (London: Macmillan, 1996), pp. 1–35.

Hunter, Adrian, *The Cambridge Introduction to the Short Story in English* (Cambridge: Cambridge University Press, 2007).

Ingram, Forrest L., *Representative Short Story Cycles of the Twentieth Century* (Paris: Mouton, 1971).

Jack, Ian, 'Introduction', 'Best of Young American Novelists 2', *Granta*, 97 (Spring 2007), 7–11.

James, Henry, *Theory of Fiction* (Lincoln, NA: University of Nebraska Press, 1972).

James, Henry, *Literary Criticism* (New York: Library of America, 1984), vol. 2.

Jen, Gish, *Typical American* (New York: Plume, 1992).

Jen, Gish, 'Who's to Judge?', *The New Republic*, 21 April 1997, pp. 18–19.

Johnson, Sarah Anne, *The Very Telling: Conversations with American Writers* (Hanover, NH: Press of New England, 2006).

Jones, Thomas, 'Mythologizing Manhattan: *The New Yorker*'s New York', *American Studies*, 28:1 (Spring 1987), 31–46.

Joyce, James, *Stephen Hero* (London: Jonathan Cape, 1944).

Joyce, James, *Dubliners* (Oxford: Oxford University Press, 2000).

Kafka, Franz, *The Great Wall of China*, trans. Malcolm Pasley (Harmondsworth: Penguin, 1991).

Kaplan, Mike and Dorr, John (dir.), *Luck Trust and Ketchup: Robert Altman in Carver Country* (1993).

Kazin, Alfred, *Writing Was Everything* (Cambridge, MA: Harvard University Press, 1995).

Keating, Peter, *The Haunted Study* (London: Secker and Warburg, 1989).

Kennedy, J. Gerald (ed.), *Modern American Short Story Sequences* (Cambridge: Cambridge University Press, 1995).

Kenner, Hugh, *Joyce's Voices* (Urbana, DC: Dalkey Archive, 2007).

Kermode, Frank, *Romantic Image* (London: Routledge, 2002).

Kermode, Frank, *The Sense of an Ending*, 2nd edn (Oxford: Oxford University Press, 2000).

Kessler, Edward, *Flannery O'Connor and the Language of Apocalypse* (Princeton, NJ: Princeton University Press, 1986).

Klinkowitz, Jerome, *The American 1960s* (Ames, IA: Iowa State University Press, 1980).

Kunkel, Thomas, *Genius in Disguise: Harold Ross of the New Yorker* (New York: Random House, 1995).

Lacey, Josh, 'Home and Away', *The Guardian*, 21 August 2004.

Lamplugh, George R., 'The Image of the Negro in Popular Magazine Fiction, 1875–1900', *Phylon*, 57:2 (1972), 177–89.

Landow, George P., *Hypertext 3.0* (Baltimore, MD: Johns Hopkins University Press, 2006).

Lardner, Ring, *The Best of Ring Lardner* (London: Everyman, 1984).

Lee, Rachel, 'Gish Jen', in King-Kok Cheung (ed.), *Words Matter* (Honolulu, HI: University of Hawaii Press, 2000), pp. 215–32.

Lentricchia, Frank, *After the New Criticism* (London: Methuen, 1983).

Levy, Andrew, *The Culture and Commerce of the American Short Story* (Cambridge: Cambridge University Press, 1993).

Lieberman, Eliah, *The American Short Story* (Ridgewood, NJ: The Editor, 1912).

Lodge, David, *The Art of Fiction* (Harmondsworth: Penguin, 1992).

Logsdon, Loren and Mayer, C. W. (eds), *Since Flannery O'Connor: Essays on the Contemporary American Short Story* (Macomb, IL: Western Illinois University Press, 1987).

Lohafer, Susan, *Coming to Terms with the Short Story* (Baton Rouge, LA: Louisiana State University Press, 1983).

Lohafer, Susan and Clarey, J. E. (eds), *Short Story Theory at a Crossroads* (Baton Rouge, LA: Louisiana State University Press, 1989).

London, Jack, *Martin Eden* (Harmondsworth: Penguin, 1980).

Lounsberry, Barbara *et al.* (eds), *The Tales We Tell* (Westport, CT: Greenwood Press, 1998).

Lowell, Robert, *Life Studies* (London: Faber, 1959).

Lundén, Rolf, *The United Stories of America* (Amsterdam: Rodopi, 1999).

Lukács, Georg, *The Theory of the Novel*, trans. Anna Bostock (London: Merlin, 1978).

Macdonald, Dwight, *Against the American Grain* (London: Victor Gollancz, 1963).

Mailer, Norman, *Cannibals and Christians* (London: Sphere, 1969).

Mailer, Norman, *Pieces and Pontifications* (London: New English Library, 1983).

Mailer, Norman, *The Armies of the Night* (Harmondsworth: Penguin, 1968).

Mailer, Norman, *Advertisements for Myself* (London: Panther, 1985).

Mann, Susan Garland, *The Short Story Cycle* (New York: Greenwood, 1989).

Mars-Jones, Adam, 'Words for the Walking Wounded', *Times Literary Supplement*, 22 January 1982, p. 76.

Mars-Jones, Adam, 'Psycho Dramas', *The Observer* (review), 6 November 2005, p. 15.

Marx, Karl and Engels, F., *The Communist Manifesto* (London: Penguin, 2002).

Matson, Esther, 'The Short Story', *Outlook*, 5 March 1919, pp. 406–9.

Matthews, Brander, *The Philosophy of the Short-Story* (New York: Peter Smith, 1931).

Maugham, W. Somerset, 'The Short Story', in *Essays on Literature* (London: New English Library, 1967), pp. 77–115.

May, Charles E. (ed.), *Short Story Theories* (Athens, OH: Ohio University Press, 1976).

May, Charles E. (ed.), *The New Short Story Theories* (Athens, OH: Ohio University Press, 1997).

May, Charles E., *The Short Story: The Reality of Artifice* (London: Routledge, 2002).

McGurl, Mark, *The Program Era: Postwar Fiction and the Rise of Creative Writing* (Cambridge, MA: Harvard University Press, 2009).

McSweeney, Kerry, *The Realist Short Story of the Powerful Glimpse* (Columbia, SC: University of South Carolina Press, 2007).

Menand, Louis, 'Saved From Drowning: Barthelme Reconsidered', *New Yorker*, 23 February 2009, pp. 68–76.

Michaels, Leonard, 'What's A Story', *Ploughshares*, 12:1 & 2 (1986), 199–204.

Milazzo, Lee (ed.), *Conversations with Joyce Carol Oates* (Jackson, MS: University Press of Mississippi, 1989).

Mills, C. Wright, *The Sociological Imagination* (Oxford: Oxford University Press, 1959).

Molesworth, Charles, *Donald Barthelme's Fiction* (Columbia, MO: University of Missouri Press, 1982)

Morrison, Toni, *Playing in the Dark* (Cambridge, MA: Harvard University Press, 1992).

Mullen, Bill, 'A Subtle Spectacle: Televisual Culture in the Short Stories of Raymond Carver', *Critique*, 39:2 (Winter 1998), 99–114

Mullen, Bill V., *Popular Fronts: Chicago and African-American Cultural Politics, 1935–46* (Urbana, IL: University of Illinois Press, 1999).

Munro, Alice, *Too Much Happiness* (London: Chatto and Windus, 2009).

Murphy, Jessica, 'Sentence by Sentence', *Atlantic*, 17 April 2006.

Myers, D. G., *The Elephants Teach: Creative Writing since 1880* (Englewood Cliffs, NJ: Prentice-Hall, 1996).

Nagel, James, *The Contemporary American Short-Story Cycle* (Baton Rouge, LA: Louisiana State University Press, 2001).

Nasso, Christine (ed.), *Contemporary Authors*, 1st Revision Series, vol. 28 (Detroit, IL: Gale, 1977).

Newlove, David, 'Fiction Briefs', *Saturday Review* (April 1981), p. 77.

Newman, Charles, *The Post-Modern Aura* (Evanston, IL: Northwestern University Press, 1985).

Norris, Frank, *Novels and Essays* (New York: Library of America, 1986).

Oates, Joyce Carol, 'The Short Story', *Southern Humanities Review* 5:3 (Summer 1971), 213–14.

Oates, Joyce Carol, *The Edge of Impossibility* (New York: Vanguard, 1972).

Oates, Joyce Carol, 'An Endangered Species', *New York Review of Books*, 29 June 2000, pp. 29–41.

O'Brien, Edward J., *The Dance of the Machines* (New York: Macauley, 1929).

O'Brien, Edward J., *The Advance of the American Short Story* (New York: Dodd, Mead, 1931).

O'Connor, Flannery, *Wise Blood* (New York: Farrar, Straus & Cudahy, 1962).

O'Connor, Flannery, *The Habit of Being* (New York: Farrar, Straus & Giroux, 1979).

O'Connor, Flannery, *Mystery and Manners* (London: Faber, 1984).

O'Connor, Frank, *The Lonely Voice* (Hoboken, NJ: Melville House, 2004).

Ohmann, Richard, *Selling Culture* (London: Verso, 1996).

Ong, Walter J., *Rhetoric, Romance and Technology* (Ithaca, NY: Cornell University Press, 1971).

O'Toole, Kristen, 'Great Online Literary Magazines', *Esquire Books Blog*, 22 January 2009, available at: www.esquire.com/blogs/books/Best-Online-Lit-Mags-Blog.

Ozick, Cynthia, 'Cheever's Yankee Heritage', *The Antioch Review*, 50:1/2 (Winter–Spring, 1992), 156–61.

Partridge, Jeffrey F. L., *Beyond Literary Chinatown* (Seattle, WA: University of Washington Press, 2007).

Passaro, Vince, 'Unlikely Voices: The Quiet Renaissance of American Short Fiction', *Harper's* (August 1999), pp. 80–9.

Pattee, Fred Lewis, *The Development of the Short Story* (New York: Harper and Row, 1923).

Patteson, Richard F. (ed), *Critical Essays on Donald Barthelme* (New York: G. K. Hall, 1992).

Peden, William, *The American Short Story: Frontline in the National Defence of Literature* (Boston, MA: Houghton Mifflin, 1964).

Peden, William, *The American Short Story: Continuity and Change, 1940–1975* (Boston, MA: Houghton Mifflin, 1975).

Penn Warren, Robert, *Selected Essays* (London: Eyre and Spottiswood, 1964).

Pérez Firmat, Gustavo, *Life on the Hyphen: The Cuban-American Way* (Austin, TX: University of Texas Press, 1994).

Plath, James (ed.), *Conversations with John Updike* (Jackson, MS: University Press of Mississippi, 1994).

Plath, Sylvia, *Letters Home* (London: Faber, 1977).

Pleynet, Marcelin, 'An Experimental Reality', *Art and Literature* (March 1964), pp. 87–94.

Poe, Edgar Allan, *Essays and Reviews* (New York: Library of America, 1984).

Pound, Ezra, *The Literary Essays*, ed. T. S. Eliot (London: Faber, 1954).

Prenshaw, Peggy Whitman (ed.), *Conversations with Eudora Welty* (New York: Washington Square Press, 1985).

Prince, Alan, 'An Interview with John Barth', *Prism* (Spring 1968), pp. 42–62.

Pynchon, Thomas, *Gravity's Rainbow* (London: Picador, 1975).

Rader, Benjamin, *In Its Own Image: How Television Transformed Sports* (New York: Free Press, 1984).

Rebein, Robert, *Hicks, Tribes, and Dirty Realists* (Lexington, KY: University Press of Kentucky, 2001).

Reid, A. D., 'On the Move', *Literary Review* (November 1996), pp. 22–3.

Reid, Ian, *The Short Story* (London: Methuen, 1977).

Riesman, David, *The Lonely Crowd* (New Haven, CT: Yale University Press, 1950).

Riesman, David, 'The Suburban Sadness', in William Dobriner (ed.), *The Suburban Community* (New York: G. P. Putnam's Sons, 1958), pp. 375–408.

Ross, Jean W., 'Interview with Grace Paley', in Linda Metzger (ed.), *Contemporary Authors*, New Revision Series, vol. 13 (Detroit, IL: Gale, 1984), pp. 399–400.

Roth, Philip, 'Iowa: A Very Far Country Indeed', *Esquire* (December 1962), pp. 19–32.

Rumbaut, Rubén, 'The Agony of Exile', in F. S. Ahearn and J. L. Athey (eds), *Refugee Children* (Baltimore, MD: Johns Hopkins University Press, 1991), pp. 53–91.

Runyon, Randolph Paul, *Reading Raymond Carver* (Syracuse, NY: Syracuse University Press, 1992).

Saroyan, William, *Sons Come and Go, Mothers Hang in Forever* (New York: McGraw-Hill, 1976).

Saunders, George, *The Brain-Dead Megaphone* (London: Bloomsbury, 2008).

Scholes, Robert, *Some Suggestions for Using Elements of Fiction* (Oxford: Oxford University Press, 1981).

Scholes, Robert, *Fabulation and Metafiction* (Urbana, IL: University of Illinois Press, 1979).

Scholes, Robert, and Kellogg, R., *The Nature of Narrative* (Oxford: Oxford University Press, 1966).

Scofield, Martin, *The Cambridge Introduction to the American Short Story* (Cambridge: Cambridge University Press, 2007).

Shaw, Valerie, *The Short Story* (London: Longman, 1983).

Showalter, Elaine, 'Piecing and Writing', in Nancy K. Miller (ed.), *The Poetics of Gender* (New York: Columbia University Press, 1986), pp. 222–47.

Silverman, Kenneth, *Edgar Allan Poe* (New York: Harper and Row, 1992).

Simmonds, Roy S., *Edward J. O'Brien and His Role in the Rise of the American Short Story in the 1920s and 1930s* (Lewiston, NY: Edwin Mellen Press, 2001).

Sklenicka, Carol, *Raymond Carver: A Writer's Life* (New York: Scribner, 2009).

Smith, Ali, *The Bridport Prize 2009*, available at: www.bridportprize.org.uk/alismithreport.htm.

Smith, C. Alphonso, *The American Short Story* (Folcroft, PA: Flocroft Library Editions, 1970).

Smith, Sarah, 'Electronic Fictions', *The New York Review of Science Fiction*, November 1993, pp. 1, 8–11.

Sollors, Werner, 'Immigrants and Other Americans', in Elliot Emory (ed.), *The Columbia Literary History of the United States* (New York: Columbia University Press, 1988), pp. 568–88.

Solotaroff, Ted, 'Writing in the Cold', *Granta*, 15 (Spring 1985), pp. 264–79.

Sontag, Susan, 'Against Interpretation', in *A Susan Sontag Reader* (Harmondsworth: Penguin, 1983), pp. 95–104.

Spencer, Elizabeth, 'Experiment is Out, Concern is In', *New York Times Book Review*, 21 November 1982, p. 7.

Sprague, Claire (ed.), *Van Wyck Brooks: The Early Years*, revised edn (Boston, MA: Northeastern University Press, 1993).

Stanton, David, 'Junot Díaz', *Poets and Writers*, 26:4 (1998), 26–38.

Stevick, Philip, *Alternative Pleasures* (Urbana, IL: University of Illinois Press, 1981).

Stull, William L. and Carroll, M. P. (eds), *Remembering Ray* (Santa Barbara, CA: Capra Press, 1993).

Tan, Amy, *The Opposite of Fate* (London: Harper Perennial, 2004).

Tanner, Tony, *City of Words: American Fiction, 1950–1970* (London: Jonathan Cape, 1971).

Tanner, Tony, *Scenes of Nature, Signs of Men* (Cambridge: Cambridge University Press, 1987).

Tate, Allen, *Essays of Four Decades*, ed. Louise Cowan (Wilmington, DE: ISI Books, 1999).

Todorov, Tzvetan, *The Poetics of Prose*, trans. Richard Howard (Oxford: Basil Blackwell, 1977).

Totten, Gary, 'Critical Reception and Cultural Capital: Edith Wharton as a Short Story Writer', *Pedagogy*, 8:1 (Winter 2008), 115–33.

Travis, Trysh, 'What We Talk About When We Talk About *The New Yorker*', *Book History*, 3 (2000), 253–85.

Trilling, Lionel, *The Liberal Imagination* (Harmondsworth: Peregrine, 1970).

Twain, Mark, *The Complete Essays*, ed. Charles Neider (New York: Doubleday, 1963).

Updike, John, *Hugging the Shore* (Harmondsworth: Penguin, 1985).

Updike, John, *More Matter* (London: Hamish Hamilton, 1999).

Walker, Alice, *In Search of Our Mothers' Gardens* (New York: Harcourt Brace Jovanovich, 1983).

Weatherby, W. J., 'Turning Life Into Great Literature', *The Guardian*, 5 August 1988, p. 33.

Weich, Dave, 'Charles Baxter Visits Old Friends in Five Oaks', Powell's Author

Interviews, 15 September 2003, available at: www.powells.com/authors/baxter.html.

Wellek, René, *A History of Modern Criticism* (New Haven, CT: Yale University Press, 1986), vol. 6.

Wellek, René and Warren, Austin, *Theory of Literature* (Harmondsworth: Penguin, 1980).

Welty, Eudora, *One Writer's Beginnings* (London: Faber, 1985).

Welty, Eudora, *The Eye of the Story* (London: Virago, 1987).

Welty, Eudora, *A Writer's Eye* (Jackson, MS: University Press of Mississippi, 2009).

[White, E. B.], 'The Talk of the Town', *The New Yorker*, 5 August 1939, p. 7.

Whittier, Anthony, 'Frank O'Connor', in Malcolm Cowley (ed.), *Writers at Work*, 1st Series (Harmondsworth: Penguin, 1977), pp. 159–82.

Wilbers, Stephen, *The Iowa Writers' Workshop* (Iowa City, IA: University of Iowa Press, 1980).

Wilde, Alan, *Middle Grounds* (Philadelphia, PA: University of Pennsylvania Press, 1987).

Williams, Blanche Colton, *How to Study 'The Best Short Stories'* (Boston, MA: Small, Maynard, 1919).

Wilson, Edmund, *Axel's Castle* (New York: Scribner, 1931).

Winther, Per, Lothe, J. and Skei, H. H. (eds), *The Art of Brevity* (Columbia, SC: University of South Carolina Press, 2004).

Wolfe, Tom, *Hooking Up* (London: Picador, 2001).

Wood, James, review of *Drown*, *The New Republic*, 16 December 1996, p. 39.

Wood, James, 'Metaphysical Parenting', *London Review of Books*, 21 June 2007, pp. 21–2.

Wroe, Nicholas, 'Breached Barrios', *GQ Magazine* (October 1996), p. 55.

Yagoda, Ben, *About Town: The New Yorker and the World It Made* (London: Duckworth, 2000)

Yardley, Jonathan, 'Chic to Chic', *The Washington Post*, 25 March 1985, C2.

Yeats, W. B., *Collected Poems* (London: Arena, 1990).

Zagarell, Sandra A., 'Narratives of Community: The Identification of a Genre', *Signs*, 13:3 (Fall 1988), 498–527.

Zeledón, Maximo, 'Dominican Dominion', *Frontera Magazine*, 5 (1998), available at: www.fronteramag.com/issue5/Díaz.

Index

The British Association for American Studies (BAAS)

The British Association for American Studies was founded in 1955 to promote the study of the United States of America. It welcomes applications for membership from anyone interested in the history, society, government and politics, economics, geography, literature, creative arts, culture and thought of the USA.

The Association publishes a newsletter twice yearly, holds an annual national conference, supports regional branches and provides other membership services, including preferential subscription rates to the *Journal of American Studies*.

Membership enquiries may be addressed to the BAAS Secretary. For contact details visit our website: www.baas.ac.uk.